AGRI SELLING

W. DAVID DOWNEY • MICHAEL A. JACKSON • CARL G. STEVENS

EDITED BY MARIE HODGE BLYSKAL

Library of Congress Card Number 82-73827

ISBN 0-930264-50-9

1184-3H

AGRI SELLING

W. David Downey
Professor
Purdue University
West Lafayette, IN

Michael A. Jackson
President
Agri Business Associates, Inc.
Indianapolis, IN

Carl G. Stevens
President
The Carl Stevens Group
Houston, TX

Edited by Marie Hodge Blyskal

To Our Wives
Deb, Kay, and Jean.

Preface

In recent years, selling has earned respectability in agriculture. Agribusiness has recognized selling as a highly important function necessary for success in the marketplace. Few agribusinesses today can rely exclusively on rapidly growing markets to build their businesses. The intensified competition that results from a maturing market brings increased emphasis on the selling function. Agrimarketers expect their sales representatives to become evermore skillful in bridging that critical "last few feet" to the customer. Very often the personal abilities and skills of the agri salesperson are the deciding factor in the purchase decision for the farmer and the agribusinessman.

Today's agri salesperson is a competent professional who combines selling skills with complex technical knowledge to catalyze change in production and marketing practices in agriculture. Customers at all levels depend heavily on the agri salesperson to bring them the latest information that will increase their yield, generate a high gross margin, reduce their costs, or provide a solution to their problem. Agri salespeople have become an integral part of the food and fiber production/marketing concept.

No longer is agri selling viewed widely by customers, management or academia with distain and distrust. Increasingly, agri salespeople are viewed as a necessary and highly productive part of the marketing and technical communication process, capable of doing great good for both the agribusiness and the customer — if they are well trained and effective.

This book gives recognition to the growingly important and professional nature of today's agri sales function.

Certainly there are a great many books and articles on selling. While many of these are very good and their concepts do apply to agriculture, few if any of these relate to the special uniqueness of the agricultural market.

This book is written by those who know and understand agriculture — and who have worked closely with field salespeople, dealing directly, to, through, and with farmers, dealers, distributors, and manufacturers of agricultural products. You will not only see agricultural examples throughout this book but will also recognize important nuances that become so important to success when dealing with the agricultural sector.

This book was intended both for the classroom *and* for the practitioner in the field. Its style should be quite useful for the undergraduate classroom at universities bold enough to offer such a practical course, and for colleges who already understand the importance of preparing their students to speak the language of their first job in agribusiness.

But this book will also be useful to those on the firing line in the real world. The everyday experiences of a great many successful salespeople are ground into the principles, concepts, and examples in this book. Many experienced salespeople will see themselves on a call just yesterday, and be reminded once again of the basics that are perpetually important to their continued success.

This book is not intended to be a model for the "right way" to sell. Its fundamental premise is that there is no *one* "right way" to do it. Each person and each situation are greatly different. It is intended to provide a framework - a guide to allow the unique personality of each individual reader to come out. Its purpose is to provide basic ideas on which to build a personal style that can be adapted to every unique circumstance encountered in the marketplace.

The philosophy throughout this book is that agri selling is, and must always be, problem solving for mutual benefit. Professional agri selling almost always involves a combination of technical agriculture with sales and marketing skills. It is this happy marriage that can generate an ethical and profitable end result for both the buyer and the seller.

Contents

Contents *(continued)*

Contents *(continued)*

ABOUT THE AUTHORS

W. DAVID DOWNEY was raised on a grain livestock farm in Wabash, Indiana. He received his B.S. in Agronomy, his M.S. in Agricultural Marketing, and his Ph.D in Agricultural Economics and Business Management from Purdue University. A Professor in the Department of Agricultural Economics at Purdue University, he teaches approximately 400 students per year "Professional Selling Skills in Agricultural Businesses." He is active in Cooperative Extension programs for several on-campus training programs including those for firms and trade associations. His research experience encompasses agricultural marketing, business management, in particular farm supplies and fertilizer and chemical distribution. He also works on a consulting basis with several agribusiness firms in various educational-training programs throughout the U.S. and Canada. Downey emphasizes the human dimension of management and marketing work in agribusinesses, in addition to more traditional areas of financial and marketing management. He has worked extensively with leadership, human relations, selling skills, farmer/consumer behavior, and group decision-making processes.

MICHAEL A. JACKSON is president of Agri Business Associates, an Indianapolis-based agricultural training and development firm. Jackson oversees agri business human resources development in areas such as business and financial management, sales and supervision, and human relations skills that have been presented to thousands of agricultural personnel. Jackson has led a pioneering effort in the agricultural training field using field research and company specific programs to serve over 140 client companies throughout the United States and abroad. A graduate of Purdue University, Jackson holds a degree in agricultural economics and has done graduate work in law and business. He has published articles on various sales and management topics in industry and company publications. Jackson is a former national secretary of the Future Farmers of America. He was raised on a family farm and grain and livestock operation near Tipton, Indiana where he is still involved in management of the farm.

CARL G. STEVENS is founder of The Carl Stevens Group, headquartered in Houston, Texas. Besides directing the company's activities, highlighted by the "Blueprint for Professional Selling" seminars, he serves as consultant to leading national and international companies and trade associations. He is one of the nation's leading authorities in the field of programmed sales education and human resource development. He graduated from Vanderbilt University with a B.A. in psychology and marketing and he has done graduate work in law and marketing. For over 15 years he has taught and was a visiting lecturer at colleges and universities throughout the U.S. He is a member of the faculty of Penton Learning System and The National Management Association. His writings have been published in Sales Management, Marketing Times, Management Forum, Transport Topics and Commerce. He has authored or co-authored several books including "Selling" published by Richard Irwin, Inc. 1978, and numerous articles in trade and professional journals.

The Definition of Selling

Few careers offer as many opportunities as sales. Yet, unethical practices on the part of some salespeople in the past has caused many customers to view sellers with suspicion. Section I will define what a salesperson does and the skills he or she should possess in order to polish the sales image and become a competent professional.

Chapter One
The Role of Selling

"...the ultimate goal is to satisfy the customer — before, during and after the sale."

Frank Richmond, a young, energetic salesperson for Miller Farm Equipment in Fargo, had had a rough day. He had just spent most of the afternoon driving from account to account, trying to sell his company's new Model A200 200-hp tractor. The machine was a good buy. It offered an engine design that raised fuel efficiency by 10 percent over the nearest competitor, had solid state silicon chip instrumentation, rode like a Cadillac, was competitively priced, and in an effort to spur sales, the company was offering a $500 rebate for those ordering the tractor before the first of the year.

For such a good deal, you'd think Frank could have done better than five "not this years," three "let me think about its," and one "leave me a brochure." It was almost a carbon copy of every day of the last week.

Frank couldn't figure out what was wrong. His prospective buyers' tractors were getting up in years, and they all agreed the A200 was a beaut.

The problem was money. Credit was tight, interest rates were outrageous, and even though breakdowns were becoming a more frequent annoyance, many of Frank's accounts felt it was wiser to ride the recession out and see whether they could "squeeze one more year" out of their ancient machinery.

As Frank's car pulled into his driveway his five-year-old son, Paul, tripped and fell, skinning his knee. "Great," thought Frank. "That puts the cap on the day."

The way Paul cried, you'd think he'd just lost his leg. In reality he just had a minor scrape, but his knee was bloody and that was the only reason he needed to bellow like a stuck hog.

Frank lifted his son up into the air as he always did and gave him a jubilant "Hi, Paul." Then, in a kidding but sensitive tone, he chided his son for crying so much and carried Paul to the house on his shoulders to repair the damage.

"Now this won't hurt much," Frank shouted above Paul's protests as he dabbed a piece of cotton with some rubbing alcohol.

"Yes it will! It's Mercurochrome," Paul cried as he fought to hold back the tears.

"It's *not* Mercurochrome, it's alcohol."

"No! It'll hurt!"

"Paul," Frank began more sternly. "Do you want your leg to get better?"

Paul did.

"Then let me clean the cut. Otherwise it could get infected, and it'll really hurt. Now this is going to sting a little bit, but not as much as Mercurochrome would."

Paul looked at his father. He was scared, but he decided to trust his dad.

****

SELLING: WHAT IT ALL MEANS

The odd thing about Frank's frustration with the A200 was that he really did know how to sell. He simply had gotten out of the practice of using the most fundamental concept in agri selling.

When Frank confronted his son's problem and applied a solution (literally and figuratively), he persuaded Paul to accept the solution. He was selling. Of course it helped that Paul really did trust his father. No one can deny that the salesperson is in many ways selling himself: his knowledge, experience and honesty. But even though he had his son's trust, Frank still had an uphill struggle to get the alcohol on his son's knee and to convince Paul he'd be better off using the alcohol. The difference between his success with Paul and his failure with potential customers can be traced to how well he is tuned to the customer's real problems and his ability to convince them he has a workable solution.

Emotion Versus Problem Solving

There was a time when books about selling stressed the emotional approach: it was assumed that successful selling depended largely upon the ability to tap the customer's emotional responses to a product or service. Today's agri selling focuses on the problem-solving aspect of the profession: the salesperson discerns a potential customer's need, provides the customer with alternatives and applies his persuasive powers to convince the customer that at least one of the proffered solutions is viable. This discernment of the customer's true problem is often hidden under a web of less important objections or hazy dissatisfactions, and usually requires a considerable amount of skilled probing on the salesperson's part, as we shall see. But to whatever lengths the salesperson must go, the ultimate goal is to satisfy the customer before, during and after the sale. Salespeople are first and foremost problem solvers and people satisfiers.

The importance to the salesperson of making a sale is obvious: his livelihood, job and most likely his self-esteem depend on it. But sales bear a fundamental relationship to the welfare of the company as well. In fact, sales are the lifeblood of any agribusiness. **SALES PAY THE BILLS**

To realize the importance of sales, we need look no further than the profit and loss statement. This barometer of a business' health begins with sales, subtracts the costs of producing or acquiring the product, further subtracts operating and overhead expenses, and hopefully winds up showing a profit. (See Figure 1.1.)

Figure 1.1 **Profit and Loss Statement**

Sales
— Cost of Goods Sold

Gross Margin
Expenses

Profit

Of course the full responsibility for sales does not rest on the sales department's shoulders alone. Backup must come from the production team, the staff and the distribution system, and may be greatly affected by the economic and competitive climate surrounding the business. But overhead expenses are generated whether sales figures are high or low, and even the selling endeavor itself will cost the company, so the aim is to keep sales high enough to turn a profit. Profit, the basic economic motive for a business' existence, is the bottom line of a story that must begin with sales.

Salespeople are usually given a high priority by most agribusinesses. A force of competent salespeople is essential in an agribusiness' battle for survival. In fact, some companies even allow their salespeople enough leeway in price negotiation to make them responsible for profits. Salespeople accomplish this by ensuring that their final price will produce a gross margin great enough to dispose of overhead expenses and still show a profit. Where direct accountability for profit is lacking, salespeople may become divorced from the company's primary reason for existence and some difficult problems can result.

SELLING AND MARKETING — NATURAL PARTNERS

"The purpose of a business is to satisfy the needs of customers. Products and services are important only to the extent that they satisfy these needs — they are means rather than ends. Therefore, marketing starts with the determination of customers' needs and ends with the repeated satisfaction of those needs.

"A business must satisfy the needs of its customers at an acceptance level of profitability. Therefore the purpose of marketing is not simply to generate sales or achieve a certain market share, but rather to produce profitable sales and a profitable market share.

"All activities of a business should be integrated and coordinated so as to satisfy customer needs at a satisfactory rate of profitability. Marketing must be coordinated with finance, production, personnel administration, engineering, and research and development. Moreover, all marketing activities must be effectively integrated and coordinated in order to achieve market impact."[1]

As you can see from the foregoing quotation, marketing embraces selling, along with all the myriad activities in which a business engages, to "satisfy customer needs at a satisfactory rate of profitability." Marketing ties together sales and profit in a neat little package that includes everything from engineering to advertising: all directed toward that bottom line of profit. Marketing activities can be summarized in four basic steps.

Figure 1.2 Four Basic Marketing Activities

1. Identifying specific segments of potential buyers, called target segments.
2. Meticulously evaluating the needs of that segment.
3. Researching and developing products or services that will answer the needs of that segment.
4. Developing a program that will make the problem-solving products or services known to the target segments.

The marketing mix is the way in which the business integrates all the diverse elements of its marketing program — according just the right emphasis to each element. This mix usually emphasizes communication with target markets (advertising, personal selling, publicity etc.); development and pricing of products or services; and distribution. It is in the first of these three areas that selling takes form.

The Process of Selling

Sales don't just happen, they're created. This creation is an active *process* making it no accident that "selling" is a verb. Sometimes the process simply makes a sale possible by offering the customer an outlet for an already-developed urge to buy. But more often, the salesperson must draw out a need (of which the customer may even be unaware) and demonstrate the product or service's usefulness in filling that need.

---

[1] From STRATEGIC MARKETING by David J. Kollat, Roger D. Blackwell and James F. Robeson. © 1972 by Holt, Rinehart and Winston, Inc. Reprinted by permission of Holt, Rinehart and Winston, CBS College Publishing.

Selling includes a wide variety of activities ranging from collecting market intelligence information about what the competition is doing, to making presentations to prospects, to providing followup service to customers. Salespeople must perform these varied activities differently depending on their product, their market, their customers and their own unique abilities. There is no one "right" process or no one "right" way to do it. But it is a process. This logical set of responsibilities and activities lead to repeated sales and profits through satisfying customers' needs.

Notice that the active selling process does not manufacture a need that didn't previously exist. Instead selling focuses on real problems and generates real solutions that benefit both buyer and seller. It creates wants in the customer that are generally strongest when tied to genuine needs. And in the event that the customer is dissatisfied with the purchase for any reason it is in the firm's best interest to find out why the customer was dissatisfied and to correct the problem so that future customers won't be dissatisfied.

SELLING IN AGRIBUSINESS

Agricultural Knowledge

While all selling has some elements in common, agri selling does have characteristics that set it apart. For one thing, the uniqueness of farmers and ranchers to agri selling cannot be overemphasized, whether the salesperson is selling to them directly or indirectly. In either case, the customer probably subscribes wholeheartedly to the traditional "agricultural ethic" of the farming community: honesty, hard work, devotion to and practical knowledge of farming, and interest in discussing every aspect of the farming experience with colleagues. This special camaraderie makes it more difficult for those who have no firsthand experience with farming, so it's generally important for agribusiness salespeople to have some familiarity with agriculture, particularly those who must work directly with producers.

Technical Knowledge

In addition to evidencing this familiarity, agribusiness salespeople have to have extensive technical knowledge in their product area. This enables them to provide the customer with complete information to make a buying decision. In fact, as agriculture becomes more and more complex technologically, salespeople find that selling depends more and more on providing the farmer or rancher with a technical solution to a difficult problem or with technical information about evermore-intricate product features. Selling a dairy farmer on a bull semen that will fit his or her needs requires thorough understanding of complex genetic strains, milk production problems and the practical aspects of dairy economics, for example.

Solid Relationships

The limited number of customers in any agricultural community also has its effect on the nature of agri selling. Maintaining longstanding relationships with steady customers in such a way that repeat business is facilitated is a challenge and necessity. News of mistreatment travels like wildfire in a tight-knit farming community. In such an environment, each customer must be valued and given exceptional service to ensure that the relationship will continue. Fierce competition generally ensues over new customer business and often one agribusiness will attempt to woo customers away from its competitor. The special nature of the salesperson/customer relationship is most evident in farm supply and marketing fields, where contact with agricultural producers is direct and agribusinesses fight for their share of the feed, chemical, machinery or seed market.

Seasonality

The seasonal nature of agriculture also has a bearing on the salesperson's job. Responsibilities vary between harvest time and planting as much for the salesperson as they do for the farmer. Adapting to these changes means that one week the salesperson may be investigating problems or complaints with products that are currently being used, and the next week filing market projections for the following year. Seasonality is present in most forms of selling to some extent, but its presence in agriculture carries even greater weight, especially for agronomic supplies. Again, this is part of the salesperson's fine tuning to agricultural moods, seasons and needs.

Biological Market

It is also unique that most agri salespeople are dealing with biological markets. They deal with living, growing organisms where timing can be the difference between life and death of the organism. Since most of these organisms are a part of the food and fiber system that feeds and clothes the nation, government regulations, policies and programs can and do dramatically impact the market and the salesperson's job. For instance, a change in regulations governing the way an animal health product can be used with livestock about ready for market can greatly impact the animal health salesperson's job.

Implied in much of the foregoing discussion is the professionalism of the agribusiness salesperson as he or she juggles the complex responsibilities of meeting customer needs and wants, satisfying requirements for profitability, dispensing technical information and knowledge, and remaining attuned to the special nuances of the agricultural field. The following chapter will take up that topic in more detail.

SUMMARY

* The fundamental concept of agri selling is convincing a prospect to accept a solution. The difference between success and failure is the salesperson's ability to understand a prospect's problem and persuade him to "buy" the salesperson's solution.

* Salespeople are first and foremost problem solvers and people satisfiers.

* Sales are a major factor in the success of a company as the income producing element. Profit is determined by subtracting Cost of Goods sold from Sales to determine Gross Margin and subtracting Expenses from Gross Margin.

* Marketing and sales go hand-in-hand as its purpose is to produce profitable sales and a profitable market share.

* Marketing activities are: identifying target segments, evaluating segment needs, researching and developing products or services to serve the needs, and developing a program to educate and inform the customers about the products or services.

* Selling is an active process comprised of many activities. Therefore, there

is no "right way" to sell. Rather the salesperson must use logic to plan his selling strategy for each customer.

* Agri selling includes several facets that are especially significant: agricultural expertise, technical knowledge, solid relationships, seasonality and a biological market.

---

1. What is the "problem-solving" approach to agri sales?

2. Define "marketing" and explain its relationship to sales.

3. What are the five characteristics that distinguish agri sales?

4. Can a salesperson create a need where none existed in order to make a sale? Explain.

**Review Questions
Chapter 1**

Chapter Two
The Profession

"Successful agri selling is like any profession — it takes careful, prolonged study."

Bill Harris, a top-notch salesman for Greenup Seeds, always looked up to his neighbor Tom Rowan, a local lawyer. Bill appreciated the years of schooling, the amount of work and the knowledge required for Tom's profession. He also happened to be fascinated by the intricacies and twists of the law. Bill's wife knew this all too well as Tom and Bill would spend hours talking about this or that lawsuit, what "stare decisis" was all about, or the strategy used to win a certain case. She once quipped that Bill was getting prepared to take the state bar exam.

So it came as a sad surprise when the Harrises found out Tom had joined a San Francisco law firm and would be moving out of Bakersfield the next month. Since the times were not the best, and people weren't buying houses, Tom decided he'd try to sell the house himself. That way, he reasoned, a real estate agent's commission wouldn't jack up the price of the house and keep buyers away.

In the meantime, there were several of those "last dinners" between the

Harrises and the Rowans. At one point during the two couple's third last dinner, the topic of conversation turned to Tom's progress in selling the house. Unfortunately, Tom couldn't be enthused. Several people had seen the place, but no one was interested in buying.

"I can't believe that," said Bill. "You've got a great house here. There's that great basement rec room with the wet bar and the fireplace. That alone would sell me on the place."

"Oh boy, no!" countered Tom. "I've been steering people away from the cellar. What with all the moving and everything, it's cluttered with junk."

"Well, what about that insulation job you did last year?"

"No one cares about that," Tom replied. "People look for luxuries. Fiberglas insulation is not what you would call a chic, in-demand item."

Bill couldn't believe his ears. Did Tom mention how quiet the neighborhood was?

"No. In fact, I warned one couple about the wild Fourth of July parties Frank Asan throws every year, keeping everyone in the neighborhood up until the fifth of July."

To Bill the problem was obvious. His intelligent lawyer friend was a wash-out at selling. For once, *Tom* needed some professional advice.

The salesman outlined what Tom was doing wrong. He pointed out that the rec room was a major selling point. No one cared about the present mess there, because that would be gone when the new owners moved in. The buyer would be more interested in the parties and fun the room would provide. However, Bill did agree that the rec room would show itself better if the boxes could be moved to the garage, and offered to help move them.

And the insulation was a distinct plus; what with the energy crisis, everyone was interested in conserving as much energy as possible. And the Asans only had one party a year. The rest of the time the neighborhood was quiet and peaceful.

Then Bill *really* got involved in coaching Tom. He put his arm around his friend, as a baseball manager would his pitcher.

"Tom, my boy, you gotta go prospecting for your most likely buyers, prepare what you want to say, move right into your presentation, target in on the house's good points, handle the buyer's objections, set up a trial close to test whether it's time to close the sale, and then if all goes well — wham! — you close."

Bill's wife couldn't believe her ears, but just smiled.

"You know what closing is, don't you?" he demanded.

"Sure," Tom replied, "that's what happens after everything is done and you get together and sign about a hundred pieces of paper. Then the house is sold."

Bill sighed and slapped his forehead.

"Tom, I think you need a crash course in the profession of salesmanship. Let's go out on the back porch."

****

Doctors, lawyers and salespeople.

Salespeople?

Some people aren't quite prepared for the third member of *that* series. Some may even reject it as nonsense. But closer examination reveals more elements in common than are immediately apparent. James Kirby, a former dean of Ohio State Law School, once defined a profession as a "learned pursuit performed for the public good." We have already seen that the salesperson performs his service for the good of customers; otherwise he is out of business, particularly in the agricultural field where repeat business is of paramount importance. Is it too far to stretch the imagination, then, to characterize selling as a "learned pursuit"?

Think about it. No one is born with the ability to sell; the salesperson learns over time what solutions will alleviate a given problem, what motivates people to behave in a certain way and what techniques will best communicate his product's usefulness in fulfilling people's needs. None of this is accidental or arbitrary. Successful selling requires careful, prolonged *study,* just as any profession does. Sometimes this study is done in a class or seminar room. Sometimes it's done on the farm or in a dealer's office in the "School of Hard Knocks." But it must be done.

A good way to see the relationship between selling and other professional pursuits is to examine more closely the elements that comprise each profession. If you dissect the aura that surrounds professionals, you will find that five factors generally contribute to that aura:

1. An accumulated body of knowledge
2. A generic language used by members of the profession
3. A structured, systematic method of procedure
4. A basis in scientific principles
5. An ascribed code of ethics

The existence of this book, and many others in the field of selling, is testimony to the fact that selling has an accumulated body of knowledge that can be written, studied and passed along from professional to professional. Some salespeople have made fortunes writing down tips and techniques to help their fellow salespeople; universities have become more and more aware of a need for courses in the academic discipline of selling; and the sum total of our knowledge is increased daily by those who distill their experience into more generalized principles.

Anyone who doubts the existence of a generic language among salespeople has only to try to interpret the conversation of two or three of them gathered together for the purpose of talking shop. As our lawyer friend Bill found, terms like "close" and "prospecting" have a meaning all their own to a salesperson, and only familiarity with the profession or its accumulated body of knowledge could convey all the specific shades of meaning they carry in a salesperson's vocabulary.

Salespeople as Professionals

Selling is Learned

ELEMENTS OF A PROFESSION

Body of Knowledge

Generic Language

Systematic Procedures   Contained within the salesperson's body of knowledge is a series of steps or procedures (with associated substeps and their procedures) that systematically capture the prospective buyer's attention and carry him through the entire sale. Again, salespeople have their own terms for each of these steps: words or phrases like "presentation," "handling objections" and "trial close." But they are *systematic,* they are necessary to the successful completion of the sale and they are part of a salesperson's professional technique. These procedures are described in detail in Section III.

Scientific Principles   Many people are surprised to learn that the art of selling is also based on scientific principles, namely, the principles of human behavorial science. Psychological theories of motivation, communication, buyer behavior, etc. play a large part in the salesperson's approach to each customer. Such scientific principles will be handled in detail in Section II.

Code of Ethics   One of the distinctly "professional" things about a profession is its adherence to a strict code of ethics, or member behavior. Lawyers, doctors and other professionals have their own review boards to ensure that members are also ethical practitioners of their profession. This is one of the areas in which salespeople have been most pointedly excluded from a professional status in some people's eyes; we have already pointed to the stereotype of the fast-talking, pushy, unethical salesperson as the culprit. But the fact is that the most successful and highly-regarded members of the selling profession are also the most ethical. A salesperson who does *not* practice ethical selling will soon be without customers. More specific information about ethics is contained in Chapter 3.

TYPES OF RESPONSI-BILITIES IN SELLING   The responsibilities of professional agribusiness salespeople tend to vary somewhat with the type of selling involved, the geographical area, the specifics of product or service, and the experience of the individual salesperson. However, most responsibilities of the profession can be broken down into either the direct or indirect kind. (See Figure 2.1.)

Figure 2.1 **Direct & Indirect Selling Responsibilities**	
DIRECT	INDIRECT
1. Prospecting	1. Handling complaints
2. Pre-call planning	2. Maintaining open communications
3. Attracting customer attention and interest	3. Market intelligence
4. Making presentations	4. Staying current on technical information
5. Handling objections	5. Handling complaints
6. Closing sales	6. Bill collection
	7. Keeping contact with experts
	8. Trade & Public Relations
	9. Paperwork
	10. Personalized Customer Service

The first and foremost function of the salesperson, and the one which people are most likely to associate with him, is that of direct selling. This involves prospecting for customers, pre-call planning, attracting the customer's attention and interest, making presentations, handling objections and closing the sale. Although all these steps seldom occur at one meeting (unless the salesperson is engaged in consumer or door-to-door sales), most will be part of the sales process over a period of time, whether they are handled in formal or informal ways. A purebred cattle breeder, for example, might work with a cattle farmer informally for several years before the farmer would actually feel the need to purchase a bull from the breeder. In such a case, most of the steps of the direct selling process will be so drawn-out and distorted that they would be virtually unrecognizable to the uninitiated.

Direct Responsibilities

Despite its relatively peripheral status in the selling process, indirect selling may take up more of the salesperson's time and effort than direct selling does. By "indirect selling" we generally mean all the service and follow-up functions performed for the customer by the agri salesperson. These include making sure the product is delivered on time and performs as expected, handling any complaints that might arise and maintaining open communications that will help ensure repeat business. Good seed salespeople know, for example, that the best time to sell next year's seed is during this year's growing and harvest season. There is no better time to discuss performance of varieties than when the salesperson is standing in the field with the grower talking about this year's crop prospects.

Indirect Responsibilities

A wide variety of other indirect selling activities are also the responsibility of the salesperson. These include market intelligence, staying current on technical information, maintaining good customer and public relations, processing paper work and providing a variety of personalized customer services.

Market intelligence is one of those selling responsibilities that is easy to overlook. Often it is not even formally acknowledged as a responsibility. But whether acknowledged or not, it is an integral task of the salesperson in the field. The expectation is that the salesperson will keep abreast of competitors' actions, prices, product performance, customers' moods, climate and crop conditions, and inventory levels. Some companies require a short written report of such factors each week. Since the salesperson *is* right there in the thick-of-things, he is the logical one to gather the information so invaluable to managers as they make far-reaching decisions in marketing, pricing, product planning etc.

Market Intelligence

Customers expect salespeople to be fully in tune with the products and services they sell. Often this requires a high degree of technical competence and product expertise, but in such cases the company normally provides intensive training to familiarize the salesperson with the product. For example, most agri chemical salespeople spend several days each year in "school" to stay current on changing technology and regulations etc. Often detailed product information notebooks accompany the salesperson in the field.

Technical Information

In some cases, salespeople will require additional education beyond high school to prepare them for technical selling jobs. Most salespeople who have been on the job for any length of time have acquired a storehouse of technical information from which to draw as they seek to answer the customer's questions and complete the sale.

Handling Complaints

Complaints are a normal part of selling, and often, customer dissatisfaction goes right back to the salesperson who sold it. Although this is seldom the most popular of the salesperson's responsibilities, most companies provide well-developed guidelines for handling complaints, so the salesperson is not alone in facing the dissatisfied customer. Some specific techniques for this aspect of indirect selling are contained in Section IV.

Bill Collection

The vast majority of customers pay their accounts on time, but there are always those few who are unable or unwilling to do so. Generally the salesperson has responsibility for at least the initial stages of collection; this usually gives him an appreciation for the need to extend credit sparingly. One account that stands uncollected can erase profits for the salesperson's entire region, so the importance of this responsibility is obvious. More details may be found in Section IV.

Keeping Contact with the Experts

Usually the salesperson is expected to maintain positive and productive contacts with county agents, university researchers and other opinion leaders in the area. Such people are not only pipelines to the most up-to-date information, but are very influential with some customers. Regular calls on such officials are in order.

Trade and Public Relations

To most people the salesperson *is* the company he represents. Thus, salespeople must always maintain an image that is consistent with the image of the company so that the general public will not become confused or misled. This is often accomplished through the salesperson's involvement in community activities: trade shows, exhibits, field plots, tests and education programs etc. Even the salesperson's conduct of personal and business affairs casts a reflection on his honesty and credibility as a salesperson. And salespeople must constantly keep this ''publicness'' in mind.

Paperwork

There's no getting around it: every salesperson's job contains some paperwork, budgeting and administrative duties. These may include a weekly report on activities, calls, market conditions etc.; order forms; inventory; and company surveys. Most salespeople prepare annual sales forecasts for their areas and make expense budget requests. At the very least, they will be required to file accurate expense statements based on meticulously kept records and/or receipts. More about this in Section IV.

Personalized Customer Service

Probably the single most time-consuming indirect selling activity is the kind of personalized customer service without which many sales would just never occur: the provision of technical advice, locating and transporting emergency supplies to help a farm customer, or advising a customer before an anticipated price increase etc. Long before the direct selling process has begun, and long after it has concluded, the salesperson is in there pitching — proving that his company can provide the service to make doing business with him worthwhile. Some specific customer services are discussed in detail in Section IV.

Predictably, the kinds of selling that can occur in agribusiness are varied, depending upon such factors as the industry and the individual firm's own structure and philosophy. Yet, selling can generally be classified according to the level of the customer within the market system.

CUSTOMERS ARE MANY AND VARIED

Manufacturing and processing firms typically take raw materials and manufactured inputs and convert them to products that can be used by farmers, ranchers, growers, producers, and even in some cases, the final consumer. Often they develop the industrial inputs used in the manufacturing of agricultural products. Feed manufacturing firms, meat packers and seed processing companies are examples of firms specializing in agricultural products. A specialty equipment manufacturing company producing automatic poultry feeding equipment uses salespeople who have a strong background in agricultural mechanics, animal science and general agriculture. This is because such salespeople usually deal with large specialized poultry producers, so they must be well-versed in the technical aspects of the field. Four years or more of higher education in poultry science or general agriculture is a common requirement for salespeople in this kind of field.

Manufacturer and Processing Firms

Salespeople in the manufacturing and processing area usually cover a wide area, some as large as several states, and they may travel by plane to save time. Sales are typically few and far between, but they are very large when they do occur. Because of the magnitude of the sale, the salesperson generally calls frequently to service the account and maintain the relationship.

The salesperson who sells to agricultural wholesalers and distributors usually travels a smaller geographical area where sales calls are reasonably regular. Contacts are also made through trade shows and conventions, where he may set up exhibits and displays. Salespeople who sell to distributors or wholesalers (who in turn move the product to retailers or farmers) usually work with the buying agents who place the orders, but spend much of their time with dealers and end users. They are usually expected to channel all field orders through an appropriate distributor and, in some cases, may never really take an order personally. All orders would then move directly from the buying agent to the manufacturing plant. Such salespeople often work out of their own homes and travel for only about one or two nights at a time.

Wholesaler/ Distributors

Agricultural pesticide distributors are an example of a wholesaler distribution system that sells to retailers. Pesticides are then re-sold directly to farmers. In some cases, the manufacturer may sell directly to the retailer,

Retailers

thus skipping a step in the process. In either case, salespeople must call on retailers fairly frequently and develop a close personal relationship working with the retailer to service the farm customer. Often they help the dealer sponsor local promotional programs, develop advertising materials, train new salespeople in technical areas and troubleshoot product complaints with customers.

Usually these salespeople cover a small geographical area from their own home offices, and report to supervisors who may be a hundred miles or more away.

In the case of large manufacturing companies that own their own retail outlets, the outlets are usually serviced or supervised by representatives of the parent company who serve a function similar to that of a salesperson except that the supervisor has more authority and concentrates on management issues as well as sales and marketing. The same is true of regional agricultural supply cooperatives, where the regional cooperative representatives assist local cooperatives in much the same way as a salesperson assists a retailer.

Farmers/ Ranchers   Selling directly to farmers is to many salespeople the ultimate in agri selling. Many find this job has distinct advantages, particularly for those who wish to remain rooted in one community and exercise little mobility. The close contact with farmers in a local area produces a closeness to farming itself. For this reason, most salespeople at this level have a strong farm background. Even those without such a background must develop a sensitivity to farm problems relevant to the product or service being sold. The salesperson at this level develops close long-term relationships with customers, sometimes for an entire professional lifetime.

The salesperson can expect to spend nights away from home very rarely. If he has access to a company vehicle, it is often a pickup truck. Long hours are demanded during the peak selling season, which depends on the product being sold.

Final Consumers   Lawn and garden shops, produce farms etc., are places where the salesperson conducts business directly with the non-farm consumer. In most cases, the consumer arrives at the business to buy much as he would at any retail store.

The main requirement for successful selling in this area is a strong technical and practical knowledge of the product. Demand is often seasonal, but within that framework hours are more or less regular (depending on the customer's needs). This is the area of involvement for those who wish to deal directly with the situations and problems of the average consumer.

SUMMARY   * Sales can be defined as a profession because it possesses the five necessary descriptive factors: a body of knowledge, a generic language, a systematic method of procedure, a basis in scientific principles and a code of ethics.
* The direct responsibility of salespeople is the selling of products and services.

* Indirect responsibilities include the service and followup functions: market intelligence, technical information, handling complaints, bill collection, keeping in contact with experts, nurturing trade and public relationships, completing paperwork and providing personalized service.

* Agri salespersons cater to many customers: manufacturing and processing firms, wholesaler/distributors, retailers, agricultural producers and consumers.

---

1. Name the five characteristics of a "professional." Why do some salespeople have "bad reputations"? What can be done to improve that reputation?

2. Which is more important, the "direct" or "indirect" selling responsibility? Why?

3. What are some of the "indirect" selling activities?

4. What is market intelligence and what are some ways an agri salesperson can provide it?

5. What levels of customers exist in agri selling? How does the salesperson's activities vary among them?

6. What responsibilities might a manufacturer's representative have who sells through distributors?

7. What is the meaning of "Personalized Customer Service"? Why does it have an effect on sales?

**Review Questions
Chapter 2**

Chapter Three
The Professional

*"A real professional is an individual who has the vital characteristics,
and who is always trying to improve"*

It was summer again, and all the salespeople from Midsouth Chemical Supply were gathering in Memphis for their annual golf outing. Most of them couldn't resist regaling each other with tales of recent victories and industry gossip. A 12000-acre plantation manager who'd come around after weeks of wooing; a manufacturer whose top selling cotton defoliant had been knocked off the market by a new EPA ruling only one day before the meeting were prime topics of conversation.

Burt Springstead was one of the best known among the sales force. He was a likeable guy from northern Mississippi who loved his work and loved to talk about his latest conquest in minute detail no matter how big or small. Funny part was, everyone loved to listen, mostly because of the way he embellished his stories with humor. Too, his sales record demanded the respect of his peers. Like Burt always said, "If you done it, it ain't braggin!"

Burt, exuberant as ever, was walking the floor, drink in hand, looking for an audience when he spotted Jim Warner.

"Uh-oh," called Jim, "looks like old Burt's back again, achin' for someone to crow to."

A slow smile spread across Burt's face as he made his way to Jim's table. Ignoring the general chorus of groans all around, he launched into his latest war story.

"Yep, Jim, really got something to crow about this time. I just heard from the head office that Morgan Brothers just came through." He paused long enough to look around the table, building up the suspense. "One hundred thousand dollars worth of our new private label CD-14, for immediate delivery to the Morgan Brothers Farm Supply stores. I've been calling on those guys for years, but never been able to get much except some specialty chemicals."

His colleagues were suitably impressed. "Say, Burt, isn't that the outfit that's been dealing exclusively with National Chem for years?" asked Hal, aware that he was fueling Burt's fire but unable to resist.

"That's right, Hal, they *used* to deal exclusively with National Chem and they've avoided private label like the plague! That's when I stopped by to see Phil Morgan, as I've been doing regularly for at least five years — but never done much with him except to fill in a few gaps. I could see right away that something was wrong. Here I was in their warehouse, a showplace that draws farmers and applicators from all over the area, and half the shelf space in the pesticide section was bare. Oh sure, they could have been restocking; but I'd heard some rumors they were having some delivery problems on some cotton insecticides, and it's not peak season yet. One look at Phil's face and I was pretty sure something was wrong. So I played a hunch and probed for information.

" 'What's the matter, Phil?' says I, 'your best man quit on ya?' Now Phil could have taken offense at that, 'cause I was implying he wasn't managing too good. But I noticed before that Phil's sort of wrapped up in the business and likely to appreciate it when someone takes time to notice that he's got troubles. I must have touched a nerve or something, because he seemed relieved to talk about it.

" 'Ah, Burt, running a business gets harder every year. I'm getting a little too old for it,' says he, waving his arm around like he's captain of a sinking ship. So of course, if I had an ounce of sympathy I would have sat down and cried into his coffee with him, right? I could have even told him how I'm getting too old for this racket too. But then all we would have had was watery coffee and the same old problem, right? So I figured I'd give my hunch a fair chance.

" 'Your problems got anything to do with those empty pallets over there?' says I, casual as you please, nodding just a little in the direction of the cotton insecticide area. Well, he hesitated a second — I could see he was deciding whether to open up — and then he caved in.

" 'Oh well, Burt, I might as well tell you,' he says. 'I got a shipment from National Chem that's already two weeks overdue and I have no idea when it'll be shipped. I keep calling and they keep stalling me — my regular salesman's on vacation or some damn thing — so the sales manager called instead. But I think he must be new or something because he told me there's some kind of mixup in their credit and accounting department he can't quite figure out.' Phil was getting more and more indignant the more he thought about it. I could see that, so I kept my cool and just kept repeating what he said, dumbfounded-like, like I never heard anything so incredible in my life.

" 'Oh, yes, that's right,' he tells me, practically shouting, 'I never had a late bill with them in my life, I always pay them on time, and now I have practically no cotton insecticide because of some stupid computer foulup. So here I am with peak season coming and no idea when the mixup's gonna be straightened out. I've threatened, complained and threatened again. It's sickening, I tell you, nobody does business the way they used to. Nobody has the pride.'

" 'Well,' says I, 'I've heard some strange things in my life but nothing quite as strange as that. Anybody who's done business with you knows that you're solid. We reconfirmed that when your financial report went through our credit check this spring. You take pride in dealing honestly with people.' With important accounts I always stay personally involved to make sure there aren't any foulups. That's the way to handle a big operation who trusts you with a lot of their business.

"I stopped for a minute to let it sink in. Then I acted like the idea just hit me. 'Say, Phil, you know I could get you some interim supplies while you're sitting here losing business with your warehouse empty. Can't have those air applicators going to your competitors can we? In fact, I could get deliveries to your other stores within 36 hours, and if your problem with National Chem isn't cleared up right away, I'd be happy to give you whatever you need to keep going. I think your customers will be more than satisfied with our private label and they'll love the price. In fact, if you like our service — and I think you will — we can talk about keeping a good thing going. What do you say?'

"Well, to make a long story short, I worked like a maniac for the next two days making sure all stores got deliveries. Phil Morgan was definitely impressed. In fact, he called me the day before yesterday to tell me that his shelves were nearly bare again — but this time it's because the product is moving! So far it's the only product line he's taken, but if we can keep it up, well it stands to reason that we're in big.

"I don't know about you guys," Burt chuckled, "But I always get all choked up at a happy ending."

****

In the previous chapter we saw how selling rates the title of "profession." Since it follows that the practitioners of a profession are professionals, let's take some time getting acquainted with the selling professional: the characteristics that make him successful, limits that govern his conduct, the rewards and disadvantages he can expect, and the formal support systems to which he can turn in times of trouble.

PROFILE OF A PROFESSIONAL

Characteristics for Success   Despite the fact that selling is a learned pursuit, it has been demonstrated time and time again that certain personal characteristics lend an invaluable boost to the salesperson's efforts. Among these are the characteristics most of us associate with the field: determination and desire, self-motivation, intelligence, articulateness, a neat appearance, an ability to deal with people, honesty and a genuine enthusiasm about whatever they are doing. In addition, recent research indicates that we should explore two other, less apparent qualities in selling: empathy and ego drive.

Determination   Among the most common traits of successful salespeople are determination and desire, which comprise the salesperson's wholehearted commitment to reach the set objective. Although technique is important, a strong mix of determination, desire and hard work has been known to overcome serious deficiencies in technique. Without the determination to sell, the salesperson won't have the concentration and motivation to keep on plugging.

Self-Motivation   Most salespeople work without close supervision on a day-to-day basis. This is both a blessing and a curse; it offers the salesperson freedom from "punching a clock," and allows him to be his own boss, but it leaves a gap in discipline. Self-motivation fills that gap. It offers the salesperson a way to meet the objectives he is determined to meet, through the development of his own self-discipline. This involves everything from getting out of bed on time in the morning to pushing yourself to make that one more call when you really feel like packing it in for a day. It is up to the salesperson to set himself on a course that will help him realize his fully internalized objective.

Intelligence   Garden-variety intelligence — the kind of commonsense qualities that help us get through the day — is indispensable to the salesperson. No form of agri selling is immune from the need for problem-solving skills: analysis, synthesis, logical decision-making etc. Sensing when to pitch in and give a farm customer a hand in finishing up the chores can give the sales call a big boost. And knowing when to say hello and leave immediately can be just as important.

Articulateness   Salespeople have to be able to communicate clearly to others in order to get their ideas across. This does not necessarily mean that all successful salespeople must be speech contest winners, but they must have the simple ability to hear what the customer is saying and be able to say what they mean so that it is understood. Excellent grammar is not a necessity for successful selling, although poor grammar can distract the customer and hurt credibility. (See Chapter 6 for more about communication.)

Appearance   Sometimes salespeople get "hung up" on the fact that they are judged "unfairly" by their appearance. Clothes, it is argued, do not make the man (or woman). But whether or not is is fair, salespeople and their products or services are often judged by appearance, so a strong effort must be made to create a good impression. Following the latest fashions or fads is not always necessary or even desirable; you should strive to match your dress to the occasion and to the community standards and be clean and well-groomed. If nothing else, this shows the customer that you have some respect for him and are willing to make an effort to keep from offending his tastes.

Diplomacy

It's no secret that selling involves dealing with people. It's also no secret that there are many different kinds of people out there, with many different personality quirks and quite a variety of perspectives and value systems. While it's natural for anybody to like some personality types better than others, the successful salesperson must be at least comfortable when dealing with many different types. And to enjoy the entire spectrum of personality types makes things a lot easier.

Honesty

"Honesty" is something of a catchall phrase that involves everything from ethical selling practices to dependability in service. The key is to have a sense of integrity and reliability that is in tune with the expectations of your particular clientele, and to keep your forthright image foremost in the public eye. What much of this comes down to is: Can you be trusted to follow through on your word? Honesty also means not shading the truth or withholding information that the customer should know, even when it might be more comfortable or more to your selfish interest to let the customer's thinking mislead him. This kind of honesty is the foundation of solid long-term relationships.

Enthusiasm

Probably nothing is so essential in the race for the sale as enthusiasm: it spreads like wildfire from salesperson to customer (in fact, the only thing that even comes close to being as contagious is its opposite, apathy). But don't be fooled by the word; enthusiasm doesn't necessarily imply or require outlandish extremes in behavior. In fact, arm-waving, backslapping, and fast-talk may send up red flags. Quiet, open sincerity will often encourage belief in your product more convincingly than anything else. Customers are often experts at perceiving your true feelings for your product and service; and since you're the expert, they will take their clue from you in forming an attitude toward what you have to offer.

Empathy and Ego Drive

What is it that distinguished Burt Springstead's efforts from those of a less alert, less successful salesperson? Many different aspects of Burt's approach could be analyzed, but two factors stand out: empathy and ego drive. Empathy is the ability to read signs and clues in such a way that you see and understand whatever another person is feeling, without becoming so emotionally involved that you take on those same feelings or that your judgment is impaired. Ego drive, on the other hand, relates to the need to perform because of the way it makes you feel about yourself, regardless of any external rewards that may also be involved (such as a commission).

In a survey reported in the *Harvard Business Review*, marketing researchers David Mayer and Herbert M. Greenberg concluded unequivocally that the single most important determinant of sales ability was a proper balance

---

[1]Jeanne Greenberg and Herbert M. Greenberg, "Job Matching for Better Sales Performance," Harvard Business Review, October, 1980.

of empathy and ego drive. Incredible as it may sound, these two seemingly opposite qualities are both necessary for effective selling; that is they actually reinforce each other.

There is a rather simple explanation for this: the virtues of either quality, when left unchecked, tend to become excessive and tip the scales away from the sale. Thus the salesperson who has plenty of empathy, but very little ego drive to counterbalance it, tends not to use his empathy persuasively. He understands what the prospect is going through, and may even know how to use that understanding to close the sale, but he simply isn't motivated to do it. If Burt Springstead had sat down and sympathized with Phil Morgan — "crying into his coffee" with him — and had very little ego drive, he might have said to himself, "This guy has enough troubles. This isn't the time to try to make a sale."

Conversely, the salesperson with a well-developed ego drive but very little empathy will have trouble making sales because he will miss many of the clues that the customer is sending about his true needs and concerns. This kind of salesperson tends to push his way through no matter what the customer's objections, because all he is concerned with is his own need to close the sale to prove that he can be successfully persuasive. If Burt Springstead had lacked empathy, he probably wouldn't have noticed that Phil Morgan looked a bit peaked and, consequently, wouldn't have expressed concern. Burt wouldn't have noticed that Phil needed to blow off steam, so he might have not probed — tactfully — about the problem, or listened intently to the problems with National Chem. Nor would he have discerned and responded to one of Phil's primary underlying concerns: the insulting implication (as Phil perceived) that his credit rating wasn't all that it should be, and that National Chem had become a big impersonal company where the customer had become a number in a computer.

The interplay of these two forces in selling could be discussed forever; but perhaps it makes more sense to examine each in more detail.

Empathy Examined   Empathy is a concept that first arrived on the scene courtesy of the psychology field. It is a staggeringly effective tool of communication, not only because it makes the person who possesses it more vividly aware of everyone around him, but because it enables others to feel that their innermost needs and concerns are of great importance to somebody. You can always tell the difference between empathy and sympathy by the degree of involvement; a sympathetic person identifies so closely with others that the boundaries between his identity and theirs are indistinct. An empathetic person, on the other hand, is able to understand and care while still retaining what might be called a respectful distance. He's the one who keeps his head long enough to help the friend or customer in trouble, instead of wringing his hands as he verifies Chicken Little's reports that the sky is falling.

This kind of understanding, as we've already indicated in passing, almost always involves reading signs or clues that the customer may give about his true feelings, either intentionally or unintentionally. Listening is truly an art to be cultivated in selling the customers. You've got to hear the words loud and clear, and also understand where the words are coming from. Each of us tends to perceive the universe through a unique filter that colors what we see on the basis of past experience, ingrained habits and attitudes etc. (more on this in Chapter 6). Not only do we have to set aside the prejudices and preconceptions that our own filter may provide in order to accurately perceive someone else's (not always an easy task for salespeople, who tend to be somewhat self-oriented); but then we have to accurately read all the influences that filter the other person's perspective.

Apart from listening to all the nuances of the words themselves, we have to be able to read the telling gesture or expression: a frown, a careworn face, fingers drumming a table absentmindedly (or is it impatiently?) etc.

The trick is to communicate your empathy, genuinely and sincerely, without going overboard. It's a good idea to use phrases like "I can certainly understand that" or "I appreciate your concern"; but it's not necessary to go into intimate details about your own problems or situation, no matter how similar. The idea is to make the customer feel that his needs and situation are of paramount concern.

Remember too, that you may recognize the empathy welling up inside you, but unless it's equally apparent to the customer, you may come close to winning them over - but fail. Work on making your empathy more obvious.

In case you've ever wondered, the need for empathy in selling is one of the chief reasons why agri salespeople are often required to come from a farm background. Apart from the obvious benefits of increased technical expertise, salespeople with such background tend to have an instinctive knowledge of how the farmer feels, and so, can get "inside" the farmer.

Ego Drive Defined

What is this amazing phenomenon called ego drive, which can be so productive when balanced by the humanness of empathy and so destructive when not? Ego drive has often been given a black eye in discussions of selling because it has been unfairly confused with such categories of motivation as ambition, greed and lust for power. It is simply (in terms of our discussion) a need to close the sale, to get the business, to achieve, because this will produce a strong improvement in self-image. The Burt Springsteads of the world view selling as something of a game, with the customer a prey to be bagged to show their prowess, even as they react empathetically to the customer's concerns. And because failure is a frequent companion in the selling profession, salespeople cannot be too thin-skinned about unsuccessful sales, else they will dry up and brood about lost opportunities instead of getting out there and selling to the next guy. As Mayer and Greenberg point out, the salesperson needs not only the correct balance of empathy and ego drive to sell well, but "a subtle balance" of forces within the ego itself: the ego must be strong enough to withstand frequent failure while being just weak enough to need the reinforcement of the sale. Truly then, the salesperson walks all kinds of tightropes; it should be more and more apparent that this agri salesperson is indeed a professional, and an extremely complicated one at that.

Ethics and Sales: A Match Made in Heaven

One of the most misleading myths about salespeople — and the most damaging to their status as professionals — is the assumption on the part of many that salespeople's best interests stand in direct contradiction to those of their customers. Thus, far from relating to each other from adversary standpoints, salesperson and customer actually work together to some extent to build the kind of relationship that will withstand the test of time.

Obviously, there is no place in a professional relationship of this nature for anything but the most ethical and aboveboard conduct. The trouble is, everybody has a different concept of ethical conduct, because we all offer highly individual interpretations of right and wrong, just and unjust, as well as different versions of actual events. Consequently a somewhat more formalized code is needed to guide salespeople as they attempt to deal with customers ethically. Although no code can provide salespeople with the day-to-day nitty-gritty details necessary for all their decisions, we will attempt to suggest an ethical framework for agri salespeople in reference to their responsibilities with the customer, the agribusiness employer, the competition, the public and with themselves.

Ethical Responsibility to the Customer

The first responsibility to the customer is to continually serve his best interests in, with and through the products and services you represent. Though a short-term gain can be made by selling a customer a product that is inferior or not quite appropriate, the tenor of your long-term relationship will be much improved if you stick to the high road.

One of the most frequently asked questions in the realm of sales ethics is: "What should I do if my competitor's product will fill the customer's need better or less expensively than my product?" The fact is that you are obligated only to show how your own products can honestly benefit the customer, not how another company's can benefit him. In fact, a case could even be made that ethical responsibility to your own firm demands that you simply deal with selling your own products and services, and leave the competitor's selling to him. Nor does the salesperson bear responsibility for making the customer's choices for him. Ethically speaking, the salesperson must provide the customer with information geared to that customer's level of understanding and interest, so that the customer will be in a position to appreciate the benefits of the product or service thoroughly and realistically.

In every case, a major difference between the competitive alternatives is the salesperson himself and the personalized service he can provide to the customer. It is very often true that this personal difference far outweighs minor price or quality disadvantages. It usually boils down to a judgment call where only the customer can weigh how important each of the attributes are in the total package being considered.

A second responsibility to the customer — and one that is tied to the first — is to refrain from the temptation to misrepresent the product or service. Overzealous promotion can sometimes lead to falsely high levels of expectation, particularly since the customer often wishes to believe that there is a magical, cheap, one-shot solution to all his troubles. The professional farm equipment salesperson who wishes to maintain the highest standards of ethical conduct may even find himself in the unusual situation of having to "unsell" the farmer who has become convinced that he will never again have to deal with a broken belt in harvest season, thanks to the magical properties of the salesperson's new harvester.

The third and final ethical responsibility to the customer, is to protect confidences and to avoid any form of unauthorized or illegal "incentives" in selling to him. Although an off-the-cuff comment to one customer about a recent disclosure made by another customer may seem innocuous to you, it may cause embarrassment or even harm both financially or personally to the customer who initially made the disclosure.

Needless to say, kickbacks (while uncommon in agriculture anyway) are totally to be avoided. Special treatment and favors outside the normal scope of service are also to be shunned, since they are both unethical, and ultimately counterproductive, because they soon get built into the normal level of expectations by customers.

Other Ethical Considerations

Sometimes it is very difficult to maintain absolute loyalty to the firm you represent. A close and frequent relationship with customers in the field builds close ties and friendships. Occasionally you may find yourself in the kind of situation where a billing or shipping problem is causing your customers and you problems. Or, your company has just announced another price increase — the third this year. In these cases, it's very tempting to lay the blame at the feet of "them." But don't do it; it's as unethical as it is ultimately destructive to your selling effort. Instead, always refer to your own organization as "we" when explaining situations. Despite the close relationships you may have carefully forged with your customers, you must remain loyal to the company when any conflict arises. In the event that proves impossible, and you cannot in good conscience support the policies of the company, there is one ethical response and one alone: resign.

The first ethical obligation to competitors is to have a healthy respect for the competitor's good name. This means not bad-mouthing his products or services (a procedure from which, incidentally, little is ever gained, since you make him the underdog — and all the world roots for the underdog). Make your sales on the merits of your own product, not on the demerits of another's. However, do not ignore the competition; be knowledgeable about their products and services without feeling compelled to criticize. Be ready to promote your relative strengths but slow to put a competitor down.

The salesperson also has a responsibility to his company to willingly participate in the total marketing strategy of his organization. This involves collecting and reporting market intelligence, developing sales forecasts, taking inventory and making special reports when called on. The tendency to increase sales by giving price concessions or other special considerations should be avoided. Anybody can sell by cutting prices, but true professionals recognize that maintaining a fair price is a fundamental responsibility. That is, their responsibility is not just to generate sales, but to generate profitable sales.

Finally, a sense of responsibility to the marketplace demands that you be informed about and uphold legal restrictions and regulations, however, they may complicate your job. If you do not vigorously uphold legal regulations, you are gambling with very high stakes — for yourself and for your company. Today the costs of improper recommendations, illegal price discussions, or delivering the wrong product can literally bankrupt a company. This is nothing to experiment with; get the facts and follow the rules scrupulously.

Responsibility to self requires that you work consistently to upgrade your professional selling skills and technical ability, regardless of the day-to-day demands of the job itself. Professional growth throughout your career will make you both more effective and more efficient, so that your self-image will be enhanced. Growth and advancement are important to your professional satisifaction, therefore ultimately to your happiness.

A more difficult ethical responsibility to self involves conducting your personal life so that it does not have unpleasant repercussions on your professional life. Many would contend that the salesperson's personal time is his own, and that if he wants to go out carousing in the wee hours of the morning, it is no one else's business. But because customers perceive the salesperson as representative of the company itself, this contention is seldom realistic. A true professional recognizes that, however unfairly, he must take responsibility for the effect his behavior and image has on his selling success, and must therefore guard against the appearance of impropriety.

The salesperson's final personal obligation is to represent himself in a way that is at all times professional, a way that will enhance the stature of agri selling. The salesperson himself, as well as his colleagues, will benefit from a truly professional status.

There are those who say that the time has come to organize professional agri salespeople in a way that will enable a code of ethics to be widely publicized and heeded. This would indeed be a step forward. When agri salespeople publicly acknowledge their adherence to a high standard of conduct, the stature of the agri selling professional will be enhanced from coast-to-coast.

REWARDING EXPERIENCE OF SALES

Generally speaking, those who enter sales are quite aware of the kinds of rewards that selling offers and are eager to receive them. Occasionally, a starry-eyed newcomer will eagerly anticipate the rewards without also considering the disadvantages of being an agri selling professional. Here we'll attempt to present both sides of the coin, with the understanding that we're likely to consider the pros more important than the cons.

Professional

The professional rewards of selling generally fall into two categories: financial and advancement opportunities.

Financial

Because selling is the "heartbeat" activity of any business — which is to say that it generates revenues directly, unlike some of the support activities — professional salespeople can expect to take home a solid paycheck, especially when they are at their most productive levels. Starting salaries in the field are particularly good when the beginning salesperson is a graduate of a university, college, or technical agricultural program, and exhibits an academic and work history that indicates such traits as leadership, ability to deal with people and agricultural experience. When a firm is seeking to hire a more experienced salesperson, past performance is generally a reliable indicator of financial renumeration.

And since motivation is a necessity in accomplishing the selling task, many firms find it useful to offer some kind of direct financial incentive, usually either a flat commission on each sale or an end-of-year bonus that is based on sales performance or company profits over the last 12 months. Many salespeople find these incentive programs appealing because they constitute a direct reward for successful efforts. However, sometimes such a program is difficult to set up; for instance, when the salesperson primarily assists dealers as they buy through a distributor, a common happenstance in agricultural chemical companies. In these cases, salespeople can expect to earn a straight salary, with all increases merited by a supervisor's evaluation. There may also be some profit-sharing incentives at the end of the year. But the point is that in almost every instance, the financial rewards are commensurate with performance — a state of affairs that many in other professions might well envy.

Advancement

Traditionally, salespeople have tended to view sales primarily as the first "dues-paying" step in a continuum leading to more "important" jobs. This attitude is disappearing somewhat, partially because more people are realizing the intrinsic worth of a sales career, and partially because firms are responding to the challenge to keep good salespeople happy by building several levels of seniority into their field sales force structure — which allows for both more status and more financial rewards even while remaining in the same local market area throughout their professional career.

The aggressive, productive and effective salesperson can move on to more and more responsible sales-related positions should they desire to do so. At first this may simply mean an increase in sales territory, or more crucial customers. But it may eventually include a move into sales management: supervising new salespeople. In the larger firms, advancement is usually well mapped out, with geographical relocations accompanying at least some of the steps. In local companies, by contrast, the chance for professional growth is less measurable, and tied to such things as increased respect (in the firm and in the community); broader market penetration; additional responsibilities within the company; and close, well-established relationships with customers.

Nor is it unheard of for successful experience in professional selling to lead to opportunities for success in the broader field of general management, or elsewhere in the business. Because sales are the heartbeat of the business, many firms put a premium on field-selling experience. In fact, some agricultural firms (particularly those in marketing) require field selling experience for important management posts, with the exception of those in the technical field. Therefore, field selling often is a good steppingstone into staff and line management, if that is your ultimate aim.

Personal Rewards

The dyed-in-the-wool professional salesperson is apt to contend that the single greatest reward from selling is personal satisfaction. Such a salesperson usually believes strongly in the kind of lifestyle he associates with his job. He enjoys immense satisfaction from meeting the challenges of making a sale. When he sees a satisfied customer or takes home a paycheck, he views it not only as his daily bread, but as tangible evidence that he has done a good job. Flexible schedules, independence to organize their own operations in the ways that suit their own individual styles, and their self-image as managers of their own sales territories, all contribute to salespeople's enchantment with the personal rewards of a selling career.

Not to be overlooked are the close personal friendships that salespeople develop with customers over time. Salespeople often receive a great deal of satisfaction out of helping their customers solve a critical problem in an area that relates to company business — the best of both worlds. And to be looked up to as an expert in their own field of agribusiness is an ego-building experience. Salespeople also like meeting and dealing with a wide spectrum of people: their interest in the human race is legendary. Perhaps most important of all in the area of personal "return on investment" in agri selling is the opportunity to work closely with agriculture, and all the good things that implies.

Disadvantages of the Profession

None of this is to say that all is milk and honey in the agri seller's land. Make no mistake about it, agri salespeople have to contend with some factors that are widely seen as disadvantages.

Rejection is a major part of the job. Let's face it, any salesperson who closes even one-fourth of the new prospects he calls on would be considered a miracle worker. Few of us find it pleasant to be told "no." You may invest a great deal of time, thought and sweat into a sales presentation — and then see it rejected out of hand by six prospects in a row!

Then there are complaints: the only thing worse than having them is not having them, because if you don't have them, it means you aren't selling anything. The hours are often punishing especially in peak season. And because every minute of the day doesn't have to be accounted for to someone, all motivation has to be self-induced; a very difficult proposition indeed when all is not going smoothly. Though salespeople generally work with many people, they are often geographically isolated from other salespeople in their own company, and even from those to whom they report. Consequently, the salesperson may begin to feel after awhile that he faces the world all by himself.

So you can see that one's decision about how "good" the selling professional's job is depends on one's innate preferences as to activities, rewards and disadvantages. It is, however, abundantly clear that the public's negative stereotype is far from warranted, particularly in agri selling.

SUPPORT MECHANISMS FOR SALES

When it comes to the individual sale, the salesperson may feel very much alone. But in the larger picture, he is supported by what sometimes seems a cast of thousands who are ready, willing and able to give him the ammunition he needs to close that sale and satisfy that customer. Just as the salesperson wishes to be recognized as a professional, he must respect the professionalism of the team of specialists who ensure an effective marketing program for the agribusiness. The number of specialists involved may vary with the size of the company and the nature of its business — from only a few to several hundred — but the need for a good two-way relationship with support staff cannot be overstressed.

Supervisors are the most common, and possibly the most helpful, of all **Supervisors** sales support personnel. They supervise a specific geographical district carrying such titles as "district manager" and "sales manager," and work closely with the salespeople in that district to ensure sales success there. Salespeople usually maintain fairly regular contact with their supervisors — at least once a week, and more if the occasion for a consultation arises. This contact is often by phone with face-to-face contact less frequent.

The supervisor generally works more closely with new salespeople, especially in the very early months. Close contact between supervisor and salesperson during this early training phase usually involves the passing along of specific procedures and product information, as well as a few days in the field introducing the new salesperson to regular customers and providing tips on selling methods and skills. The supervisor is ultimately accountable for success in his district, so he is almost always anxious to be as supportive and helpful to his salespeople as possible. He is the direct pipeline to the company, and so must be treated respectfully.

The existence of this book is testimony to the fact that formal training in **Training** selling skills is becoming more widespread. Sometimes such training is ac- **Programs** complished through self-study materials that companies may pass along to new salespeople — product information, general company orientation, fundamental selling tips etc. — while at other times the company may devote a few days or weeks at headquarters to such basics before sending new salespeople off to the field. It is useful to remember, however, that nearly all companies expect on-the-job training to be the core of their training program.

But more and more companies are also recognizing the value of regular periodic training even for their more experienced sales staff. Some have professional company trainers or outside consultants to provide useful brushups on skills and techniques.

Whenever customers have a special problem that is beyond the scope of a salesperson's expertise, the salesperson can count on technologists from the home or regional office to act as troubleshooters. Most farm equipment companies, for example, assign agricultural engineers to this task, while the equivalent in an agricultural chemical company might be the entomologist or agronomist. Likewise, when a cattle feeder is grappling with problems of slow rate of gain, he can count on his feed salesperson to bring in the feed nutritionist when necessary to help determine any nutrition problem.

The salesperson's job is made easier when the customer's awareness of **Advertising** products and services has been sparked by a company advertising and promotion campaign. This is true in the case of both national and local campaigns. In some agricultural industries, such as animal health products, the advertising department even personalizes its copy to fit individual dealers, and then runs the copy in the dealer's local newspaper. In such cases the parent company may split the cost of local advertising with the dealer, but whoever foots the bill, the ultimate winner is the salesperson whose job is made easier.

Marketing   The marketing department often aids the selling process by developing special incentives and programs that the salesperson can use to enhance the desirability of the product or service in the customer's eyes. The seed industry often develops travel incentive programs while other manufacturers tend to stick to special discounts on early orders and other price incentives to generate business. Where customers earn trips to exotic resorts from manufacturers, it is common for salespeople to accompany their customers — an incentive for the salesperson as well as for the customer and provides the opportunity for the salesperson to further develop relationships with key customers.

Indirect support for the selling effort may come through efforts of the research and development team, who hopefully develop saleable products and services for the salesperson to sell. The better their job, the easier the job for the salesperson. The research department that develops a superior new variety of wheat can make the seed salesperson's job far easier.

Credit   The credit department has the responsibility for insuring "collectable" sales. The salesperson can make the mistake of viewing this department as more of an obstacle than a help. Yet because the sale has not been completed until the money is in hand, the credit department often saves the salesperson from unnecessary headaches. One uncollectable bad debt can cancel out all the profit made from dozens, perhaps hundreds, of sales, so follow your credit department's credit approval guidelines carefully.

Outside Agencies   Besides the internal support services offered for salespeople, there are outside agencies that can be tapped by an alert and dedicated professional for information, problem-solving techniques, or other sales support. These agencies include universities, the various trade presses, government agencies, the cooperative extension service, and even dealers or customers themselves. (One customer may just have solved a low rate of gain problem that can provide the solution for another cattle feeder in your area — with you as the catalyst.) Most salespeople in the agricultural field use all these sources at one time or another in their career, so become familiar with them and learn how to get the most out of them.

What we've attempted in this chapter is to portray the major facets of the selling professional's world. In the next section we'll move on from the salesperson to the customer: what motivates him, why and how he buys, and what the salesperson must do to keep the lines of communication open.

* A successful salesperson has characteristics which ensure his effectiveness: determination, self-motivation, intelligence, articulateness, neat appearance, diplomacy, honesty, enthusiasm, empathy and ego drive.

* Empathy can be defined as the ability to understand what a person is feeling without becoming emotionally involved. Ego drive relates to the personal need of a salesperson to perform because of his attitude about himself, despite external rewards. The two attributes combined in the correct proportions make way for the accurate gauging of a customer's need.

* The presence of unethical sales practices has earned a tarnished image for some salespeople. The sales industry has not adopted a formal code of ethics. Yet each person owes it to himself to keep in mind these considerations: honesty and considering the customer's best interests along with keeping confidences and avoiding unethical sales approaches. An ethical salesperson should also respect his competitors, be well-versed in legal restrictions and regulations, and devote himself to represent the company and product in the proper way.

* Sales contains positive and negative aspects. The rewards may be defined as financial, advancement and personal, while the negatives may be discouragement and handling rejection and complaints.

* The salesperson usually doesn't have to shoulder the sales burden alone. Supervisors, training programs to increase effectiveness and advertising to promote the product or service all help. Other aids may include an effective credit department, marketing department and outside agencies.

SUMMARY

---

1. List the characteristics that make a successful salesperson.

2. Define empathy and ego drive. What is the result when either characteristic is in excess?

3. What are the salesperson's ethical responsibilities to a customer? To his company?

4. What are the two types of rewards that await a salesperson? Is sales considered a "lifetime" career or a "stepping stone" to a more advanced position?

5. What is the role of the supervisor in the sales process?

6. How important are the "support" groups which assist the sales function?

**Review Questions
Chapter 3**

The Psychology of Selling

Sales is an intricate process because it relies on the salesperson's ability to understand customers and relate to their needs. That ability may be one of the most difficult to develop because of the complexity of human beings. Section II examines basic buying behavior of agricultural customers and the communications skills a salesperson should possess.

Chapter Four
Understanding People

*"Very few sales offer a problem-solving situation where
there is no human involvement or interest."*

Walt Workman, a heavyset, bushy-browed man, has been running
Workman's Farm Supply for the past 23 years. Even though there are
several competing hardware chains and a co-op outlet in the area, he and his
balding younger brother Max make up one of the most prolific selling teams
in southeast Iowa. Supplier salespeople who deal with the pair love them.
They move merchandise like there's no tomorrow.

But, watching the pair in action could give the most open-minded company
rep cause for alarm. Max and Walt are more than a little unorthodox in their
relationship with customers.

When a customer walks into Workman's, he is generally met by Walt or
Max, who yells a first name greeting and a "What can I do for you today?"
That's when the action begins.

"MAX!" Walt will yell to his brother, who always seems to be ferreting
around the shelves along one merchandise-choked aisle or another, "36-inch
bicycle wheels?" Max pops his head out from behind a pile of boxes and

ambles over to Walt, nodding a hello to the customer and looking at him for an explanation.

"Bobby left his bike behind the pickup and then I backed right over it this morning," explains the customer, Hank Baxter from Four-Mile.

"How d'ya like kids today?" Walt asks Max, shaking his head. "You wonder if they know how to take care of their belongings."

"I ask that boy a hundred times a week not to leave that thing there where I might run over it, but he still does it," Hank moans.

"Kids!" agrees Walt, now turning with Hank to receive Max's verdict.

"Why didn't you look before you backed up over it?" Max asks with more than just a little implication of fault.

Somewhat taken aback, Hank replies, "Well, Max, I was in a rush this morning. I usually check for that kid's bike — being that it always seems to be right behind my rear wheel — but I was in a rush."

"It's partly your own fault, then," says Max, launching into a sermon, "You got to watch kids like a hawk if you *really* don't want these things to happen."

Now Walt has to jump in again. "Max!" he pleads, "Hank doesn't need a lecture from you, he needs a new wheel. He's here for our help."

"You can't be on these kids all the time, y'know," says Hank, "You've got two of your own. You know what it's like. And besides, Max, do I have to remind you whose son locked his father in the farm supply store restroom and left, while customers were waiting to be helped?"

Max threw up his hands. "Ahhhh! Where's the wheel? Maybe we can just rebend it into shape instead of getting a new one."

Hank holds up the severely bent wheel. Max looks at it. "I think we have one in the back," he says and disappears.

Walt takes the bent wheel. "Will you look at that?" he says disbelievingly.

"I'm going to take it out of his allowance," warns Hank.

"That's the only way kids'll learn," Walt concludes.

****

Transactional Analysis as a Way to Understand Customers   In the previous chapter, we learned of the role that empathy plays in sales success; good salespeople must be able to "read" their prospects to understand their underlying motives or needs. Here we will offer a simple, yet accurate, system for understanding the vagaries of customers' wills. First introduced by the late Eric Berne, and popularized by Tom Harris in his book *I'm OK — You're OK*, transactional analysis—or TA—is a valuable tool for anyone, particularly a salesperson, who wishes to gain insight into human behavior. TA is not a value system and so doesn't imply that a particular type of behavior is best. Its basic premise is that people can control and are responsible for their feelings, thoughts and behavior.

While quite logical and acceptable on the surface, this premise is difficult to operate by. It's much easier to blame someone else for our feelings and behavior than to recognize we can choose responses to others from alternatives. Thus, someone doesn't "make you mad!" Rather you chose to get angry and you can control your response. After all, you could have laughed it off, right? It might not be easy, but according to TA, it is possible to control and be responsible for our behavior.

Why did Max Workman yell at his customer for backing up over his son's bike? After all, one might reason, it shouldn't matter to Max; he's making a sale. And why did Hank offer excuses for his actions? Surely he didn't owe Max an explanation.

TA Ego States

The fact is that very few sales offer a problem-solving opportunity, devoid of human involvement and interest. If Hank were to walk into Workman's and state flatly that he needed a bicycle wheel, and Walt or Max were simply to ask what size and hand it over, something would be missing. Though indeed, sales are occasionally made this way, it's not the norm in rural communities where people are expected to be more interested in one another. Human interaction is a complex process that meets many needs simultaneously. In order to understand more about the mysteries of that process, we need a particular language with which to analyze it. TA, and specifically its ego states—Parent, Adult, and Child—provide that language. Not related to chronological age, each ego state represents an *attitude* that exists in the human brain. You might say it represents the real-life role with which a person identifies at a given moment. And the proportion of time any one person spends relating to others from a particular ego state varies from one individual to another, although all ego states are common to everyone in some measure.

Figure 4.1 **The Three Ego States**

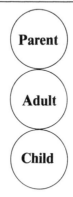

The Parent

The Parent state represents the internalized voice of the authoritarian figures you have come to know and emulate throughout a lifetime, particularly your parents as you saw them in the early years. This means that your behavior and attitudes are in part a reflection of behavior and attitudes you absorbed before you were old enough and experienced enough to examine them rationally and knowledgeably. If your parents told you that all salesmen are shifty-eyed, chances are some part of you still harbors that message. This is why the Parent is often referred to as "the learned concepts of life"; somewhere along the line, you *learned* the values and beliefs you now hold. These beliefs may have been transmitted verbally or nonverbally;

they may involve such categories as shoulds and oughts, priorities and the kinds of people to admire or like; but regardless of what is transmitted or how, Berne says the message is indelibly recorded in your brain in much the same way a cassette is tape-recorded. They are played back later in life at the subconscious level as we enter circumstances that trigger them. Salespeople should be particularly mindful of hidden parental messages in the buying decision; they must be brought out in the open and dealt with wherever possible to avoid a stalemate.

Mottoes are Parent Messages

Often parent messages are cloaked in the guise of a wise old folk saying or motto that is so well-known it can't *possibly* warrant criticism. One customer may have been treated to the insight "money doesn't grow on trees," while another may have absorbed the attitude "you can't take it with you." The former may drive an extremely hard bargain, while the latter may never even think to ask the price. To make matters worse, you may deal with each in turn, one after another, which takes some fancy mental gear-switching.

Nurturing Parent Behavior

Another aspect of the Parent state is the prevailing mode of behavior we absorb from watching our parents in action. Generally we see two kinds of Parent behavior in varying degrees: nurturing and critical.

The nurturing Parent is the behavior state which yearns to "take care of." When someone shows interest in or concern for another's well-being, he is said to be expressing nurturing Parent behavior. While the passerby who rushes into the street to whisk a toddler to safety is a nurturing Parent, so too is the salesperson who does whatever he can to solve his customer's problems and make that customer content. The astute salesperson nurtures not only by seeing that the buyer gets everything he needs, but also by watching for and responding to clues that are subtle cries for help. The farmer who says he "just doesn't know" whether he should settle for the bulk-blended fertilizer or spend the extra money for a premium grade, may be giving you a verbal clue that he is in need of a "nurturing Parent." Subtle clues are the furrowed brow and pursed lips, the half-hour of deliberation with arms folded and chin resting on hand, or the sharing of troubles and frustrations. By realizing that the unsure customer may be looking for an expert to come to his rescue and help him make a decision the salesperson can be sympathetic to the customer's needs, ask the right questions, and perhaps even weigh the farmer's stated pros and cons. Once a bond of trust is established, some customers are quite responsive to letting the salesperson "take care of" them. Of course, some customers enjoy playing nurturing Parent toward salespeople. (Recognize and deal positively with this human need too.)

Critical Parent Behavior

The other Parent state, as one might expect, is just the opposite of the nurturing Parent. This is the critical Parent, with its absolute judgments about anything and everything. As mentioned above, these judgments are learned from watching how your own parents operated when you were a child. They manifest themselves in a particular person as built-up criticism.

The overly critical person blowing off steam about the government, the weather, big companies, and even you the salesperson is in fact venting the collection of bad feelings within himself. As the saying goes, when someone points the finger of accusation, three fingers are always pointing right back at him. This type of customer is no picnic for the unwary, or even wary, salesperson; but the important thing to realize is that the customer will probably find fault no matter what the salesperson does, so it's best not to take his criticism personally.

The Adult

The next ego state Berne describes is the Adult. Imagine a computer which takes factual, objective information; runs it through its analysis and comes out with the best possible answer, given the input. The Adult works in much the same manner, taking facts and probability estimates, analyzing them without being dominated by what daddy always said was "the right way," then arriving at an objective conclusion. It is the link with reality that tells you, among other things, that the red apple in your hand is simply a red apple and not necessarily a poisoned gift from one of your competitors.

The Adult ego state is becoming more and more important to agri salespeople. Why? Today, with the always growing influence of government regulation, the facts of life about tight money and recession, and such common factors as crop yield and profit margins, a farmer must use rational thinking to keep his business afloat and thriving. Growingly more and more purchases are being made from the Adult ego state. The salesperson must be able to deal objectively and logically with this businesslike breed of prospects.

The Child

The Child state is that which involves feelings and emotions. But this is not necessarily a "bad" state to deal with; there's a difference between "childlike" and "childish." Childish is an emotive word which stirs up images of temper tantrums and stomping feet. Childlike, on the other hand, encompasses *everything* to do with the way children behave, from those hot temper tantrums to the wondering innocence of a four-year-old watching ants cart off bits-and-pieces of a dropped cookie.

The Child ego state, when present in a grown-up's ego framework, also contains simple recordings of early life experiences and how we felt about them. That's why a smile will spread across the face of someone who suddenly realizes he's stumbled upon the old swimming hole and swing tree, and why the smile will be swept away when he realizes no one swims there any more.

If these examples strike a chord, you will understand that when a person is in the Child state, he is not thinking logically, or in an adult fashion. He is fancifully caught up in melancholy or glee, or recklessly impulsive and automatic. On the other hand, he is also quite predictable. Some childlike emotions for a good salesperson to watch for are fear, anger, happiness, impulsiveness, sadness and affection.

Fear plays an important part in the selling relationships. The fear of failing, being laughed at, being wrong are key reasons for certain human behaviors. The entire time you're trying to make a sale, a prospect may be worried about a number of things: his budget, your product and what the neighbors are buying. The problem is, kids can express their emotions and grown-ups can't (except in certain acceptable ways) and your sales prospect may be disguising his fears. His talk about *really* wanting "the best money can buy" may be a cover-up for not wanting to come out on the short-end of a deal. So the salesperson may need to assume a nurturing or reassuring stance to "comfort" the fear emotion. Don't forget too, that for many men, fear is also a sign of weakness, and for a man that may be camouflaged in a more manly, acceptable emotion — anger. Consequently, impulsiveness, which sometimes goes hand-in-hand with happiness, is also an important element of any sale. The impulsive customer may buy intuitively rather than logically. That does not necessarily mean a bad decision; it's just a decision made in a different way and you might do well to target your efforts accordingly. Perhaps the Child state of our personality has always been tacitly recognized. It might account for the popularity of such sayings as "The only difference between men and boys is the size of their toys."

Natural Child   Child ego state types can be put into three general categories. First among these is the natural child. Herein lies the child that feels the whole spectrum of emotions, from happiness to fear, sadness and anger. And the natural child generally *does* what he feels. Grown-ups operating in the Child state, of course, do not throw themselves on the floor kicking their feet and screaming. Impulsiveness, intuitiveness and rebellious acts are generally billboard announcements that the natural child is in control. In fact, whenever someone is baring his or her emotions without repressing them, the natural child state is probably present. For the salesperson, the natural child provides an open window through which to view exactly what the customer is thinking. The natural child is also the state to which the salesperson directs a good deal of his efforts getting to know the prospect. Good feelings, after all, are born in the Child.

The Little Professor   The second Child ego state is the so-called little professor. This one represents the creativity that dwells in all people to one extent or another. It is the one that finds joy in figuring out a riddle or puzzle and will spend hours taking apart the tractor radio to see how it works. Luckily, because of his nature, having once taken apart the radio, the little professor will probably be able to put it back together again without much trouble. Such ego state types may require special attention from a salesperson because his needs may be based on unorthodox ideas. You may have to help him figure out what products would help him with a new idea about soil conditioning. However you are likely to have help from him, since the little professor's mind is always working, always figuring, always looking at the problem from a thousand different angles.

Adapted Child   The third major part of the Child ego state is the adapted child, probably the easiest one to deal with because he is eager to please. This state results from suppression of the natural child in the early years; the child does only what he is supposed to do. Why? The adapted child strongly yearns for the approval of the authority figure and for that reason is glad to follow orders, as well as to agree with you often. Such a child, however, requires plenty of positive feedback or reinforcement. Criticism, while it can drive the adapted child to work harder to please, can also have a crushing impact and can cause great harm. The salesperson can easily win the heart of this "child" with plenty of positive stroking — but he must also be sure he does not let himself take unfair advantage and view this customer as a complete pushover.

Contamination

Sometimes a prospect will be so tightly tied to unfounded parent messages, that his Adult may not be able to function purely logically and objectively. In other words, beliefs and learned prejudices about suppliers, products, brands etc. may be so strong that the facts and performance won't change the prospect's opinions very easily, if at all. This situation is referred to as contamination of the Adult.

Some prospects frequent given suppliers of brands without serious thought given to alternatives, just because that's the way it's been. Any salesperson who suggests a departure from the norm with one of these individuals must move cautiously, building trust gradually over time, even though the facts suggest otherwise.

Which ego state is best? As mentioned earlier, TA isn't a value system and so doesn't suggest relative value of behavior from each ego state. Likewise, no one ego state is better all the time. Yet, since the Adult ego state is the only position from which logical choices about behavioral style can be made, it may make sense to maintain the Adult as our "executive of behavior." From that posture a salesperson can choose nurturing or childlike behavior, or something in between, as situations and circumstances warrant, rather than purely emoting and losing sales as a result.

TA IN TRANS-ACTIONS

Now let's go back to Max and Walt's farm supply store to take a look at the transactions that took place between the two store owners and their customer. A careful look through the eyes of transactional analytical techniques can shed some light on how Max and Walt move so much merchandise out the door.

Communicate on the Channels

One of the key applications of TA is in the analysis of communication channels between people. When one person talks to another, he is talking from a specific ego state. Remember, the states are Parent, Adult and Child, more simply, P-A-C. But that person is also addressing the other person's ego state(s). For example, when Walt Workman asked Hank Baxter, "What can I do for you today?" Walt's Adult state was addressing Hank's Adult state. This provoked a response, of course, from Hank:

[1]"What can I do for you today?"   [2]I need a new bicycle
                                                      wheel, 36-inch rim."

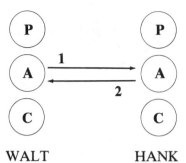

Hank's reply, because he was dispassionately supplying the requested information, is also Adult, directed to Walt's Adult ego state. This exchange is a *complementary transaction*: Walt's Adult asked Hank's Adult a question, and Hank's Adult replied appropriately and as expected.

Next, Walt and Hank have a good time complementing each other with more complementary transactions:

[1]"...and then I backed right over   [2]"How d'ya like kids today?
it this morning."   You wonder if they know how to
                                             take care of their belongings."

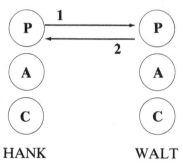

[1]"I ask that boy a hundred times a week
not to leave that thing where I   [2]"Kids!"
might run over it, but he still
does it."

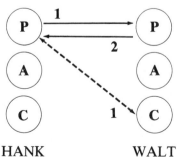

Walt and Hank are playing Parent, and are happily reinforcing each other's truisms and disgust. But look at that exchange carefully. Although Hank is verbally addressing Parent to Parent, such exaggerated phrases as "a hundred times a week," and the expression of helplessness, "but he still does it," are tip-offs that the emotional Child is also talking in the subtext of the conversation. A subtext is an implied or hinted thought, expressed in tone or perhaps in specific words chosen. In TA this is called an *ulterior transaction.* While the straightforward verbal conversation is taking place, some sort of subtext or hidden message is conveyed, too. This subtext is what upsets Max, and causes him to get right to the point.

[1] "Why didn't you look before you backed up over it?"

[2] "Well, Max, I was in a rush this morning. I usually check . . . being that it always seems to be right behind my rear wheel—but I was in a rush."

```
        P  ╲ 1        P
             ╲
        A     ╲      A
               ╲
        C    2  ╲ C
       MAX      HANK
```

Max and Hank are still involved in a complementary transaction, but the ego states doing the talking have switched. Max uses the strong parent phrase, "why didn't you" and Hank responds with an explanation from his Child state. Max got his expected response. Luckily for Hank, Max, Walt, and the sale, Walt jumps into the conversation before things go too far. After Max's Parent assails Hank's Child, (1, below) Walt's Parent comes to the rescue and chides Max's Child (2, below). Hank retains the truisms of the Parent role, with a subtext of the defensive child (3, below).

"Max! Hank doesn't need a lecture from you, he needs a new wheel."

"It's partly your own fault, then. You've got to watch kids like a hawk."

"You can't be on these kids all the time y'know."

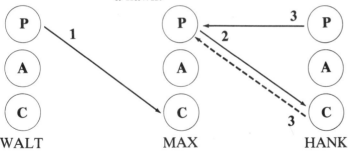

What happened? Walt's move averted any problems caused by the *crossed transaction* between Max and Hank. The so-called crossed transaction resulted from Max's Parent addressing Hank's Child but Hank's Parent seeming to respond in return.

But Hank of course, seeing Max outnumbered two Parents to one, can't resist getting one shot back: *His* Parent attacks Max's Child, (1, below). Max gives up, and instead of trying to oppress Hank's Parent (he's outnumbered, don't forget, and besides, the sale is the thing that's important), responds Adult-Adult (2). (Note, however, that there is an ulterior transaction or subtext message of nurturing Parent hoping to help out Hank's Child by saving him a little money.)

[1]"And besides Max, do I have to remind you whose son locked his father in the farm supply store restroom and left, while customers were waiting to be helped?"

[2]"Ahhhh! Where's the wheel? Maybe we can just rebend it into shape instead of getting a new one."

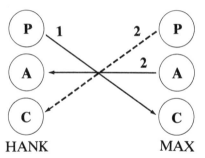

HANK   MAX

Finally, after Max realizes the wheel is hopelessly bent and heads for the store room to get a new one, Walt and Hank revert to playing Parent again. "Will you look at that (wheel)?" says Walt's disbelieving Parent. "I'm going to take it out of his allowance," replies Hank's lecturing Parent. "That's the only way kids'll learn," concludes Walt's Parent.

So what's Max's and Walt's secret to sales success? Although they probably don't know it, together they are correctly addressing their customers' Parent-Adult-Child ego states. As we saw, when Max fell down by improperly chastising Hank's Child when Hank was clearly operating for the most part in the Parental state, Walt picked it up. With another customer, Max's always-bothered Parent-to-Child ego is just the ticket to make the sale and Walt takes a back seat. What the team of Max and Walt inadvertently do, every salesperson should do intentionally. Stay in tune with the ego state your customer is using at a given moment and work toward creating complementary transactions. Keep crossed transaction lines to a minimum, or risk losing communication and sales.

Had Walt not come to the rescue when Max's Parent was accusing Hank's Child of being negligent, the outcome might have been devastating.

Hank could have become "hooked" into a serious Parent put-down message to Max, and then guessing about Max's personality, things could really have snowballed with more crossed transactions. Max and Walt would surely lose in that kind of encounter, perhaps to the point of losing Hank's business entirely.

How can a salesperson avoid getting "hooked" into reciprocal Parent put-down behavior? He must maintain the Adult ego as executor of behavior. That is, delegate control of your behavior to the logical, reasoning, thinking Adult. That doesn't mean always functioning in the Adult, but to allow the Adult to choose behavior. Sometimes it's better to listen as a nurturing parent, or to respond more childlike, depending on the situation. The Adult can make the appropriate selection. Importantly, the objective of using the Adult as executor of behavior isn't always to avoid conflict. Sometimes open disagreement is healthy. Yet with the Adult in control, the salesperson is more likely to maintain control of his behavior even in a conflict situation. Maintaining control over the direction of a selling relationship in a professional manner is the end result of effective Adult-controlled communication.

Let's see how TA can be used to the agri salesperson's benefit. One of the **USING TA** most important transactional analysis tools is that known as a "stroke." A **IN SALES** stroke is any recognition of another person's presence and can take a number of forms: the words you use, a particular gesture, body language, a simple touch, or anything that tells someone "I know you're there." When two people meet on the street, their faces may suddenly light up expressing pleasant surprise at the chance meeting. Next come the warm greetings and the handshakes. "How you doin', John? Never thought I'd run into you here." These are all strokes. And they are, of course, positive strokes which compliment the person and let him know he's welcome and that you're glad to see him.

There are negative strokes, too. For example, if it were a mortal enemy you ran into on the street; the sudden look of surprise, then the angry scowl as you refused to acknowledge each other with a nod or even say hello. These strokes, while clearly negative, are strokes nonetheless.

Receiving strokes is one of the most important needs humans have. From the time of birth and the first wild flailing of the arms and crying out as mother passes the crib, humans exhibit signs of this desire to be recognized; to be told, as mentioned above, "I know you're there." The way a child is brought up — the kind of strokes he receives — has a very powerful influence on his emotional and physical development.

And that upbringing may also greatly affect the decisions he makes throughout life. The child who receives positive strokes — and perhaps even a toy football before he can walk — from parents who value excellence in sports, is more likely to grow up working toward excellence in athletics to maintain his parent's pride in his accomplishments.

Or innovation may be an important way for some farmers to receive and continue receiving strokes. Those farmers in the county who buy the latest in harvesting equipment technology may be getting important strokes in being seen as leader, calculated risk-taker, or innovator (more about this in Chapter 5).

Discounting Strokes

If life were that simple, however, people would just parcel out the appropriate strokes to each other and everyone would be happy. Unfortunately, this is not the case. The great need for positive strokes and the things we do to get them is counterbalanced by "Parent" messages which warn that we should also be modest. This tends to confuse the business of stroking. For instance, while you may praise a retailer for moving a large amount of merchandise last month, that positive stroke will be tempered by the recipient's "Well, everybody is getting good business this spring..." That modesty is called "discounting" the stroke.

This characteristic is especially evident in rural people. They downplay the open expression of their need for strokes. But because strokes are so important to *all* people — including those who discount them — this downplaying must not be misinterpreted as a lack of need. It is merely one more obstacle the salesperson must be careful not to trip over. The salesperson must be alert even to the disguised need for strokes and be able to respond appropriately to fulfill the ever-present need for a good positive stroke. Being able to recognize these needs can be the critical factor in making a salesperson highly successful, moderately successful, or a failure.

Being able to provide the right kind of strokes in a selling situation is quite important. Recognition of the need for stroking and fulfillment of that need is one of the basic cogs in the selling wheel. Luckily, fulfillment of the customer's "ego" need helps meet the needs of the salesperson through the business they transact. Of course, an overuse or misuse of stroking behavior can cause the salesperson to appear manipulative. The key here is sincerity and an understanding of the relative need for strokes from different prospects.

Different people need different amounts of strokes. You must know people whose whole day is made with just one compliment. For them, a little stroking goes a long way. They already feel good about themselves because, perhaps, they have a long history of receiving positive strokes. But though your stroke is just one more on the pile, never assume that it is unwelcome. Your compliment on a particular morning may chase away a temporary case of the blues or lack of confidence, and thus will be greeted with open arms.

At the other end of the spectrum, you must also know people who can get a hundred positive strokes in one day but even *that* seems not to be enough. Perhaps all their lives they have felt "undernourished" in positive strokes, and consequently they try to make up that deficit by seeking more strokes than they can possibly get in any one situation. Watch out. That type tends to constantly demand attention from those around them, and salespeople become a prime target.

Yes, positive strokes are probably the best kind of all. They make the customer feel important and significant as long as they are genuine. It is risky to give strokes which lack sincerity. Done genuinely though, positive strokes are also good for the salesperson. He exercises total control over their disbursement and usually their direct impact can be quickly and easily seen. But believe it or not, negative strokes can help people feel important too. They make a person feel significant to some extent and in effect say: "You're complaining and whining is so important and bothersome that it makes me mad enough to spend my energy giving you a negative stroke." While negative strokes are not nearly so productive as positive ones, they are far better than no stroke or recognition at all.

Positive strokes — which tend to make people feel good about themselves — and negative strokes — which tend to reinforce already present bad feelings about the self — come in a variety of types.   **Types of Strokes**

Warm fuzzies, probably some of the best strokes of all, are completely genuine and totally unconditional. They are freely given compliments or warm feelings of friendship that do not require anything in return. And they are also not necessarily connected to the sale. For example, if you happened to pick up a book about the application of computers to the farm business for a customer who mentioned that he was thinking about getting one, that would be a warm fuzzy. These strokes are some of the best tools for forging a good relationship between salesperson and customer, even though they may be discounted. The only thing better than a warm fuzzy is something called a *Super Stroke* — recognition from a very special person for something you consider important.   **Warm Fuzzies**

Plastic fuzzies are positive strokes — but with intentional strings attached. The main idea behind these positive conditional strokes is to encourage people into behaving in a particular manner. A vacation in Hawaii for retailers who have moved X-thousand dollars of your company's product for the previous year are plastic fuzzies. Because one of the primary functions of a salesperson is to "manipulate" customer behavior, these strokes are quite useful, ethical and essential. Of course, there are risks in using plastic fuzzies should the prospect or customer resent being manipulated in that way. Some customers may resent what might appear to be open attempts at behavior modification. Others, meanwhile, come to expect the windbreakers, caps, pens, calendars and special services that regular customers generally get. Yet recognition and rewards for desirable behavior will remain an important sales tool.   **Plastic Fuzzies**

Cotton candy is a positive stroke that appears to have substance but is actually mostly air. "Hey, how are you doing?" is a cotton candy stroke. It sounds good but has little meaning.   **Cotton Candy and Maintenance Strokes**

Maintenance strokes are positive strokes that have little real meaning but are primarily used to keep a conversation or relationship going. The routine sales call, for example, gives recognition to the customer that you know he's out there and you're thinking of him, even though you may know no real business will be transacted. The customer may have enough of your product inventoried, but he still needs the strokes your call supplies.

Communications channels remain open and the customer feels important.

Cold Pricklies   *Cold pricklies* are negative strokes designed to help a person feel bad about himself. When Oliver Hardy calls Stan Laurel "a nitwit," that's a cold pricklie. Other forms include laughing at people, cursing them, even physical abuse. Curiously enough, however, some people just love to get negative strokes. They almost seem to go out of their way to set things up so that a negative stroke is guaranteed. Why? Eric Berne offers this explanation. When the cold pricklies fans were growing up, the great preponderance of strokes they received from parents were negative, so much so that negative strokes became virtually the only evidence to themselves that they existed. Thus, because we all like the reassurance that we indeed are alive and living, cold pricklie lovers structure their world so that they constantly receive a steady stream of existence-confirming negative strokes. Too, negative strokes are easier to get than positive ones. Simply raise a ruckus, rub someone the wrong way, and presto! Here come the negative strokes. Ahh, it's great to be alive!

Such people are tough customers for salespeople. While you may reassure the person with *positive* strokes, this may make the chronic complainer uneasy and frustrate him because he is not quite sure how to handle this strange stroke. Thus the best method for dealing with a cold pricklie addict is for the salesperson to simply realize what he's dealing with — which will, hopefully, help him keep his cool under fire. Give him honest, positive strokes — but don't expect miracles.

Touching   *Touching* is another kind of stroke which sends very strong messages to the other person. It adds a special dimension to the attention given. Television interviewer Barbara Walters uses touching to a great benefit. Many times she successfully draws out the interviewee's deepest feelings with a simple touch of the forearm as she asks some personal question. Although men in our culture are not really permitted to touch each other except through a handshake, a pat on the back, or a well-targeted fist, touching is still important. Think of all the indications you receive from a simple handshake. Is the grip a bone-crushing, intimidating one, or firm, sincere and friendly? Is it accompanied by a pat on the back and an arm on the shoulder? Is it terse and businesslike, moderate in duration, or too long and presumptuously more friendly than a first meeting should warrant? In this narrow band wherein touching is allowed, the salesperson must be aware of the kind of emotional strokes he is expressing through physical contact.

Listening   *Listening,* too, is a kind of stroking. The attentive active listener who is actually taking in the import of what the speaker is saying and perhaps nodding in understanding, is broadcasting one of the most welcome strokes. Repeating the main points in your own words, further reinforces the customer's realization that you indeed understand and, like other positive strokes, says "I know you're there." You've confirmed that the feelings behind the words have been heard too. While active listening is often a time-consuming, difficult task, it can have a high payoff because it concentrates on the customer. People like good listeners!

In fact all stroking, appropriately and wisely used, is beneficial to the salesperson. People like other people who make them feel good about themselves, and a salesperson who is adept at stroking will be well liked by the customer. That translates into sales. Salespeople who recognize and fulfill the *human* needs of their customers add a success-producing dimension to their job of filling the customer's *business* needs. It's that personalized service which keeps Workman Farm Supply and hundreds of other local agri-businesses formidable competitors to national outlets whose employees are often less motivated to give that personal attention.

As we have seen, transactional analysis can provide insight into why people act the way they do. TA helps explain another phenomenon all too familiar to salespeople: the collection of "trading stamps."

STAMP COLLECTING

No, they're not the type you pick up at the grocery with your purchases. These stamps are quite different.

Ever have "one of those days" when everything goes wrong? You get up 15 minutes late and cut yourself while shaving in a rush. Then your brother-in-law, who you don't care much for anyway, forgot to put gas in your car after he borrowed it last night, forcing you to stop on the way to your first call. A big order to your best dealer was shipped two weeks late and you just found out about it now — a month later — from the angry customer. The brochures on the new model your company introduced, and which everybody is dying to find out about, had to be recalled because of a major printing error. And then to top it off, the waitress at lunch brought you a ham-and-cheese sandwich with mustard — which you hate! That did it, and you blew up, even though a new sandwich, without mustard, was whisked to you immediately. That's stamp collecting.

From the time you first got up, you started collecting trading stamps, one for each bit of bad news. You filled up at least half a book's worth — metaphorically speaking — in just three hours, and by the time you bit into that offending mustard you cashed in all the stamps for a nice *psychological prize* — an angry blowup at the waitress which was out of proportion to her "crime." *That* is trading-stamp collecting and cashing in.

Everyone who fails to deal with the day's frustrations *when* they happen collects trading stamps. Salespeople are no exception. And, more importantly to the salesperson, neither are customers, which explains why Joe Jones really let you have it last week for what anyone else would have seen as a minor oversight. So you forgot the calendar you promised to bring over with you. Big deal.

Salespeople are especially vulnerable to those who are ripe for cashing in trading stamps, primarily because they have to take a certain amount of abuse if they want to keep their customers. Unfortunately, customers know that salespeople are likely targets to dump books of trading stamps onto. Luckily, TA can help you understand stamp collecting and teach you to avoid getting stuck.

An important point to remember about stamp collecting is that at the moment of cashing them in, the person feels justified in doing so. He feels OK about unloading on you at that time, even if you don't personally deserve it; which is why you've got to watch your step. Thus, if you can recognize a bulging stamp book while it's still burning a hole in someone's pocket, you can possibly avoid an unnecessary argument, maintain control of the selling situation, not lose a customer, and not get dumped on. That's the purpose for understanding TA trading stamps.

Stamp collectors generally tend to send off a warning flare that they're about ready to cash in for a blowup. Phrases like "That's it..." or "I've just about had it" are signals of an approaching storm. Unfortunately, at that point, it's like looking at a locomotive's cow catcher to find out you're about to be run over by the train. If things have gone that far, you may not have been paying attention. It is essential that you be aware of the numerous tipoffs that tell you your customer has been collecting stamps today. A history of blowups for relatively insignificant mistakes would be one warning to be on your guard against. A mean disposition, or angry scowl and one-word answers are other tipoffs. Too, if your customer actually tells you about how so-and-so tried to rob him out of ten dollars when he went to buy a pack of cigarettes, and how the mechanic still hasn't fixed the Ford after three tries, you can rest assured he's ready to blowup.

The best way to handle the situation is with kid gloves. Move cautiously, avoiding any inadvertent provocation. Try to remain in the neutral position and ease the customer along. Some careful stroking through active and empathetic listening might help defuse the powder keg. If the collector starts opening up and telling you about his feelings it helps build your relationship with him even further.

The important thing to remember, however, is not to get "hooked." If the person does start cashing in stamps, be aware that his verbal attacks on you, your company, and the tie you're wearing are overreactions to the emotion of the moment. At all costs, don't get into a shouting match or argument. The blowup is likely to dissipate soon and the stamp collector who has just thrown several dozen books at you may feel embarrassed for having done so. At this point, help him save face by not drawing attention to the blowup. You will not only gain respect, but possibly win some points.

People collect a number of different types of stamps. Farmers tend to collect stamps over a long period of time in different ways. The collection generally coincides with you and your company's track record with him and the service he gets. Thus, an unfriendly secretary at your office may count as one stamp; poor equipment in July, three stamps; your being late for an appointment in August, five stamps. And a sales call just as dinner was beginning in October, may be worth two stamps. Finally, when enough stamps have been collected, the farmer can point to a good long list of charges which justify his changing suppliers. Without that list "as long as my arm," he might feel guilty for changing.

Of course, customers are not the only stamp collectors. Salespeople collect them too. And this is especially dangerous if it goes unrecognized by you for any length of time and so continues to grow. You may save up 10 or 20 books of stamps from all the abuse heaped upon you and other seeming assaults on your integrity until finally, when that certain "problem" customer fails to tell you he intended to cancel an order *before* it was actually delivered to his warehouse, you can really feel justified in letting him have it. You can rant and rave and scream — and say goodbye to that account too. But that's not what you're in business for, even though "he deserved every bit of it."

Everybody collects stamps to some degree or another and it is not necessarily bad, as long as it doesn't interfere with your control of the sales situation or damage customer relations. One way to see that it doesn't get out of hand is to dissipate the bad feelings in nonharmful, constructive ways. Get rid of a couple of stamps at a time by calmly talking your frustrations or problems out with a spouse, friend or associate. Exercising or strenuous work like chopping wood is another way to shake stamps out of your book. Some people prefer a game of golf or tennis, or simply a quiet walk in the woods. Getting rid of stamps in this way will help your salesmanship as well as your personal life. After all, your spouse, who has been collecting stamps from the day's chores; your children, who have been collecting *their* own stamps from teachers and peers; and even Fido who's been collecting *his* own stamps from the bulldog across the street, don't need *your* stamps to top everything off.

RITUALS AND PASS-TIMES

Let's move our attention to the beginning of a sales call. More often than not, the first several minutes of any sales call are spent on small talk that establishes a rapport with the customer and creates a common ground or bond on which the sale can be launched. Consequently, this is highly important and must be handled carefully, so as not to appear phony. This small talk is called a *ritual,* which by definition is a transaction that is habitual and may lack real meaning. "How're you doing today?" is one opening line ritual that may lead into a discussion about the wife, kids, farm or home. Opening rituals frequently move into a type of small talk called a *pass-time.* The salesperson doesn't want to launch right into his purpose — and for that matter the customer doesn't want to appear unfriendly by jumping right to "So what do you want?" — so the pass-time is a bridge between the first hello and actually getting down to business. Some common pass-times used in agri selling are:

"Ain't it awful how..."
"Why don't they..."
"Whatever became of..."
"Cars..."
"Politics..."
"Did you hear the one about..."

But don't be mistaken. Pass-times are not just a necessary evil or total waste of time. Much meaningful information can be gleaned from them about people in your sales territory, perhaps. Or you may be able to pick up clues about how your customer is feeling today, which could be helpful in telling you which particular approach to use. This "activity," using TA terms, is a function performed to meet a specific objective. Such a utilization of pass-time to gather information on market conditions, what the competitors are doing and consumer thinking patterns are, must be distinguished from wasted pass-time talking about the weather. The customer may not be able to distinguish when the expert salesperson is wrapped up completely in a pass-time and when he's involved in an intelligence-gathering activity that only looks like pass-time. The professional salesperson, however, should be fully aware.

However, pass-times sometimes become so ritualistic that you may find yourself spending half-an-hour having a great time talking about a common interest but getting no selling done. The alert salesman must judge each situation on its own merits and decide whether maybe it *is* justifiable to spend 20 minutes on a game of "Whatever became of..." because this particular prospect is potentially a big customer who values socializing with his suppliers. But the salesperson who spends half of most calls on pass-times may be using his valuable time poorly. Such an occupational hazard should be avoided, especially by those who love to talk.

It's important to remember that transactional analysis in total doesn't provide all the answers for dealing with human beings in selling situations. Yet the logic behind understanding more about why people act as they do is clear. TA offers a chance for salespeople to put some handles on human behavior and learn more about this most important variable in successful agri selling.

SUMMARY

* Transactional Analysis, a valuable tool for salespeople, is based on the premise that people can control and are responsible for their behavior.

* There are three ego states that represent attitudes that exist in the human brain. The Parent represents the internalized voice of an authoritarian figure people emulate throughout a lifetime. The Adult is a logical analytical state that takes information and processes it to determine an answer. The third, or Child state, is that which involves feelings and emotions.

* The Parent state includes concepts like the "nurturing state" in which people yearn to care for others and the "critical" parent who judges their actions.

* The Child ego state also includes some varied aspects. The "natural" child does what he feels, the "little professor" represents the creativity that dwells in all people and the "adapted child" who yearns for the approval of an authority figure and is glad to follow orders.

* "Contamination of the Adult" means a prospect will be so tightly tied to the Parent messages that his Adult state doesn't act logically.

* A salesperson can take advantage of the ego states by utilizing them, yet not getting lost in them to the extent that he offends a customer.

* One important TA tool is the stroke, a recognition of another person — either negatively or positively. Positive strokes compliment the person while negative strokes, such as an unfriendly statement, may alienate them.

* More accurately defined, strokes may be: Warm Fuzzies — completely

genuine; Plastic Fuzzies — positive with strings attached; Cotton Candy — mostly air; Maintenance — little meaning but used to keep a conversation or relationship going; Cold Pricklies — negative strokes designed to make a person feel poorly about himself; Touching — indicates its meaning by its sincerity of form; and Listening — presence or lack of may be quite important.

* Stamp Collecting is defined as failing to deal with the day's frustrations when they happen, resulting in an outpouring of emotion which is sometimes harmful.

* "Ritual" is a transaction that is habitual and may lack real meaning. Ritual frequently turns into "Pass Time," a type of small talk which may yield useful information or be meaningless.

---

1. Name the three TA ego states and define them.

2. What are "Parent messages" and how do they affect a person's perceptions?

3. Which ego state is viewed as the most logical and businesslike?

4. Name and define the three types of the Child ego state.

5. What is a crossed transaction?

6. Define negative and positive strokes. Why do farm people tend to discount the positive strokes they receive?

7. What is a "maintenance stroke" and is it an important part of the sales process?

8. Define "stamp collecting." How can it be controlled?

9. Why are "pass times" a valuable tool for the salesperson? When do they become a negative force?

**Review Questions
Chapter 4**

Chapter Five
Why and How People Buy

"Before anyone can hope to sell something to another person, he must first understand what that person wants and why they want it."

As he read the phone message, George Brady's worst fears were confirmed. Bob Steller had cancelled his order for the new cattle feeding system and feed grinding-mixer unit. George had been working on that sale for the last seven months. He'd given it a lot of effort — detailed engineering plans, complete economic analysis using three different price assumptions, and even went with Bob to the PCA to talk about financing. "Darn," thought George, "not only would that setup have helped Bob expand his operation, that sale would have given me enough points for the Hawaii trip this winter. I can't give up that easily. I'm going over to talk to Bob anyway."

Over coffee in Bob's kitchen, Bob explained further. "Sure, I'd like to go ahead — with Gary in college, hauling feed from the elevator is more than I can handle. But you know as well as I do, George, that credit is really getting tight. I was really hoping to expand into the larger setup because Gary's going to get out of college year after next. And that would give us the best setup around here. But with the variable interest rates on my land moving up and cattle prices at rock bottom and falling — well, I'm just afraid I can't swing it. My PCA man says he would go along with me on this if I wanted to, but he's got second thoughts with the beef outlook the way it is. The payments on that system are just too much with these depressed markets.

"Phyllis says she could get a job in town if it came to that," Bob continued. "But I don't want to get us so strapped that she's got to go to work to keep Gary in college. Sure I want to expand — and maybe it's the best thing in the long run. But I just can't see it the way things are now. When it comes to choosing between keeping my kids in college or expanding — well, I can expand later."

Bob obviously had been doing a lot of thinking. His farm wasn't about to go under, George knew that. But his PCA man had really gotten to him. George was sure this was a postponement rather than a permanent decision. And maybe, George reasoned, he could come up with another plan that would be within Bob's grasp. If he could solve Bob's most immediate need for an improved feed grinding system, he could salvage part of the sale. Moving ahead with the new grinder-mixer would give him the efficiency he needs now and would fit into a new feeding system in another year or so, he figured.

"Say Bob, I've got an idea that might fit into your budget and keep you on track for the new operation. I think you deserve the ease and efficiency that our grinder-mixer can give you. Let's take another look at your setup."

****

As our look at transactional analysis proved, there is usually more going on between two people than meets the eye. In the previous chapter we discussed the fundamentals of human transactions. Now we will see how those nuts and bolts fit together to support a buying decision.

WHY DO PEOPLE BUY?   Before anyone can hope to sell something to another person, he must first understand what that person wants and why they want it. Why do people buy? Simply put, people buy to satisfy their needs. Think back to caveman days when selling or bartering first began. The first prehistoric "salesperson" did not make that initial deal just because he had worked out a slick presentation. He had some *thing* — an extra club, an excess amount of antelope meat, a strange new thing called fire — that another caveman wanted. And the potential customer had something he wanted. Although the real trick in those days was to come to some mutually beneficial exchange agreement so that the other person wouldn't just slug you on the head and take your antelope meat, the basic element of a sale was there. Both people had something the other person *needed,* and the one who was aggressive enough to initiate the exchange was the salesman.

Although there are many different kinds of needs, they are prioritized in order of their importance. A farmer does not suddenly think, "I'm going to have to replace those hoses on my anhydrous ammonia tank before they

break. Wonder where I should buy them?'' and in the next moment forget
that thought and decide he can impress his neighbors with a new grain
truck. The pioneer in recognizing this prioritized ranking order of needs is
the respected psychologist, Abraham Maslow.

Maslow suggested that human needs are arranged into a five-level hierar-   **The Hierarchy of**
chy, with the most important needs, physiological needs, coming first. (See   **Human Needs**
Figure 5.1.) The most basic requirements are those things necessary for survival like air, water, food, shelter, warmth, sleep and sexual fulfillment.
Unless these most important needs have been met, a person will not be motivated to seek fulfillment of needs on the next levels. For example, when
smoke begins to fill a room causing a person to choke and gasp for air, that
person's highest and perhaps only need is to get out of there quickly. He
isn't going to be very concerned about his finances or reputation at a moment like that.

Figure 5.1 **Maslow's Hierarchy of Human Needs**

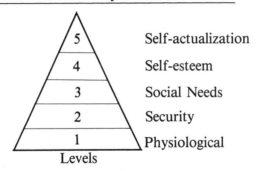

Feeling secure about the physiological necessities that threaten survival is
what the second level of needs is all about. Once a person is no longer immediately threatened, he begins to think about safety and security in the future. "How can I keep myself free from injury or being hurt,'' he asks.

At level three, people start dealing with more complex social needs. They
want to be accepted by other people and find enjoyment in belonging to a
group. Families, social cliques, clubs and agricultural organizations help fill
this need. Peer acceptance is a strong motivator for some people and they
are motivated to "keep up with the neighbors'' or at least choose a course
of action that is accepted by their friends.

Level four, self-esteem needs, are even more complicated. These needs involve the desire for respect by others and a need to feel important. Once a
farmer feels reasonably comfortable with his acceptance by peers, he may
be motivated to do something to help himself be noticed by others in his
group or that will give him status. Being elected to a leadership position, being recognized as a top farmer, or driving a late model car can all help fill
this need.

Finally, the needs at level five are the most complex of all. These involve
the need for self-actualization — a sense of self-worth or personal accomplishment. Self-actualization comes about not because others note a per-

son's accomplishments, but from the good feeling a person gets about him or herself from doing something *he or she* believes is important. A Peace Corp volunteer, a school board president, or a person who contributes to local charities — those who provide a service not for prestige, but because they feel it is important and worthwhile, are fulfilling their needs for self-actualization.

How does the Maslow hierarchy of needs apply to you, the salesperson? In the circles you're likely to frequent, people will probably have their basic needs for physical survival already met. While making ends meet may sometimes be a problem for all of us, people generally have enough food on the table or know how to get some in a pinch. People in this category spend a lot of time seeking out social and self-esteem fulfillment. This can be an important factor in how you tailor your sales presentation or approach a prospect.

But safety and security can also be important motivators for a customer, especially when the product involves significant physical or financial risk. For example, selling chemicals that can be applied in a variety of weather conditions over a relatively long period in the growing season is really appealing to a farmer's need for security and safety. Or a commodity broker can appeal to financial security when trying to sell a hedging program to a feed manufacturer or a grain producer.

Let's go back to salesperson George Brady and cattleman Bob Steller to see how the recognition and fulfillment of these various needs played a part in the sales call. Bob unknowingly confirmed the basis of Maslow's hierarchy with his statement, "When it comes to choosing between keeping my kids in college or expanding — well, I can expand later."

Bob's need for economic survival and need to feel secure in his survival (level two) had taken precedence over his need to grow into a father-son operation that is "the best setup around here" (level four). By recognizing that his customers safety and security needs have taken precedence over the desire to expand, George was able to adjust his selling strategy and maintain the possibility of making an immediate — and perhaps a longer-term sale. And he had the foresight to appeal to Bob's need for self-esteem by saying, "You *deserve* the ease and efficiency that our grinder-mixer can give you."

But don't forget, regardless of what needs your product may fulfill, buyers almost always behave rationally in one respect: they always expect to gain more by buying something than they expect to give up. What they gain may be measurable economic benefits, emotional satisfaction, or a combination of the two. But if that requirement is not met, there is no sale. After all, why should the buyer give up something of value to get less value in return? Although time may prove them right or wrong, both buyer and seller *expect* to gain from every transaction.

Wants And Needs And How You Feel

Going along with this, is the realization that customers often equate needs with wants and vice versa. They almost always *want* a product they think they *need,* but they will also believe they *need* many products that they in fact only *want.* The argument about the difference between needs and wants is purely academic. In either case, the get-more-than-you-give ration-ale still applies. The sale will occur only when the fulfillment of needs — or wants — will provide the customer with more than the cost of buying the product.

And who decides when the benefits are higher than the cost? In our socie-ty it is the customer who chooses. Of course, there are some areas where laws and government regulations limit consumer choices, but the decision by and large is left to the customer. Only he knows his needs and desires in-timately enough to make a buying decision, and as long as the salesperson is ethical and honest in what he says about the product, the burden of making a correct buying decision rests squarely on the customer's shoulders.

While a good part of the buying decision in agribusinesses is increasingly based on rational thinking, humans are not completely clear-thinking, logi-cal creatures. Emotions do play a part — a big part in many cases. In sur-veys of salespeople from coast-to-coast, selling all types of products, some feel that as much as 90 percent of the buying decision is based on emotional rather than logical reasoning! These results may sound a bit extreme, since farmers today are indeed relying more and more on sound business judg-ments when they make purchases. But the point is that the salesperson can-not ignore the emotional aspects of the buying decision.

According to consulting psychologist Gail Elridge:

"All behavior is caused — goal directed — and a salesman is in some way satisfying some need at some level...man only acts when moved through fear, hope, love or greed. Human beings are basically emoting creatures. Emotions arouse, sustain and direct behavior."[1]

What Elridge is saying is that no matter what the superficial needs or de-sires expressed by the customer, beneath them lie powerful emotions. When a farmer trades harvest machines, it is true he needs that machine to harvest his crops. But behind that primary reason lies some emotions. Perhaps he fears break-downs on his old machine and the inability to complete harvest before bad weather. Perhaps the prestige of having a new model is a factor. Or perhaps new safety features make him feel better about his son helping with harvest. If the salesperson can find the underlying drive or need, he has gone a long way toward making a sale.

There is a tie-in here, also, to transactional analysis. As we learned, peo-ple can generally be found in one of three ego states: Parent, Adult or Child. If you can identify what ego state predominates in your sales call, you can get some clue as to underlying motives. A person primarily in-fluenced by the Child state may be motivated to action by strong emotional needs common to childhood: happiness, fear or stubbornness, for example. A Parent type, on the other hand, might be driven by the need for com-manding authority, taking care of others, or doing things the old traditional comfortable way. Even beneath the Adult may lie some basic driving emo-tions. Don't forget, although the Adult is the dispassionate, computerlike ego state which enjoys freedom from emotion, it can sometimes be used by either a sophisticated Parent or Child to rationalize or justify the desires of either of those two states.

[1]Gail Elridge, Industrial Psychologist-Blueprint for Professional Selling Seminar, San Antonio, TX, 1972.

THE FACTORS THAT MOTIVATE

Another important school of thought revolves around something called "motivational selling." Motivational selling, as its name suggests, taps into a person's powerful motivating drives to generate the sale. It's something like placing your prospect on a raft on the "emotional current" of the Mississippi River and letting the river do the work of moving him from Point A — being a prospect — to Point B — being a customer.

First: Primary Factors

Psychologists have broken down human motivating factors into two categories. The first are the *primary* human drives: hunger, thirst and sex, for example. This can be related to Maslow's first level of physiological needs, but be aware of the distinction. Maslow spoke of the needs themselves, food is an example. A person needs food to live and knows he needs it. Motivational selling is concerned with the internal forces which almost automatically press human beings into action. You may *know* you need food in an abstract sense, and you will set out to get food often long before you really need to eat it. But the drive that arises from hunger is far stronger than the drive that arises from knowledge that food is a necessity. It is a biological switch that clicks inside your body to get your feet moving and your eyes searching for food to quench the hunger. When you are hungry, you automatically see and smell things that might otherwise go unnoticed.

Second: Acquired Factors

The second set of motives are those that are *acquired*. These motives do differ from community-to-community or family-to-family because they are drives that are learned. Some acquired motives are status and prestige, being a good "breadwinner" for your family, being a community leader, being highly organized, being independent or being religious. Because a good many people's primary motives are well or adequately satisfied, acquired motives are often elevated to the importance of primary motives. Although it's fair to say that if famine suddenly struck, things would quickly return to their proper places, acquired and primary motives are virtual equals in everyday life. Because of that, a salesperson can appeal to these acquired motives with great effect.

The Hidden Buying Urge

The customer's motives are often called *hidden buying urges*. Through a predetermined set of questions, a salesperson can get down to brass tacks and discover which of these hidden buying urges is the most important one. A dealer who wants to be recognized as an innovator is not hard for the experienced salesperson to identify, for example.

The one overriding, most important motive is called the "dominant buying urge." Motivational selling therefore requires that the salesperson first discover what the dominant buying urge is, then tailor his approach and presentation to address that drive. We will discuss motivational selling and various techniques the salesperson can use to motivate prospects in a later chapter.

HOW DO PEOPLE BUY?

Now we must approach the question of how farmers and agribusiness customers buy. First of all, the salesperson must understand that no purchase is ever made unless some sort of problem or need is perceived. If you do not believe you are sick, it isn't likely you will be in the market for medicine. But suppose a new vitamin supplement is discovered that can remarkably increase your stamina and greatly reduce the frequency of colds. If someone is to sell this new vitamin to you, they will first have to make you aware of its existence and then convince you that it can in fact increase your stamina and reduce your colds. That is, you first must become aware of the product and your need for it.

A farm store salesperson may have a preventive medicine for a disease in baby pigs. But before it can be sold, the salesperson must identify the disease, its probability of occurrence, and its consequence to the hog producer before he can present his solution and possibly make the sale. That is, he must convince the farmer there is a problem and his solution will make the farmer appreciably better off. Unless the farmer perceives the problem, he is not likely to be interested in a solution. That is the salesperson's job. Since many times the customer is not aware of a problem or need, you must show the customer his problem or the additional potential that is possible and then present a solution.

The buying decision procedure is a problem-solving procedure:

Solving the Problem

1. What is the problem?
2. What is causing the problem?
3. What are the possible solutions to the problem?
4. What is the one best possible solution?

Once the problem is recognized, we get to the "How" of buying. How does the buyer make his purchase decision? The first thing a farmer with a problem does is to look for information that will help him understand the problem and provide him with alternative solutions. The extensiveness of that search depends on a number of factors. For example, the farmer may want to take his time and look at every possible solution before making large, infrequent purchases such as buildings or major pieces of agricultural machinery. Or when money is tight, the farmer may want to extensively search out the one solution that stretches his dollar as far as it will go. And some customers are just extremely cautious and simply by their own nature do not make hasty decisions.

In other situations, the information search may be short, for example, if the items being bought are small, frequently purchased things such as tools or lubricants. The customer's deliberation may also be short when there is a high level of trust in the supplier or salesperson; when the trust level is high the farmer says, "Why waste time looking around. I know he'll treat me right." Or the farmer may simply be an impulsive, extroverted sort who often makes quick decisions.

The farmer first brings his own attitudes, characteristics and information — obtained, perhaps, from a magazine or neighbor — when he enters the buying situation. From there he seeks a dealer or salesperson who will give him further information that will educate him and help him rationalize or justify the purchase. Throughout the whole process, the farmer is influ-

The Farmer's Buying Decision Model

enced by the attributes of the dealer, the manufacturer and the product. Finally, once he has bought the product, its continued use and repurchase depends on product performance and the kind of service he gets.

The most important of these influencing factors, especially in the purchase of a specific product such as herbicide or seed, is the dealer; of course, dealers and salespeople are often seen by the farmer as one and the same. The farmer tends to choose a person to deal with first and choice of product or brand follows. So you can see what a large part the human relationship plays in helping the customer choose a product that will best serve his needs. Therefore the characteristics of the dealer become a strong influence on the farmer's buying decision.

The third influencing factor is product performance, though the dealer still has a strong impact. In fact, the farmer is so dependent on the dealer that if the farmer finds that the product is unsatisfactory he may question his choice of dealers as much as the product. This points up the importance of following ethical selling practices and not trying to "put one over" on the customer or "sell him a bill of goods." You may fool someone once, and maybe even twice, but the dishonest agribusiness salesperson will not likely see that same farmer a third time.

INSIDE THE FARMER'S BUYING DECISION MODEL   What kind of influences affect the farmer's buying decision? As previously mentioned, the farmer already brings with him his own attitudes based on his cultural, economic, social, legal, environmental and technical background. Some of his major attitudes are:

Farmer Attitudes

1. Confidence in the dealer
2. Desire to buy products that are complementary or go together
3. Desire for a nearby supplier
4. Concern about safety hazards and dangerous chemical misuse
5. Need for technical knowledge
6. Need for economic knowledge
7. Desire for services
8. Desire to be well-regarded by friends and neighbors
9. Degree of habitualness
10. Need for respect or recognition
11. Degree of aversion to risk

With these concerns in his back pocket, the farmer then sets out to find a good dealer, even before he tries to decide which is the best product or brand. Some of the things the farmer looks for in a "good" dealer are:

Dealer Attributes

1. High quality products
2. Reputation for credibility
3. Accurate and dependable information

4. Good management at the dealer's store
5. Dealer support of product
6. Prompt, satisfactory handling of complaints
7. Complementary or backup services
8. Convenient location
9. Good personal relationships with customers
10. Understanding of farmers' problems
11. A broad product line
12. Neat and attractive store
13. Reasonable credit policies
14. Fair pricing

Once the farmer is ready to choose a product, manufacturer and product itself influence the decision:

Manufacturer Attributes
1. Recognized name with a good reputation
2. Company support of product
3. Product quality
4. Readily available supplies
5. Credible company representatives
6. Factual product information
7. Access to representatives for problem solving
8. Good appearance and attitude of sales representatives

Product Attributes
1. Good quality
2. Dependability
3. Good performance
4. Safety
5. Product availability
6. Safe, sturdy containers

Dealer Loyalty

The average farmer-buyer also tends to be loyal to one or a few dealers. Because of that, he will depend heavily on information supplied by the dealer and will often rely on dealer recommendations of product type or brand. As previously mentioned, the dealer — and thus dealer loyalty — is one of the most important influencing factors of the sale to farmers. Why so much loyalty?

For one, the farmer likes to do business with people whom he can depend on and trust. The closeness of relationship between farmer and the manager of a farm supply unit appears to be the most important element of dealer loyalty. Farmers do business with their "friends" and keep doing business with them. As shown in the list of dealer attributes a farmer looks for, the farmer's "friend" will be reliable and can be trusted, and he will often be able to provide services and offer credit.

Too, the farmer's needs almost mandate he have a dependable dealer to back him up. Technology changes faster than farmers can keep pace without the help of a specialist. They must depend on the dealer for that information. Such a dependence requires the farmer to stick with dealers they trust.

Other characteristics of the farmer-buyer which are also directly related to the dealer, include the desire for a nearby supplier. While farmers prefer to buy nearby, they will travel farther in the off-season. But during the busy season, they are far more concerned with convenience and availability. The farmer also likes a supplier with a wide selection of products, but that does not always mean he will be a one-stop shopper: many times he will split purchases between two or more dealers.

With an increasing awareness of the environmental and health dangers of powerful fertilizers, herbicides and pesticides, and with the attendant increasing legal liability, more and more farmers want to ensure proper handling of such chemicals. Thus they expect the dealers to advise them correctly on amounts to be used, as well as on handling and storage precautions and dangers. Farmers believe that the dangers from chemicals do not arise so much from the powerfulness of the chemicals themselves as from improper handling and usage. This fear, so to speak, of mishandling is what has sparked the interest in custom application. The number of liability suits has also had a similar effect and there appears to be no letup in sight for them. Thus the dealer must be more knowledgeable about these products and their handling not only to satisfy the customers, but also because custom application shifts damage liabilities to the dealer.

Because of a lack of time and lack of understanding about broad economic/technological connections and their aversion to risk, farmers highly value information about products and their use. They get information from a number of sources. Magazines, government publications, dealers, neighbors and county agents are the farmer's primary sources of information. But there is a distinction to be made here. While an initial source of information, such as a magazine or government pamphlet, may spark a farmer's curiosity about a certain technique or product, the source that helps him rationalize an ultimate purchase will probably be either a dealer or neighbor.

In fact, farmers need information that falls into three categories:

1. News of new technology, products, services and techniques.

2. Information that will persuade the farmer that Product X will actually benefit him.

3. Post-purchase information that will reinforce the sale and deal with any product-use problems that might have cropped up.

The salesperson, of course, plays a primary role in all three information needs. As previously mentioned, though farmers learn of new products from magazines or neighbors, the dealer must keep up-to-date on that same information because it is likely the farmer will be coming to him if he is interested in the new product. The dealer, of course, must also have the information needed for the farmer to rationalize his purchase, and he must be available with still more information to handle customer complaints or misunderstandings.

The manufacturer's representative, interestingly enough, does not appear to be a major source of information for the farmer except in the case where the problem is very technical. Manufacturer representatives are therefore viewed more as a backup for the dealers, who the farmers see as the real representatives for the product.

Finally, farmer-buyers exhibit certain common characteristics based on the size of their operations, income, age etc. As can be seen in Figure 5.2, those characteristics can play an important part in determining the farmer's degree of progressiveness: his willingness to accept new ideas, methods, technologies and products.

Figure 5.2 **Characteristics Determining Farmer's Progressiveness**

Characteristic	Less Progressive	More Progressive
Size of farm	Smaller	Larger
Level of income	Lower	Higher
Age	Older	Younger
Views farm as business	Weaker Agreement	Stronger Agreement
Views farm as way of life	Stronger Agreement	Weaker Agreement
Level of education	Lower	Higher
Level of technological knowledge	Lower	Higher

In turn, the level of progressiveness of the farmer can also determine a number of associated behavior traits. For example, as can be seen in Figure 5.3, the less progressive farmers, who also tend to have smaller farms, do not do as much price shopping as their more progressive, larger counterparts who make high-volume purchases.

Figure 5.3 **Progressiveness Determines Characteristics**

Behavior Trait	**Less Progressive**	**More Progressive**
Reads farm publications	Less	More
Shops around	Less	More
Loyal to dealer	More	Less
Price conscious	Less	More
Willing to travel to make purchases	Less	More
Buys dealer services	Less	More
Does not like cooperatives	Less	More
Involved in community	Less	More

SELLING TO OPINION LEADERS

Another wide-ranging category of personality types of which the salesperson and dealer should be fully aware is determined by how likely the farmer is to easily adopt a new idea or technology. This categorization is based on the pioneering work of Joe Bohlen of Iowa State University, who studied how farmers react to new ideas and developed a set of product adoption theories. Subsequent work done as recent as 1982 by other researchers, among them Everett Rogers also of Iowa State University, and industry specialists have confirmed this "adoption theory."

Product Adoption

Roger's book, *Diffusion of Innovations,* was first published in 1962, but it has proven to be sound in numerous research projects since then. Rogers reported that the adoption of a new product or service is a five-step process:

1. The customer has an awareness of the product.
2. Interest in the product builds.
3. The product is evaluated.
4. Trial usage of the product takes place.
5. Adoption of the product results if the customer is satisfied.

The first step, awareness, takes place during the company's initial advertising and promotional campaign for the product at farm shows, field trials, county fairs and through the media. At this point, the prospect is getting his first look at the new product and his curiosity is hopefully aroused.

Let's use an example—a small computer. In step two, consumer interest in the computer is generated. This may happen as soon as the customer first encounters the product, but it can also develop later on in the promotional campaign. When the prospective buyer stops by the store to get a closer look or sends in a request for pamphlets or other information, the interest is present.

Next, the customer will evaluate the product and consider how a personal business computer might work in his operation whether it is necessary, and what it can do to save money and boost productivity. If this evaluation takes place at a sales call, the salesperson's visit can be critical in clearing up misconceptions, providing information and driving home the benefits of the product.

Finally, in step five, the product is adopted, assuming the customer has come to believe it will fit into everyday use he decides to buy it. But even after the farmer has paid his money for the computer, he will continue to look for reinforcement of his buying decision. Here's where follow-up calls to see how the product is performing are important. Too, the purchaser will closely follow the continued ad campaign, voraciously reading the magazine ads and articles on the product.

Idea Adoption

But in his studies, Rogers noted that different farmers vary in their eagerness to adopt new ideas. Just sit back for a moment and think about how quickly *you* might put down $4000 to $10000 (or more) to buy a small computer to aid your selling job. Most of you would probably rather wait and see whether the idea catches on or whether fellow salespeople had purchased such a machine and were happy with it. Still, there would be a few brave souls who decided that buying the computer would be a good idea.

Rogers placed farmers into five groups: innovators, early adopters, early majority, late majority, and laggards. Only about 2.5 percent of farmers are anxious to try an untried brand or idea. These are called *innovators.*

Innovators

Innovators are risk-takers. As Christopher Columbus types, they see themselves keeping in touch with new ideas, and are well-read. They often thoroughly read research bulletins, are well-educated, have a scientific approach to problem solving, and have an ability to deal with abstract ideas. Often enough too, they tend to hold leadership positions in regional, state and national farm organizations rather than in more local groups. While they enjoy a high social status, they are often viewed skeptically by the folks around home and may *not* have a great deal of influence locally.

> Figure 5.4 **Farmers as ag idea adopters**
>
> **% of all farmers**
>
> Innovators 2.5
> Early Adopters 13.5
> Early Majority 34
> Late Majority 34
> Laggards 16

Early Adopters   The next of Rogers' grouping is that of *early adopters.* This group, while not the very first in the county to embrace a new product or idea, is surely in the "first wave" of adopters. They comprise 13.5 percent of all farmers. They are alert to the possibilities in new ideas being tried by the innovators, and consequently have a higher success rate at adopting "good" ideas because they learn from the success and failures of the innovators. Like the innovators, early adopters are well-educated and keep up-to-date by attending extension meetings, subscribing to farm publications and reading extension bulletins. Early adopters' farms are slightly smaller, less specialized and slightly less efficient than those of the innovators. But their peers see them as "good farmers," and they enjoy high social status. They are involved in many community organizations.

A key factor for salespeople to know about early adopters is that they are well-respected in their community. And while they often are aware of the fact, they are not the sort to broadcast to everyone that they're trying out the new idea. They often maintain a low profile. Nevertheless they are generally watched closely by other, less-bold farmers, and they enjoy having influence in the community, viewing it as a responsibility. Because early adopters are well regarded they are good target customers. Consider the possibilities of selling to the "leader" who's playing follow the leader with a hundred followers.

Early Majority   The next group to adopt a new idea, about 34 percent of the farmer population, is called the *early majority.* These socially-oriented people, with many contacts in the community, begin to see a successful pattern developing with the innovator's and early adopter's acceptance of the new product, and have decided there is enough evidence for them to jump aboard ship too. When they switch to the new method, they are making a deliberate decision to break with tradition. The members of the early majority also rely on neighbors and friends for information and of course read the farm publications. Their education is slightly above average, and their farms are slightly larger than average.

Late Majority   Group number four is the *late majority,* the next 34 percent to adopt the product. As can be seen from their position, they have a wait-and-see attitude. They are often skeptical about new ideas, and that tends to dominate their thinking. They are also further along on the spectrum of less-progressive farmers: less well-educated, less well-read, they have smaller farms, rely more on friends and neighbors for information, and travel outside the community less frequently.

Laggards   Finally, the last people to get in line in the adoption of a new idea are the so-called *laggards* — the remaining 16 percent of farmers. These are the least progressive farmers, averse to taking risks, less educated, afraid of debt, and their feet are firmly planted — maybe cemented — in tradition. The only time they come around is when adoption becomes necessary for survival or when the product is so widely used that they *have* to switch over. Laggards are not heavily involved in community groups — and almost never in a leadership capacity. They are less well-read than almost everyone else, depending mostly on friends and neighbors and on the broadcast media for information.

It should be fairly easy to realize how important the early adopters can be to any selling strategy. For any company introducing a brand new technology or for those interested in shoring up a weak market area, the early adopters should be a primary objective. Sell to them and you virtually are selling to everyone else without taking another step. But how do you find opinion leaders?

Actually the job of recognizing these people is not so hard as one might first think. Take another look at the description of the early adopters, then at your sales territory. Opinion leaders can be found on the boards of directors of cooperatives, school boards and churches, and attend a wide variety of public meetings. Or a salesperson not familiar with the territory need only ask people who the "best farmers" in the community are. Most of the fingers will be pointing at early adopters. Other good sources of information for pinning down opinion leaders are county agents, PCA managers, extension specialists, bankers and farm suppliers.

Searching Out Opinion Leaders

But while it may be easy to find the early adopters, it may *not* be so easy to sell to them. Don't forget, they are high-profile people — that's how you probably uncovered their whereabouts in the first place — and there are quite a few salespeople banging on their doors for the same reason you are. Because they are approached by so many people, they are often wary of strangers. Then too, because they feel a responsibility to their community as leaders, and because they do not want to ruin their reputation with too many foolish choices, they are not easily swayed.

However, opinion leaders are curious about better ways to do things and sometimes seek out the information on their own. They are willing to examine ideas and listen to a salesperson who knows what he's talking about. In most cases, they won't waste their time with a salesperson who's unprepared.

Opinion leaders also have egos that could use stroking, even though they maintain a posture of modesty. The salesperson must carefully approach the opinion leader, admiring his accomplishments but not overdoing it. The salesperson should also listen to the early adopter for he may have some useful advice about how the manufacturer, dealer or salesperson might better serve the area.

The more sophisticated approach involves an established advisory group of opinion leaders. These early adopters enjoy getting together with others of their kind to trade ideas, and everybody comes out a winner.

It is a good idea for the salesperson to develop a good relationship with the opinion leader for a number of reasons. For one, he will prove helpful as a source of extremely well-respected testimonials. But a salesperson must be careful to prepare himself fully for a call on an opinion leader. As mentioned, they enjoy speaking with someone who knows what he's talking about and thus you should be ready.

Special attention must also be paid to them, for if they are not well-serviced, the hoped for influential source of positive, community-wide recommendations can become a powerful negative force which warns other community members away.

Because opinion leaders seem to revel in adopting good new ideas and products, it is a poor idea to offer special rewards or deals to get opinion leaders to use and recommend the product. It is sufficient to offer the opinion leader what he wants: a good new idea. To do otherwise might cause him to feel manipulated, which could result in a negative, often vocal reaction.

Thus, because of their great influence, opinion leaders' business should be a prime objective of the successful salesperson. Developing a good relationship with these farmers will certainly give the salesperson a distinct edge over the competition.

SUMMARY

* People buy to satisfy their needs — either real or perceived. They almost always want a product they think they need and need products that they only want.

* The Maslow Hierarchy of Needs suggests that human needs occur in five levels and that the first need must be fulfilled before the person progresses to the next level. The levels are: physiological, safety and security, social, self-esteem, and self-actualization. The alert salesperson should determine at what level the prospect is operating and address his individual need.

* Behind needs lie powerful emotions, and a direct application of the transactional analysis theory. Prospects' ego states can determine how they should be approached.

* Motivational selling is based on the human tendency to be urged into action by internal factors (primary factors) or learned motives (acquired factors). Motives are often called "hidden buying urges." A "dominant buying urge" probably exists and the salesperson should tailor his presentation towards satisfying that urge.

* The decision to buy is a problem-solving move. Identification of a problem, its cause, possible solutions and the best solution are parts of the process for solving the problem.

* The prospect is influenced by many factors, the most important being the dealer. Farmers tend to be dependent upon their dealers and choose a person to work with rather than a particular product.

* The farmer's buying decision hinges upon his cultural, economic, social, legal, environmental and technical background.

* A farmer will tend to choose his dealer based on the following: reputation, accurate information, service, quality and personal relationship.

* Another influencing factor may be the manufacturer's attributes, such as company reputation, service, credibility, information availability and quality.

* A product is generally judged by its dependability, safety, availability and quality.

* The more progressive farmers tend to have larger farms, higher incomes, higher education and technical knowledge, are younger and view farming as a business venture rather than as a lifestyle. They also show less dealer loyalty than their less progressive peers and are well-read, price conscious and involved in the community.

* Farmers may also be categorized by their willingness to adopt new ideas. Innovators, Early Adopters, Early Majority, Late Majority and Laggards each tend to adopt ideas with different frequencies. Agri salespeople may find that Early Adopters are a prime target because others may follow their lead.

**Review Questions
Chapter 5**

1. Describe Maslow's Hierarchy of Needs and its five steps. Who will be more apt to buy something to compete with others, a farmer at level three or level four?

2. Why are buying decisions based on emotion rather than logic? In what transactional analysis state are most emotional decisions made?

3. What is the difference between an "acquired motivational factor" and a "primary factor"?

4. What is the most influential factor in a farmer's decision to choose a product? Why?

5. Since farmers depend on dealers as a primary information source, what kinds of information should the dealer provide?

6. List the five steps in the Idea Adoption Process. Why are "Innovators" more apt to complete the process more quickly than "Early Adopters"?

Chapter Six
How People Communicate

"How a salesperson handles communication both as a sender and receiver has a greater effect on his life than any other thing he does."

S alesperson Steve Conway should have sensed the problem the moment he walked up to Jim Dvorak. The 45-year-old farmer appeared disinterested in talking to Steve and proceeded with his work as the salesperson started talking and following him around his shop. Finally, Jim stopped what he was doing, folded his arms over his chest and asked Steve what he wanted. Steve explained that he was visiting farmers in the area and dropping off pamphlets and materials to let them know about National Breeders' entry into the western Iowa market.

"Well, son," Jim began, "I don't think I'd be interested in what you have to sell."

Steve interrupted. "I know what you're going to say Mr., Mr. ...."

"Dvorak," his prospect prompted.

"I know what you're going to say, Mr. Dvorak. You're already dealing with Platte Valley Company. I've encountered that problem with a number of farmers in the county."

"Son, I don't need National Breeders."

"Mr. Dvorak, you may not *need* National Breeders, but I think after you've looked at our track record compared to the competition's, you'll *want* National Breeders to be your supplier." Steve went on. "Our hybrid swine are bred for improved feed efficiency. Feeders from National Breeder sows and boars on the average achieve a pound of gain on 2.7 pounds of feed compared to Platte Valley's feed efficiency ratio of 1 pound of gain to 3.6 pounds of feed. And that compares favorably to the results of an Iowa State University survey of 500 farms throughout the state. Their summary showed an average feed efficiency of 1 pound of gain to 4.3 pounds of feed."

"Son," Jim began again, "You don't seem to understand. I am not interested in sows or boars. I don't have hogs here!"

"Ahhh," said Steve. "Well National Breeders does not just deal in swine. Let me give you this information package on our excellent high efficiency white-and-brown egg layers. As you can see, our birds are extremely feed efficient and also respond well to sophisticated husbandry."

Steve looked expectantly at Jim with a broad smile.

Jim, all this time frowning, finally could take no more and exploded. "Look around you, boy! D'you see any pigs, chickens, sheep, cows, giraffe, ANYTHING? This isn't a livestock farm, it's strictly a cash grain operation. Now get the message! That's why I don't need National Breeders and don't *want* you either!"

****

SELLING VS. COMMUNICATION

While Steve clearly violated more than one tenet of good salesmanship — such as not first establishing a need for his product — he also made a major glaring mistake: he failed to effectively communicate with Jim. Steve was saying things Jim had no need to listen to, and he was also refusing to correctly read the signals Jim was sending: the defensively folded hands, the frown, the disinterest in talking, and his verbal protests. As we can plainly see from Steve's example, good communication is absolutely mandatory for selling success.

In fact, many people describe communication and selling as being *the same thing,* and they are right. The selling process is a communications process. The salesperson is communicating his thoughts or messages about a product to a prospect. If he does a poor job in getting that message across, how can he possibly get the prospect to realize that he should buy the product? The answer is, he can't. The success of any sale is closely tied to the salesperson's ability to successfully explain the product and its benefits to the consumer and to read the customer's favorable and unfavorable cues.

Everyday Communications

Each and every one of us is involved in the communications process all day long. We talk with family, friends, business associates and prospects. We read the newspaper and watch television. We write letters. But there is a problem. Because people communicate all the time, they mistakenly believe that all that "practice" *guarantees* that they will communicate clearly and effectively. For most people nothing could be farther from the truth. The main difficulty can be seen in this transaction between a father and his four-year-old daughter after she asked him what a cemetery was. "A cemetery is a place where they bury people's bodies when they die," the father explained. After a few moments of puzzlement, the girl wanted to know more: "But daddy, what do they do with their heads?"

All kinds of communication derailments are continually occurring in the sales process too. The salesperson may use words or jargon that the prospect is not familiar with and therefore does not understand; one of the conversation's two participants may have left out a key bit of information quite by accident, making a particular conclusion either confusing or illogical; words with double meaning may be used and each person derives a different definition from the word; the salesperson may be so worried about covering every point in his presentation that he may not be listening to the customer and is missing vital information; or someone may assume the other person is very knowledgeable about a process or technique that he has never heard about.

According to Dr. DeWitt C. Reddick, dean of the University of Texas School of Communication, "How an individual handles communication both as a receiver and as a sender has a greater effect on his life than any other thing he does." The child who listens and understands the teacher and effectively communicates in front of the class is more successful in school than the child who can't understand the teacher and has the answer on the tip of his tongue, but can't quite put it into the right words because he is nervous about answering out loud. Is there any reason the same shouldn't hold true for salespeople?

Unfortunately, while all salespeople are taught the basics of what to tell the prospects about their product, what to watch for in the prospect's reactions and even how people interact, many never learn how to communicate effectively with people. That is taken for granted. Such a necessary education must start with an understanding of how communication takes place.

The act of communicating is a process in which one person creates an idea, puts that idea into a special form or code for transmission and sends the message through some channel. At the other end of the channel, another person picks up the message, decodes it so he can understand it and finally receives the message. This process can be seen in Figure 6.1 below.

THE COMMUNICA-TIONS PROCESS

Figure 6.1 **The Communications Process**

All communication has a source, and where humans are concerned this source is generally the thoughts, ideas, needs or desires which one person wishes to convey to another person. At this point, those thoughts are simply a series of electrical charges within the brain. Since human beings can't read each other's minds, the thoughts must be changed into a form that another person can see or hear. This form is a common language. The needs, thought or desire is put into a special "code," whereby, for example, the code C-A-R means a certain type of transportation vehicle.

Now the communication sender must choose an appropriate channel through which to send his encoded message. This channel can be a spoken conversation, a written memo, a telephone call or a pantomime. Or it could take other forms, such as a pat on the back, a smile or an angry scowl. And still other channels of communication might take the form of a painting, sculpture or symphony. All of these are means of expressing an idea or thought.

Once the recipient gets the message via his senses, he sets about decoding it based on his experiences, background and shared knowledge of the common language. If the person can "relate" to the message received, he can then understand the thoughts of the other person. If he does not understand, he will try to formulate his own coded message which says, "I am confused." The original sender will then have to repackage his thoughts into a different form, or channel them to the recipient via another, more understandable medium. Perhaps the pat on the back was mistaken for an aggressive swat. The communicator will then switch mediums from tactile to verbal and explain, "No, I was just congratulating you."

With so many break-points in the process — source to encoding, encoding to channel, channel to decoding, decoding to understanding — it's no wonder so many mistakes occur. Multiply that by the number of messages sent and received by you each day, and communication misunderstandings become almost a fact of life.

That is why everyone, especially the salesperson, should strive for something called *total communication*. Total communication is that perfect communication which transfers the exact image you had in your mind intact to the other person's mind, something like a photocopy machine — an exact reproduction is made. Total communication, of course, is not a rare beast on a per-unit level. Many individual communications you send and receive do reach this perfect state. But the concept of total communication deals with all communication: the 10,000 different messages you've sent out all day long, all week, all your life. When we step-up to this longer-range perspective, most people never get near total communication. In fact, it is a fair guess that only about 60 percent of your image gets through to the other person, or in different words, you achieve total communication only 60 percent of the time.

Making an attempt to achieve something approaching total communication is important for the salesperson because communication is the primary vehicle through which human relations operate. Since selling is based firmly in human relations, unless a better interaction (communication) between salesperson and customer is reached, the establishment of that human relationship suffers. How much more effective would your selling efforts and time be if you were "with the customer" and getting your message across just as you intended 70 percent, 80 percent, or even 90 percent of the time instead of just 60 percent or even less? But before we can start moving in the right direction, we must know what it is that causes us to move in the wrong direction.

Since communication is a person-to-person activity, the "system" has two main elements: a sender and a recipient. Each one encodes and decodes messages by way of their language skills and senses. But what if all the parts of the communication system are not in tiptop working order? When that happens, communication becomes more garbled, signals are missed and misunderstandings occur. Such system failures, most obviously, can be caused by external noises, such as the roar of grain elevators, or by hearing deficiencies. But other "bugs" cause havoc and make communication more difficult. The recipient may have a headache, may have just had an argument with his wife or her husband, or he may be under pressure from the boss to improve performance. In any case, his or her mind is preoccupied. The signals you are broadcasting are being interfered with by signals from another "transmitting station." When this is the problem, it is hard for you to recognize it. But when you do suspect such outside interference you can compensate by maintaining a professional posture as someone there to help, not to add to the problems. Likewise, if the communication problem is caused by something such as a noisy environment, it is a good idea to seek some refuge by moving elsewhere.

PROBLEMS OF COMMUNICA-TION

Another major problem area which causes sometimes massive communications breakdown is the commonality of the sender's and recipient's coding system: the common language. You would never try to get a point across in English to a Frenchman who spoke only French. The same goes even for people who share a common language. One of the most striking examples is the word "bad." Not too long ago bad — to a teenager — meant good, as in "Boy, he plays a bad guitar." But to the parent nodding in agreement about the bad rock-and-roll guitar music, "bad" held an entirely different meaning. But words are only part of the "common language."

The Common Language

Words are only symbols that trigger pictures in your mind, based on the things you have experienced and remembered in your lifetime and on things about which you hold an opinion. Just sit back a moment and consider these: Describe a beautiful woman, a handsome man. What's your favorite food? What does your dream house look like?

Chances are, a hundred different people would describe each of those things a hundred different ways. People understand what you say, based on what they know. If the salesperson is trying to convey the idea that his product will provide a benefit, such as "you'll now have time to raise more livestock," he will never make the customer understand the "benefit" if he has never in fact wanted to raise more livestock because the markets are bad, the investment's too high or some other reason.

The best communication takes place between people who share the same field of experience. Children, for example, who have the same interests, live in the same environment, have a similar socio-economic status, share common attitudes and vocabulary, and who have a lot of experiences in common are perhaps the best communicators. But as children grow up, they start moving apart and away from this world of almost perfect commonality. One child's parents fall extremely ill. Another child moves out of state. A third chooses to attend a college on the other side of the country. A fourth child joins the military. And in all this activity, the commonality eventually disintegrates and a 30-year-old man who returns to his hometown as a successful doctor can't seem to establish the same old bonds and communication with his childhood friend who never ventured outside the home area.

Schramm's Diagram and Overlap   Wilbut Schramm, in his book, *The Process and Effects of Mass Communication,* illustrated this problem with the diagram in Figure 6.2.

Figure 6.2 **Process and Effects of Mass Communication**

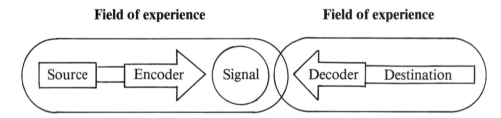

In Schramm's diagram, the "field of experience" of the source encompasses everything in the world that he has come in contact with. And the same for the destination's or recipient's field of experience. Where these two fields overlap, the source and recipient share common denominators or experiences. It is in this area that communication can take place. The only way an experience that is not shared *can* be shared is if that uncommon experience can be somehow related to a commonly shared experience. For example, if the source wants to make the recipient understand Chemical X, and the recipient has never heard of Chemical X, the salesperson will have to explain that Chemical X is a herbicide, something like Herbicide Y, with which the customer *is* familiar.

If the areas of overlap are large, communication is easy. If the overlap is small, communication will be more difficult and will involve a lot of work bringing the uncommon experiences into the realm of common experience. If there is absolutely no overlap, communication cannot take place. Thus, the source and recipient below who have grown up together in the same town find it easier to communicate with each other as seen in A.

Figure 6.3 **Communication's "Field of Experience" Overlap**

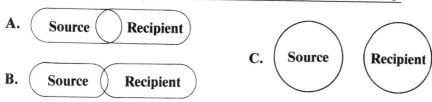

But a nonfarm newcomer to a small town who has lived most of his life in Chicago will have a harder time (at least in the beginning) finding a common ground on which to communicate with the people in a rural farm community as seen in B.

And the salesperson from North Dakota will have an almost impossible task in trying to make a Chinese rice grower understand what he has to say (as in C of Figure 6.3).

An important theory of communication for salespeople to understand revolves around the so-called *mental filter,* which explains the varied potential of human beings to understand and communicate messages. As can be seen in Figure 6.4, the five sensory inputs pick up external signals and transmit them to the brain where they are filtered in much the same way a municipal water system purifies water: the large rocks remove big impurities and the smaller rocks remove progressively smaller pollutants until finally the water is completely pure. If we were to draw off the "water" at each level of the human psychological filter, we would notice progressively sophisticated levels of understanding.

The Mental Filter

Figure 6.4 **The Psychological Filter**

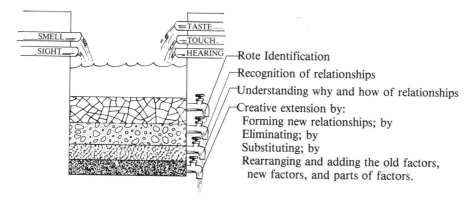

By Rote   The first level of filtration is able to produce simple rote or memorized understanding. Such things as the alphabet, numbers and words are examples of the level of understanding that is possible here. No relationships are drawn, just rudimentary identification of various codes.

Relationship Recognition   Level two gives us the ability to put things together and draw relationships between simple elements. For example, we know at level two that the numeral 1 comes before the numeral 2, or that the sun rises in the east, climbs up into the sky, then sinks into the west. We don't know why these relationships exist, just that they do.

Understanding What You Recognize   At level three, we have the capacity to understand why the relationships are such. We can comprehend that the sun rises in the east and sets in the west because the earth is revolving in the counterclockwise motion (assuming the south pole is the center point).

Creatively Extending Your Understanding   The fourth level of understanding allows us to creatively extend the elements and their relationships that we know about and form potential new relationships. It is this level of understanding that let Copernicus conclude that indeed the whole solar system and universe did not have to revolve around the earth but that the universe may only *appear* to revolve around us. Either the earth is stationary and the whole universe moves or the earth moves and the universe stays still; in either case the appearance of the universe's movement would be the same. It is more likely the smaller body — earth — is doing the moving. As can be seen with Copernicus, thinking at this level involves elimination, substitution, addition, rearrangement and combination.

What does this mean for the salesperson? First of all, it will give you a greater understanding of your customer's psychological capacity for understanding what you have to explain to him so you may tailor your communication accordingly. If a potential customer seems to be able to only understand relationships, but not why the relationships exists, you are probably wasting your time explaining why a particular hybrid produces more wheat per acre than another and why a particular feature of your product is beneficial; and thus you must be extra careful in your presentation.

Other prospects, operating at the higher level three may be quite willing and able to understand relationships and the why's and how's of those relationships, but they might have difficulty extending their knowledge to new, unfamiliar relationships. Thus, you will have a hard time bringing them into the common ground of experience overlap if they are unfamiliar with something you want them to understand.

Linking Filters and Needs   Simple enough, perhaps, but let's take things one step further and we can thus get a very detailed picture of the person we want to get our message to. By linking our psychological filter with the customer's needs as well as his field of experience, we can make a determination as to whether or not a particular communication recipient understands us. But more importantly, we can see possible hotspots or danger points of misunderstanding. This linkage is shown in the following diagram.

Figure 6.5 **Linking Filters and Needs**

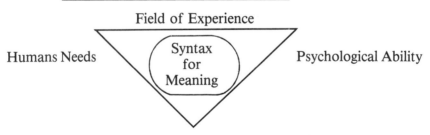

Based on how much each of these three forces is tugging the recipient's thoughts, you can find his frame of reference. For example, a person who has apparently realized he should finally buy his own combine, and who is on level three of Maslow's Hierarchy of Human Needs (Chapter 5), requires social approval. In the psychological ability department, he is a level three also: able to understand the why and how of relationships, and his field of experience does not cover ownership of such equipment as he has always had custom harvesting service do the work for him. If you were to just look at his field of experience, you might believe he would be extremely averse to the risk of buying a combine, probably not knowing how to run it, worried about repairs and worried about the expense.

But the desire for peer approval is pulling him away from that aversion to risk, and his ability to understand relationships — "Those farmers who own their own equipment are respected by their neighbors and viewed as more successful and by buying a combine I can gain respect and appear more successful" — which will aid you in throwing the psychological tug-of-war between risk aversion and the need for peer approval to the latter's favor.

But now suppose the farmer already felt secure in his standing in the community and was at Maslow's fourth level — the need for ego gratification or self-esteem. If you tried selling the combine based on the peer approval it would provide, the customer would never see a need. You have failed to communicate. Sales communication would be more effective by explaining how ownership would give him total control over his farm operations, fulfilling a personal need to be more self-sufficient. You would have found the common ground on which to communicate.

Now that you have seen the interworkings of communication, what can be done to aid the process of communicating? Anything that limits communication effectiveness can be considered a "noise." Such noises can be reduced by remembering a few basic principles when you are trying to communicate:

BASIC PRIN-CIPLES OF COMMUNICA-TION

1. Don't ever assume the recipient of your message is an impartial collector of information. All information is viewed in relation to a person's needs, experiences and ability to comprehend.

2. With the assumption that everything you communicate has subjective implications regardless of how objective you think it may be, empathize with the prospect — put yourself in his shoes — and give the prospect your message in a form he can understand and relate to. Switch places and communicate to them as you would have them communicate to you.

3. Because communication breaks down where there is little overlap of each person's field of experience, it is *your* job to bring as much of what you want your subject to understand into the common arena. You must connect with the things your prospect does understand and relate the elements he does not understand.

4. Don't assume that simplicity in the encoding phase will eliminate problems of understanding. Even the simplest words can have many and varied meanings which could become sources of confusion.

Basic Goals

With a solid understanding of how people communicate, the salesperson can now proceed to put that tool of the trade to work fulfilling the goal of selling. The four basic goals the salesperson wants to accomplish with communication are:

1. To create an awareness of the product
2. To help the prospect develop an understanding of the product and what it can do for him
3. To gain prospect conviction that the product is indeed good and will fulfill his needs
4. To cause the prospect to actually buy the product

How these are accomplished will be dealt with in the following four-chapter block covering the selling process.

FORMAL SALES COMMUNICA-TIONS

A majority of the communication experiences agri salespeople partake in are "one on one." Personalized selling requires such a communication approach. Often appearing informal in nature, this interpersonal communication is socially acceptable and puts prospects at ease. However, there are many instances where a more formal communication style is necessary: prospect or customer meetings, presentations to peers or management, civic or community group meetings. This "speechmaking" requires much of the same kind of preparation as does personalized selling. Further, the same jitters develop in a salesperson just beginning the process of formal speaking as occur when the first few sales calls are made. The professional sales person must develop competencies in *both* one on one and formal communication styles to be most effective. Consequently, making presentations is a skill which must be cultivated rather than avoided.

There's really very little to be afraid of if you know how to develop a good presentation and if you are prepared. And while it may be of little solace the first time you stand in front of a group, remember what Emerson said, "All good speakers were bad speakers at first." The moral? Practice makes perfect.

Every presentation is designed to achieve one or more of four goals: **GOALS**

1. To educate the audience
2. To persuade the audience to agree with your thoughts
3. To relax or entertain the audience with something interesting
4. To motivate the audience to act on your suggestions

The cornerstone of good public speaking, as with good salesmanship, is **PREPARATION** preparation. If you adequately prepare yourself, you will convey your message effectively and you be will self-confident. This will contribute to the audience's relaxation. No one wants to watch a nervous, terrified person for 30 minutes. Preparation tips include:

1. Allow adequate time for research, study and reflection. Don't put this work off until the last minute, for then you'll be less comfortable in front of the group to whom you're speaking.

2. Speak only about subjects about which you are familiar and excited. No one enjoys a speaker who's stumbling through unfamiliar territory and is bored too.

3. Make your points by using examples of your own personal experiences as they relate to your topic.

4. Don't write up a word-for-word speech. Work from brief notes or an outline so that you are "there" with the people instead of "somewhere else" — involved in reading. Take Bishop Fulton Sheen's advice, "Never submit your active mind to a dead sheet of paper."

5. Don't memorize. That's harder anyway, but you also run the risk of having to search your memory for what you are about to say, which looks foolish.

6. Don't tell them everything you know. Give the audience only the cream off the top. That way you'll feel more confident, you'll give them only the best and most important information, and you won't swamp the listeners with an overabundance of information.

7. Relax. Be yourself. As anyone knows from a simple job interview, you will appear much more confident, knowledgeable and believable if you are calm and collected.

8. Finally, don't speak if you have nothing to say.

During the presentation you will want to follow the basic principles of good speaking. You should first have a vivid picture of what you want to say in your mind before you open your mouth.

You should also use words that the listeners can understand and relate to. Never speak "over their heads."

You will want to use the most concise, specific, correct words to convey your ideas. Action words put color into your speech and bring the pictures you are drawing to life.

Many speakers, in an effort to get through this tension-producing exercise and off the stage, rush through the speech as if they were meeting the President of the United States in just three minutes. Speak distinctly and slowly for the listeners. This allows time for what you are saying to sink in, and it also gives the listeners time to digest what you are saying.

Every good speech requires a good opening and a good "snapper," or closing thought. You have only about 30 seconds to capture your audience, make a good impression on them and make them want to listen to *you*. Following are some good opening techniques:

Openers

1. Ask a question. Nothing can get the wheels turning and generate interest like a question — as long as the question is important, pertinent and relevent to the audience.

2. Ask the audience to participate, perhaps with a show of hands of all people who have had a particular problem last year. Their physical involvement breaks the tension and opens them up to what you have to say.

3. Arouse the audience's curiousity by, for example, telling them your presentation will show them how to get something they want. Psychologists tell us that a curious person cannot keep a closed mind. He will be receptive to you.

4. Use showmanship. You try to bring your presentation to life when you're trying to sell something to one individual, why not use some of the same techniques — an exciting exhibit, an interesting demonstration — to liven up the speech?

5. Begin with an interesting example, such as the tale of a farmer who could not get his cows to eat. Everyone loves a story that fits their purpose and interests in attending the meeting.

The Body

With your speech underway, take the opportunity to give your audience some solid information.

If you're giving a speech to inform, outline two or three points you wish to convey and back up those points with illustrations. For example, if you're talking about the necessity of vaccinating cattle for disease, think through the reasons for vaccinating: 1) profit from healthy animals, 2) stopping the spread of disease from animal to animal and from farm to farm, and 3) responsibility of each farmer to be a good manager. In talking about each point, you can cite cases of what happened to farmers who didn't vaccinate versus ones who did and give figures to back up your points.

A speech to entertain or "greetings" from a company are a different story. This type of speech may be harder to create because the thoughts are more abstract. Still, it needs to be as organized as any other presentation. Perhaps your message is to thank your customers for a successful year. Again, think of all the reasons you appreciate their patronage (i.e. successful year for the company allowing continued service, community prosperity, improved agriculture in the area etc.) Use examples and personal experiences. People understand day-to-day problems and will probably enjoy hearing about the rainy morning you got stuck three times and had to be pulled out by the same farmer.

Once you have successfully opened and delivered your speech, how do **The Closing**
you close? Some possibilities include:

1. Summarize what you have said, the points you have raised and the ideas you want to get across briefly, logically and succinctly.

2. If you have the talent for developing jokes or funny stories — close with a good one. This leaves the audience in a happy frame of mind, and that happiness helps provide a pleasant reinforcing agent for your point.

3. Close with a quotation or verse that really sums up the point of your speech. *But* whatever quote you use, it must be relevant to your point, be short, contain a complete thought, be clearly humorous, serious or inspiring, and should be authored by someone your audience will accept and agree with.

4. Motivate your audience by clearly summing up what action they have to take in order to reap the rewards about which you have told them.

With all this information backing you up, you should have the con- **Additional Hints**
fidence to go up there and "knock 'em dead." But if you feel really confident, let's take one more step. Here's how you can be a "hit" in your public
address:

1. Be appreciative. If you're glad to be there, tell them and show them.

2. Make the audience feel important. Tell them why they were important enough to get you behind the lectern.

3. Play yourself down rather than brag about how smart you are. People don't enjoy a braggart, and you may alienate your audience immediately. By being low-key, you create a realistic expectation. When you really deliver, the audience gets much more than they bargained for.

4. Unless you're late, don't apologize. Why is that? Your apology is merely a plea for sympathy because you aren't prepared. There's no excuse. Instead, prepare, or don't accept a speaking engagement for which you are not willing to prepare.

5. Don't preach to your audience and certainly don't criticize them. That is not your right or responsibility. Remember the Biblical verse, "Judge not that ye be not judged, for whosoever judgment ye judge so shall be meted unto you."

6. Last, enjoy yourself! The audience can sense your attitude. And why not? You're right up there for them all to see. If *you're* having fun, *they'll* have fun; if you're uptight or bored, the audience will be too.

Now go out and "knock 'em dead!"

* Good communication is mandatory for selling success. Salespeople not **SUMMARY**
in tune with a prospect's signals may lose sales.

* The communication process includes a source, who sends a message and a

receiver, who takes the message and decodes it. The message is sent through a channel, which may be oral, written or nonverbal.

* Breaks in the communication process cause mistakes frequently, so communicators should strive for "total communication" in which the receiver gets the exact message the course sent.

* Despite effectiveness of the parts of sender and recipient, mistakes can still occur. External noise and the common language may prevent the reception of accurate signals.

* Schramm's Overlap Diagram illustrates the principle that the more common experiences people share, the more effective their communication. If overlap is large, communication is easy. If a small overlap, difficult communication ensues.

* The Mental Filter illustrates tiers of understanding that vary from person to person. Level one is ability to memorize information and level two is ability to draw relationships between elements. Understanding those relationships is level three, while level four allows creation of new relationships based on knowledge of existing relationships.

* Linking the needs of a prospect with knowledge of the filter system can allow a salesperson to understand at what level the prospect is operating and provide for a sale.

* Basic goals of communication are to: create an awareness of the product, help the prospect develop an understanding of the product and what it can do for him, gain prospect conviction that the product will fill his needs and to cause the prospect to purchase the product.

* Normal communication may mean a speech or presentation. Adequate preparation will spell the difference between success and failure when talking with an audience.

* Goals of a presentation are: to educate the audience, persuade the audience to agree with your thoughts, to relax or entertain and to motivate to action.

* A presentation includes three parts: an attention-getting opening, an informational body and a snappy closing.

Review Questions
Chapter 6

1. Why can effective communication be difficult to achieve?

2. Describe the communication process. Where can breakdowns in the process occur?

3. Explain "total communication." How can a salesperson accomplish it?

4. What effect does a person's "field of experience" have on the communication process?

5. Name the four levels of the "mental filter." How can this knowledge help a salesperson do a better job of selling?

6. What are the four goals of communication for a salesperson?

7. Should a formal speech be memorized? Why or why not?

8. List three ways to get the audience's attention in the opening.

9. Should you tell jokes in a speech? Why or why not?

10. How do one-on-one communication and formal presentations to larger groups complement one another?

The Sales Process

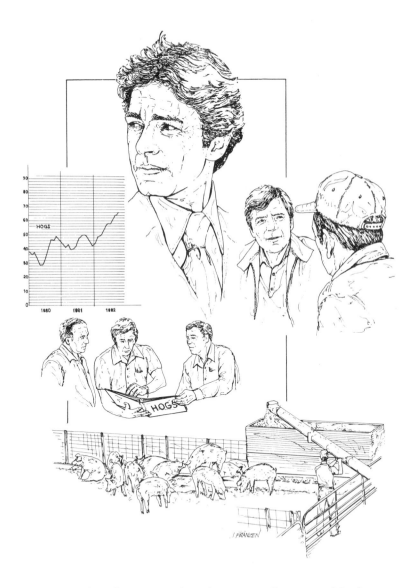

The actual selling process involves several major steps. Success with the most widely known step — closing — will come only with the careful and professional execution of the other parts of the process. Section III examines each step as it follows the progress of one agri salesperson.

Chapter Seven
The Preparation

"Preparation is simply the work an agri salesperson does
to gear up for a professional sales call."

Mike was so absorbed in thought that he almost missed his exit off the interstate toward home. His regional manager had really been adamant about expanding direct sales to producers — not just in his district, but throughout the whole region. His company gave the toughest talk he had ever heard from them, and he had the distinct impression that it was going to get a lot tougher if their market share trend didn't turn around soon.

Mike Adams had been representing Fast-Grow Feeds since he finished his ag degree two years ago. He really liked the feed business and livestock production, especially hogs which dominated his area. He had mostly worked with dealers in a six-county area, occasionally calling on farmers with a feed store or elevator manager. He had developed some good friends among his 20 accounts.

It was easy to understand where the company was coming from. Sales through dealers and elevators had dropped noticeably, even in the brief two years Mike had been in the district. His customers were having a tough time. One of his dealers had even gone out of business earlier this year.

Interestingly enough, though, hog numbers were up — concentrated in larger operations that sometimes used more feed than some of Mike's smaller dealers sold. Several of the larger farrow-to-finish producers had installed elaborate feed mixing systems that allowed them to combine highly concentrated "premixes" containing vitamins, minerals and animal health products directly with their own grain to produce their feed almost like a prescription.

In fact, it was just this market that Mike's regional manager was so strong on. Fast-Grow had introduced a complete line of premixes. "We've got to go after that large producer premix business or we'll be completely out of the market in five years!" he'd emphasized.

Frankly, the idea of selling directly to these large hog producers was pretty scary. "Why they'll eat me alive," Mike thought as he negotiated the curves on North River Road. "Most of those guys have been in business 25 years and have forgotten more about hogs than I'll ever know," he worried aloud. He knew, however, that he had a good product and Fast-Grow had had him in the home office for at least three weeks of training since he started. He should be ready for the challenge.

That night, Mike began to think about how he should get started. He knew that he had better have some progress to report at next month's sales meeting. He worried about how he should proceed.

****

Mike Adams has his work cut out for him if he is to succeed. He is facing the challenge of entering a market that is relatively new and somewhat threatening. His job will be easier and have a significantly higher probability of success if he follows a few basic rules about preparing for sales calls.

DEFINING PREPARATION   In a nut shell, preparation is simply that work you do which prepares you for a professional sales call. The process involves: knowing your product, finding out who your prospects are, what their needs are, why they need your product and why they should buy from you. Planning selling strategy — an important part of preparation — becomes relatively simple once we know our product, market and prospects.

THE ROLE OF KNOWLEDGE IN SELLING   To begin with, the basis for any successful selling relationship with agricultural customers is the salesperson's technical competency and knowledge of the product and its use. All farm supplies and services either directly or ultimately become part of a highly-complex production process. If products are misused, the customer cannot gain their full benefits and will likely be dissatisfied with the results. Research has proven repeatedly that farm customers are increasingly relying on suppliers at both the dealer and manufacturer level to inform, advise, recommend, suggest and troubleshoot for them. A salesperson or company representative who cannot perform these functions will have a difficult time selling. No matter how polished a person's selling skills are, if product knowledge is inadequate or technical questions about their product and its use can't be handled, a salesperson will have trouble getting sales — and even more difficulty getting repeat business.

Most agribusinesses recognize the importance of technical expertise in selling to dealers and farmers. They hold regular training sessions to ensure that field salespeople are current on everyday technical problems. Technical specialists are sometimes assigned to specific geographical areas to support field salespeople when difficult problems arise. Further, field salespeople are expected to study new technical information that relates to their product as it becomes available from their own company, university research publications and industry trade magazines.

Upgrading one's technical and product knowledge is a perpetual process. Not only does the information base keep changing and growing, but the successful salesperson knows that customers continually demand more from them. The better equipped he can be, the more successful he will be with his customers.

With product knowledge as a footing, the cornerstone of the preparation process is prospecting.

PROSPECTING — LOOKING FOR CUSTOMERS

Like the crusty old-timer crouched by the stream panning for gold in the creekbed, salespeople too have to be prospectors — actually getting out in the field, sifting and sorting prospects, and looking for customers — before they ever find any gold. Expanding sales usually means gaining *new* customers. Increasing your sales as your regular customers expand their own businesses is effective, but takes time. Many agribusinesses are not patient enough to wait on this alternative as the exclusive method to increase sales. Even if you already have a good business, you must continually work for new and better accounts because a host of natural events will always work to shrink your list. People die, move out of the area, retire from the business and go bankrupt. No matter how good a salesperson you are, or how conscientious, your customer ranks will naturally become depleted through no fault of your own. And the only way to stem the tide of attrition is to prospect for more customers to take the place of those that are lost. This can be accomplished in a number of ways.

Know Your Market

Effective selling and prospecting require a good understanding of your market area. What is the total potential for your product? What share of the market do you currently have? Who uses your products and why? Who doesn't and why? Who are your competitors and why are they successful? What trends are important in your market? Answers to these questions and a host of others are important in doing a good selling job.

Although some of this understanding is gained during the initial training period when the salesperson first breaks into a new company or area, the world is ever changing and so is the market. This means the successful salesperson must keep abreast of what's going on. Information must be gleaned from current customers, colleagues, newspapers and magazines, and visits with public officials and community leaders. With this essential information, the salesperson can begin to take aim on the most likely targets.

A bird's-eye view of your sales area can initially be overwhelming. Close examination may reveal possibilities everywhere you look. While it varies among different agribusiness industries and among market areas in the same industry, in most cases there are large numbers of farmers or dealers who are potential customers. In fact, the sheer number of possibilities intimidates some salespeople to the point that they don't know how or where to begin.

On the other hand, when a salesperson has been in a territory for a while it's easy to fall into the trap of failing to see potential customers who may be all around. While the salesperson working for a farm store intellectually knows a great deal about his market area, he may get so used to dealing with the same farmers that he forgets about the wide variety of prospects that are all around: part-time farmers, suburban homeowners and other farmers who he doesn't normally deal with. Just because a big farmer turned him down three years ago, does not mean that farmer isn't a good prospect today. Things change, and so do prospects. So it's important to look objectively at your potential.

Finding Prospects   Finding choice prospects is not as difficult as it might first seem. All it takes is a little creativity and some work. There are any number of sources from which to build a good prospect list. Here are some ideas which might work for you:

1. Get a map of your sales territory and locate all your present accounts with pushpins of varying colors according to volume of sales. This is a good way to find holes in your coverage, whereupon you can investigate why those areas are empty and how you can go about filling them.

2. Join up with memberships in community organizations and services clubs. These activities provide lots of opportunities to meet people and keep tabs on what's going on. You often make friends, develop trust and credibility that ends up in sales to other members or leads to other prospects. Simply attending public meetings such as university extension programs, field days or trade shows can also provide valuable contacts with prospective customers as it builds your general knowledge level and creates additional credibility.

3. Keep yourself in the "public light" by letting it be known you're interested in speaking before local groups who are always looking for qualified speakers; for example, 4-H clubs, farmers' groups, sales meetings and civic organizations. By presenting yourself as a spokesperson or authority, you will gain respect and contacts.

4. Keep a close eye on the press, and on trade and professional journals to find out what company is expanding its territory, who's moving up the corporate ladder, what farmers are buying, new store openings and new companies locating in the area. All this information provides opportunities for the alert salesperson.

5. Other salespeople who are not competing with you and are in other

fields, can sometimes provide leads to prospective customers.

6. Customers are also a good source for finding *new* prospects who might be interested in what you are offering. In fact new accounts are even an excellent source because they are usually proud of their decision and are anxious to share their good ideas with others. Be sure to ask your new account diplomatically whether you are free to mention his name as recommending that you talk to a suggested prospect. Established accounts are also good sources for new prospect suggestions. Your accounts should be combed over regularly for this purpose. Your customers are constantly following the trade just as you are, and they may have picked up a lead you missed.

7. After a prospect has turned you down, don't close your case and walk away. Ask him whether he might know someone else who *would* be interested in what you have to offer. He might actually know, and because people often feel a little guilty about turning you away, he may be inclined to give you *something*. That something could be a lead which produces one or several customers.

8. Above all, stay alert as you move through your day. Clues from a casual conversation at the coffee shop with a new friend, noticing Pete Johnson hauling his tractor in for repairs the second time in a month, or seeing some blueprints and equipment brochures on your dealer's desk can suggest some very fruitful opportunities for the smart salesperson. Opportunities are everywhere. You can find them so long as you constantly keep your eyes open.

As seen in the "Selling Scenario" at the beginning of the chapter, prospecting for customers will be an important part of the job for Mike Adams. In his six county area he must get in touch with a new segment of the market, and then be ready to make contact with them. There is a lot of territory to cover, but his two years in the area will be of great help to him.

Making Calls

One of the most productive ways of finding prospects is to go directly to the field and look for them yourself — making calls on people who you believe might become customers. These can either be cold calls, cool calls, lead followups or targeted calls.

Cold Calls

Cold calling is something like scattering buckshot: the law of percentages dictates that at least some of the pellets will hit the target. Simply enough, cold calling involves a salesperson's stopping at every prospective farm or agribusiness in an area without any prior information about the prospect. It recognizes that many, probably most, of the calls will not result in a sale. But in the process of canvassing the territory, prospects will be uncovered that will be interested and ultimately become actual customers — prospects that would not likely be reached in any other way. Research and practical experience prove that it works — particularly with products where demand is widespread. In the seed industry for example, it is commonly believed that the more farmers called on, the more sales will be made. Some seed companies report sales call to order ratios that are quite consistent over time. The order may not always be a large one, but even a trial order can have a good long-term payoff. It's a start.

Many salespeople don't particularly enjoy cold calling. After all, it's flying blind into the market. You are calling on strangers who did not ask you to come to their farm or business. The success rate will likely be low. That terrible two letter word, "No!" may be heard frequently and no one likes rejection. Yet it does uncover new and highly profitable customers. Even if the success ratio of cold calls would only be five percent, that could add up to a very *productive* use of time. Consequently, many agribusinesses encourage or even require their salespeople to spend part of their time systematically cold calling in their territory. Why? Because it works!

Cool Calls

The next step up the prospecting ladder is *cool calling*. Rather than blanketing the area, cool calls involve a directed approach to prospects that generally have characteristics that the salesperson believes increase the likelihood of success. A salesperson selling a new type of automatic hog feeding system might well decide he will do better with larger, high technology producers. Cool calling in this case might mean identifying all producers marketing over 2000 hogs per year who have a hog confinement system — and then systematically calling on all of them over a 12 month period. This approach would be very appropriate for Mike Adams.

Cool call prospects might be identified by examining membership lists in trade organizations, current owners of other products sold by your company, conversations with people who know the area, or simply visually observing the prospect's place of business as you drive by. No matter what source of information is used, the success rate can be expected to be higher than cold calling — but it will miss some prospects who may go unnoticed or do not fit the criterion.

Following Leads

A third and more productive method of coming up with good prospects is to *followup on leads* generated when compiling prospect lists. Earlier, several different sources of prospects were discussed, but those are of no value until they are used and followed up on. You will likely be able to characterize some leads as "hot" while other are a shot in the dark. Even though many leads won't pan out, they often direct you to something else that ultimately pays off.

PRIORITIZING TARGET PROSPECTS

We have established that simply making more sales calls can result in more sales. There is no doubt that cold call selling is effective to tap prospects not easily reached any other way. But where information is available that can direct selling effort — well, it just makes sense to use it. Once prospects have been identified, it is smart to prioritize them so that efforts can be concentrated on those who show the highest probability of payoff...a *targeted* selling approach.

Many experts believe that concentrating selling efforts on a few select prospects has a higher probability of payoff than dissipating time and resources over a larger number of prospects. They argue that working on a dozen desirable prospects is a lot better than trying to call on fifty — not only because you are more likely to close on a much higher proportion of the small select group, but also because it costs less, will detract less from the quality of service provided to regular customers, and will not be as visible to or antagonize competitors as would a broad frontal attack on many of their customers. Concentrating efforts can make a greater impact — just as a 95-pound woman in spike heels can make an "impression" on a linoleum kitchen floor while her 200-pound husband in street shoes makes no mark at all.

A *high-potential* prospect is, in general, one who has a relatively high probability of buying, who will likely stay with you over a period of time if you serve him well and who will be profitable for you to serve. Each industry and market area has other more specific characteristics of high-potential prospects. A little thinking can usually identify these characteristics. Familiarity with your market area will even allow you to identify and evaluate specific high-potential prospects that might be targeted for concentrated effort.

High-Potential Prospects

One method for targeting the high potential prospects is to rate probable candidates on a series of those factors you believe are important to predicting selling success.[1] Then, prospects with the highest total rating become the prospects who get the first and most concentrated selling attention. For example, Figure 7.1 shows the factors a fertilizer salesperson might use in prioritizing retail customers. Each agribusiness will need to determine what characteristics to include. With factors identified, the salesperson chooses several prospects that he intuitively believes would be good bets. Each prospect is rated on a 1-10 scale (10 being highly favorable and 0 being highly unfavorable) on each characteristic. Be sure to rate all prospects on one characteristic before moving on to the next so that a comparative effect from prospect to prospect is achieved. For example, item one relates to the potential business each customer could give you. If the first customer is quite large, then award him a 9 or 10 for potential account size. If the next prospect is only "average" size, then award him a 5 or 6 for this factor.

---

[1]The numerical rating system for high potential prospects is attributed to Agri Business Associates, an Indianapolis based agribusiness training and development company.

Figure 7.1 **Prospect Priority Index**

Prospect

Prospect Priority Index					
Factor					
1. Potential account size	___	___	___	___	___
2. Credit evaluation	___	___	___	___	___
3. Current business	___	___	___	___	___
4. Product match	___	___	___	___	___
5. Service match	___	___	___	___	___
6. Time complementarity	___	___	___	___	___
7. Location	___	___	___	___	___
8. Opinion leader	___	___	___	___	___
9. Current vulnerability	___	___	___	___	___
10. Loyalty	___	___	___	___	___
11. Price philosophy	___	___	___	___	___
12. Potential profitability	___	___	___	___	___
13.	___	___	___	___	___
14.	___	___	___	___	___
Total for Final Prospect Priority Index					

Prospect Prioity Index Explanation:

1. How much potential business could this prospect give me?
2. How likely is this prospect to pay?
3. How much of this prospect's business am I now getting?
4. Do my products match this prospect's needs?
5. Do my services match this prospect's needs?
6. Do I have time to serve this prospect?
7. How conveniently is this prospect located?
8. How well is this prospect recognized as an opinion leader in the market?
9. How vulnerable is this prospect in his relationship with his current supplier?
10. How loyal will this prospect likely be?
11. How closely does the price philosophy of this prospect match my own?
12. What is the potential profitability of this account?

Finally, total all these factors for a final PPI (Prospect Priority Index) for each prospect. The maximum PPI possible, of course, will vary with the number of characteristics you decide to include, but the higher the score, the better the prospect. The PPI approach might be extremely valuable to Mike Adams. Using PPI would help him zero in on the most likely prospects to concentrate on.

Don't abandon all common sense in favor of this mathematical approach to prioritizing prospects. It's simply a scaling approach to thinking strategically about how and where you should spend your time. If a given PPI does not match your "gut" instinct for that prospect's potential, then rethink the situation. Recheck your ratings. Perhaps some were inaccurate and need to be revised. Or perhaps your "gut feel" was way off base and you were on the wrong track to begin with. In any event, rational examination of the facts is an invaluable part of high potential prospect selling.

QUALIFYING PROSPECTS

Remember that once you are on the trail of a prospect you must determine whether you're after a truly "qualified" buyer. By that we mean, does the prospect have the authority to make the purchase decision and is he able to pay, and will your product or service fill a need for your prospect.

Each of the prospecting methods just discussed provides the professional salesperson an opportunity to check for these important characteristics at some point in the sales process. However, a distinct advantage of high potential prospecting is that these qualities are often taken into account in considering top prospects. Whatever the prospecting method you use, though, qualifying prospects is an essential task.

Identifying the Decision Maker

It is silly to spend an inordinate amount of time trying to sell your product to someone who is merely carrying out a preliminary study of purchase options for a committee that will then make recommendations to a purchasing head who must then get approval from the president of the company. Not that you should avoid meeting "front" people, or demand to see the top person immediately. But you must apply your efforts to the situation accordingly, perhaps saving the real bargaining for your meeting with the president. Too, be aware of who makes the decisions in a farm family agribusiness. The traditional view has been that farming and ranching purchasing decisions were dominated by the husband. Now, however, it is becoming increasingly evident that the farm/wife often has an important voice in the ultimate decision of whether the family should take on a significant debt to finance a hundred-thousand-dollar combine.

Ability to Pay

Another factor that figures importantly in whether a prospect will qualify as a customer is the ability to pay. One who is not able to pay, even though he may greatly desire and need your product, should be considered unqualified. Making a sale to a customer with financial problems can create serious difficulties and usually isn't worth it. Follow the recommendations of your company's credit representatives in determining a customer's financial ability to pay. Many agribusinesses, especially those selling to dealers and distributors, require a formal credit check of the prospect before an account is established or any product can be delivered. It's usually a good idea to do a credit check any time a significant expenditure is expected.

Product Appropriateness

It is also essential that there be a good fit between your product or service and the prospective customer's needs. A product that will not squarely fulfill the customers needs will almost surely detract from your product, your company and you. You are selling the solutions to problems. When your solution is not a very good one, you might be better off to resist the temptation to make the sale. Better that you pass up the deal than sell a herbicide to a farmer for use on a crop for which the herbicide was marginally suitable at best. Passing up such a sale can build an image of credibility and honesty that can really help you later.

PLANNING YOUR SELLING STRATEGY

Once prospects have been identified, a plan for getting their business and developing a long-term mutually beneficial relationship must be created. In general, *strategy* is an action plan for accomplishing these objectives. It is useful for the agri salesperson to consider strategy at two levels, however; first an overall selling strategy for getting the prospect's business over a period of time; second, the strategy or action plan for an individual sales call. While it's possible that a salesperson might get all of a farmer's or dealer's business on the first call, it's unlikely. The overall selling strategy requires significant followup work over a period of time.

Overall Strategy

For example, the seed corn dealer's overall selling strategy to capture a high-priority prospect might include an initial call to discover or confirm prospect profile information, find out more about his farming practices and problems, and get the prospect to attend a field day where some of their hybrids are demonstrated. Then a followup call might be planned for a few days after the field day with the hope of getting a trial order of at least ten units of three different hybrids to be planted next spring. Next, the overall strategy might be to make three to four calls during the planting and growing season to monitor planting methods and hybrid performance. Finally, depending on how the season progresses, a strong attempt might be made in late July and August of next year to increase the next order to at least 75 percent of the prospect's hybrid seed purchases.

No one would logically expect the flow of events laid out by the overall selling strategy to follow exactly as planned — although it's amazing how often an experienced professional can plan and execute such a plan to reap the predicted result on schedule. Yet circumstances and prospects often do not behave in a completely predictable manner. As a result, the agri salesperson must be ready to make adjustments in the selling plan as circumstances demand it. But, even in this case, the plan or strategy is useful for it gives logical direction and serves as a point of intentional departure. Those without an overall selling strategy are aimless in their approach and when they succeed it's more in spite of their efforts than because of them.

An overall selling strategy is begun by gathering information about prospects, then formulating a sales objective, followed by working out individual sales call strategies. This detailed preparation can make the difference between a successful sale and no sale at all. The amount of preparation needed, of course, varies from call to call and prospect to prospect. But even selling to existing customers with whom the salesperson has already had a long, close relationship may require some preparation.

Profiling Prospects

What kind of information must you develop about the prospect in order to do a good job? Of course that depends greatly on what you are selling and who you are trying to sell it to. But, in every case, you'll want some nitty-gritty information like your prospect's name and the name of the business. You'll want to know something about its size, who is in charge and some idea of how much of the product they have been buying in the past and from whom. More complex information you'll want to try to acquire about the business includes an indication of its financial health, credit rating philosophies, long-term goals and immediate plans, the power-structure within the organization, and any current problems or needs they might be experiencing within their organization or with their current supplier.

Beyond that, you will also want to gather information about key people in the organization — especially the individual you'll be dealing with. Finding out about his/her age, education, background, experience, family and personal interests could turn up some common ground: so you're both graduates of the state college, class of '65. Knowing what the buyer does with any spare time — fishing, hunting, basketball, travel — can also result in the discovery of common interests. But even if you don't find direct interests in common, you may still win some points. By understanding what makes your prospect tick, you're more likely to be able to lock in on the same wavelength and develop a good rapport on which to build a good relationship.

Most importantly you'll want to know the personality type and value structure you'll be dealing with so that you can be prepared to relate to your prospect more effectively. If you are young and fresh out of ag school, it can be very helpful to know ahead of time about your prospect's profile: he's a 64-year-old poultry producer who founded the business 42 years ago, has two sons in the business, is very proud of his operation, has a big ego, loves football and hunting, but hates salesmen. In fact, this kind of information about a new prospect is helpful no matter how long you've been selling, and it becomes invaluable when it comes to designing your opening, building interest, and making your presentation. It will also be helpful in knowing how to handle potential objections and what might lie behind those protests. Being forewarned that your prospect "hates salesmen" can be a big help!

Gathering Information

Having this information is one thing. Getting it, in light of the fact that rural people generally don't like salespeople "snooping around," is another thing. Still, there *are* ways to gather information. A good bit of it can be gleaned just by visual observation. Is the agribusiness' inventory bulging out of its storage space? What's the physical condition of the buildings and machinery? Does the dealer have an extensive ad campaign? What is it like? Is the farm always bustling with activity — and is that activity overexcited, tense and hyperactive with tools and equipment in constant disarray, or is it coordinated and under control with everything organized and in its place?

As we mentioned before, those customers with whom you have an established relationship are good sources of prospect information. Farmers to whom you sell or other business people in the community generally keep track of and will probably have some information about their neighbors. It goes without saying, of course, that you should not try to gather information from business associates or neighboring farmers who don't know *you*. It could send them running to their friend — your prospect — to set off the alarm that someone is "snooping around." But tactful questions in casual conversations with those whom you have developed a trusting relationship can reveal much about priority prospects.

Salespeople who deal with your prospect in noncompeting fields can also be valuable sources of information. You should get several different points of view by talking to a few of your current customers and non-competing salespeople to draw a balanced character sketch of your prospective client.

You can also learn a bit from other sources mentioned earlier in this chapter from which you could have also compiled your original list of good prospects. You'll learn a lot, for example, from being active in community organizations. Too, if you are dealing with a larger company, whose stock is publicly traded on a stock exchange, annual and quarterly reports, press releases and government filings can also be wellsprings of information. The county courthouse records property transfers and mortgages that are public information. County plat maps often are available to reveal landownership. Smaller local companies may have brochures, fact booklets and advertisements from which you can learn more about the company. If your prospect list includes cooperatives, it's easy to get a copy of their annual report and learn a lot about this quasi-public organization from members or employees.

And there is always the potential customer, himself, whom you might approach for information. Since so much of agribusiness centers on the solving of some technical problem, it is perfectly appropriate for the salesperson to forgo the detective bit and go straight to the customer or prospect for data which will help him in making a worthwhile and realistic proposal. Nonetheless, any prior information can be helpful.

Organizing Information   Much profile information may be accumulated by aggressive salespeople. Not only can there be a great deal of information about new potential prospects, but similar data may be kept for existing customers. In fact, many agribusinesses require their salespeople to keep files of just this kind of information on each and every customer so if you are promoted, or for some reason are no longer around, your replacement has important information to work with. For this reason and because facts can be easily confused or forgotten when you try to keep them all in your head, it makes a lot of sense to keep a file on each priority prospect (and customer).

Develop a format that will help you organize this information similar to the one in figure 7.2. Design one to suit your own needs. This will be of great help in preparing for your first call and will help you stay organized.

Figure 7.2 **Prospect Profile Worksheet**

1. Prospect Name _____ Age (approx) _____
2. Address _____ Phone _____
3. Family Situation_____
   _____

4. Personality Description _____
   _____

5. Interests, Hobbies, etc. _____
   _____
   _____

6. Educational Backgrounds_____
   _____

7. Business Situation:
   Acres Owned, by crop _____
   Acres Rented, by crop _____
   Livestock Program _____
   Labor Situation-Employees _____
   Major Equipment Line _____
   Current Lender _____
   Years With Lender _____
   Problems With Lender _____
   _____

   Other Farm Input Suppliers _____
   _____

8. Factors Likely To Be Important To This Prospect In Selecting A Lender
   _____
   _____

9. Past Experiences With Prospect _____
   _____
   _____

10. Anticipated Problems In Servicing This Prospect _____
    _____
    _____

From Strategic Agri Selling for Agricultural Lenders, a program developed by Agribusiness Associates, Indianapolis, IN.

Objectives of the Call

Before you make your initial call on a prospective customer, you should define the objectives of the call. The sales call objective is a measurable goal which will more clearly direct the manner you handle the call and serve to gage to what extent you were successful. While the ultimate objective of any selling strategy is to sell something, and you should always be ready to do so, the normal course of events in agri selling often requires more than one call perhaps many, to conclude the sale. The objective of the initial call often emphasizes information gathering — information that is necessary to uncover problems or needs of the customer so that you can determine and suggest how your product or service can help them. Too, obtaining credit application information is a frequent objective of an initial call on a prospect.

The sales call objective should be quite specific rather than general. Nonspecific call objectives like "to learn more about the customer" or "to get better acquainted" are just not very useful. They are so intangible that it's difficult to know what you are really trying to accomplish and whether you were successful. Instead, ask yourself, "What specifically do I want to learn about my prospect? What do I want to happen as a direct result of the call?" On a first call, a seed dealer may want to confirm information he has on his prospect profile, uncover what specific hybrids the prospect planted last year, and find out how well they performed. His objectives may also include learning the prospect's yield goals, major soil types, fertility program, population rate, and whether he has a preference for early or late hybrids. Clearly, when the seed dealer knows precisely what he wants to find out ahead of time, the chances of getting the information are greatly enhanced.

It's a good idea to write out the sales call objective. Putting the objective on paper serves several purposes, the first of which is that it helps you be better prepared and organized to get exactly what you want done. Secondly, the act of putting it on paper places it more firmly in your mind and reduces the likelihood that major items might be forgotten — especially if it's not feasible to use any notes in the call. And when your objective is written, its much easier to judge later how you lived up to it. After all, the memory has a way of playing tricks; once a salesperson sees what he's accomplished it's easy for him to think *that* was what he intended to accomplish all along. Continuous evaluation of how we are doing is necessary to becoming more effective salespeople.

Followup Call Objective

So far we have been discussing the importance of having a well-defined sales call objective on the initial call. But it is equally important to have a stated objective for *every* sales call you make on a prospect *and* well-established customers. Some sales managers even require their salespeople to write out their call objectives each day before they begin their calls because they believe their salespeople will be more efficient, more businesslike and more successful if they have their goals well-in-mind before they make the call. This is an excellent idea! Busy customers often have an uncanny intuitive ability to know when their time is being wasted by a salesperson who "just stopped by." The point is, you should have a well-defined call objective on *all* sales calls. It's the written sales call objective that helps you keep track of your activity, avoid wasting time and increase productivity.

An individual sales call strategy is also a plan of action but it focuses only on what is planned for a specific sales call. The call strategy should of course fit within and be consistent with the overall selling strategy; but more specifically it directs the flow of the action within the call so that the objective of that call will be accomplished. **Sales Call Strategy**

For example, the hybrid seed corn dealer planning for his first call on that high-potential prospect might decide it would be best to call the farmer around lunchtime to see if it would be okay to stop by early afternoon "to show you a summary of yield checks that were just released for the area." Then he might plan to open his call by asking how his son is doing at state college and what his plans are for the future; next he might ask him how the dry weather is affecting crops, gradually moving into a discussion of various hybrids. It will be important, he may calculate, to get as much information as possible about agronomic practices to see which of the hybrids he might be most interested in. If the dealer has enough prior information about the farmer, he may even be ready to talk about some specific hybrids in detail, just to whet his appetite. If possible, he will hold the invitation for attending the field day demonstration until the end of the conversation, after he has learned which hybrids the farmer will likely be most interested in. Finally, he may plan to leave a calling card with the date, time and location of the field day and get a verbal commitment of attendance. If for some reason the farmer can't make it, the dealer may have a contingency plan to set up a special time when he might personally show the field plots to the prospect.

With a specific strategy in mind, this dealer has a better than average chance of getting results. A format similar to figure 7.3 (on following page) may be an excellent way to organize and prepare an individual sales call strategy.

Note that strategy is not technique-oriented. It does not suggest exactly what to say, how to say it or how to act. Selling techniques will be discussed later. But strategy does give you the plan of attack — a logical flow of events that will lead to accomplishing results that are mutually beneficial for both you and your prospect.

As mentioned before, some people, especially those from close-knit rural areas, are sometimes suspicious of strangers who know "too much" about them. Thus you must use what you *know* in a subtle manner. You don't want to come on like an investigative reporter with statements like: "I've checked around to find out a little about your operation here and it looks to me like you've got some serious problems," or "Luckily we're much more reliable than that fly-by-night outfit that got you into this mess." That will definitely scare the prospect away. It must be kept in mind that all of the available information you have gathered up to this point is for *your* benefit. You might impress the farmer with the fact that you know his operation inside out but that impression could easily backfire. You benefit by using the information to discreetly guide the sales conversation in the direction you want it to go. But the natural discovery process of your sales call must be allowed to flow freely as the conversation develops. **Customer Caution**

Figure 7.3 **Sales Call Strategy Worksheet**

1. The most likely problem or need this prospect has that I could help with is _____

2. I can help meet that need by selling _____

3. This will meet the need by _____

4. Important personal characteristics that I need to consider in calling on this prospect are _____

   I should take these into account by _____

5. Important characteristcs of the operation that I need to consider are ___

   I should take these into account by _____

6. This prospect's current supplier is _____
   I can (do what?) _____
   better than the current supplier, and I can prove it to the prospect by ___

7. Other information I need to get from the prospect as I probe is_____

8. Two subjects that I can start out with to build rapport are: (1) _____

   and (2)_____
9. I think I can arouse interest in my organization by _____

10. My own behavioral style with this prospect should be _____

11. One problem I expect to have with this prospect is _____

    And I will counter this by _____

Preparing Selling Aids   The development of a sales call strategy leads to preparing supportive material — selling aids — for use in helping you tell your story. A selling aid can be virtually anything — so long as it helps convince a prospect that you're a knowledgeable, competent professional. Obviously, some selling aids are more effective than others. Reports, samples, research data, demonstration kits, personalized examples are among the most common. Whatever the selling aids, they must be well-prepared, easy to understand, and easy to use!

A key point regarding the use of selling aids is that they are most effective when prepared by the user for a specific prospect. Company-prepared aids are fine so long as the salesperson takes time to practice using them instead of purely "learning by doing." There's no question that lack of familiarity with your selling aids defeats the purpose for having them.

More on selling aids and their use in Section IV, so suffice it to say here that developing personalized sales aids is an important part of preparing for calls on high-potential prospects.

MAKING CONTACT

Finally, you must establish contact with the prospect in order to put all the preparation and planning to good use. This can sometimes be a difficult task. Many people — and those in agribusiness are no exception — carry strong prejudices against salespeople which are often hurled directly at them. There are also numerous barricades surrounding your prospect which must be overcome: secretaries, assistants, junior executives and spouses all attempt to shield the people you must contact. And there is also the matter of time. Obviously the buyer is not just sitting around waiting for a salesperson to call him up so he can buy something. Your customer's days are just as filled as yours with phone calls, meetings, production problems and loads of other things. How do you deal with all these roadblocks?

Roadblocks

These days, receptionists and secretaries are more than people who take dictation and answer the phone. Farm wives also have become an intricate part of the farm business. Therefore, they are an important part of a salesperson's road to success. They key to dealing with them is to work along *with* them as the intermediaries they are, rather than trying to get around them. They should be treated with respect and courtesy because, quite simply, they hold the keys to the decision-maker's door. In some cases, they may even help make the decision. If you make an effort to be nice, most of the time they will reciprocate. Secretaries or farm wives need to know why you want to see the boss, or their husband. If your strategy is clearly fixed in your mind, you will simply have to refer to a specific plan or problem that must be discussed. If the call is a followup call, you should point that out. And by all means, mention it when you are returning *his* call — if that is in fact the case. A successful sales call could result in a long-term relationship with that particular person and company, and that means a long-term and repetitive relationship with the secretary, receptionist or farm wife, too.

Using Telephones

The telephone is the ticket to getting around some of the problems presented by your time constraints and those of the buyer. Too few salespeople recognize the value and efficiency of the telephone. It allows you to "visit" prospects over a hundred square mile area in a matter of minutes. If the person you want to talk to is busy, the only time lost is that spent on the phone — you can always call back later. The phone is such a valuable tool that a growing number of salespeople have a mobile telephone in their car to keep them in constant contact with their office and with customers, particularly in highly concentrated agricultural areas like California or the mid-South.

This also allows the salesperson to be productive between calls.

Making Appointments   It is usually desirable to phone ahead and make an appointment with your prospect. This shows that you value his/her time. It also makes the best use of your time so that you are seldom left waiting in an office to see the buyer because of three other *appointments* ahead of you.

Waiting is one game played by those who have various prejudices against salespeople. Of course, some delays and waiting are unavoidable, but when they go on for too long a time or happen every time you walk in the door, something must be done, for a salesperson's time is valuable too. If you find you are spending too much time in an outer office where it seems you are always left to sit and wait, you have two choices. You can constructively use the time to prepare the ideas you are about to deliver, or familiarize yourself with the calls that will take place later in the day. But if you find it's getting perilously late for you to make *this* call and stay on schedule for your next one, you can alert the customer or prospect to the importance of your time by suggesting that the appointment be rescheduled because you must get on to business elsewhere. That generally notifies the customer that you have been kept waiting too long and may alleviate the problem somewhat in the future.

VALUE OF PREPARATION   All this preparation may sound like lots of messing around to the uninitiated, or to experienced salespeople who have gotten into the habit of simply going out "to talk to people." But, the fact is, preparation pays off handsomely for both the beginner and the experienced salesperson.

For those in their first year or two of agri selling, proper preparation pays off in self-confidence, better effectiveness and, ultimately, in more sales. For experienced salespeople, the payoff comes via more purposeful calls on the right prospects — breaking up the routine that comes from knowing the territory "like the back of your hand." New doors can be opened and tough nuts can finally be cracked.

It's certainly true that more experienced salespeople can and should approach the preparation process somewhat differently. Experience does give some professionals the intuitive ability to know what questions to ask and what to do next. The experienced salesperson may not need to do quite as much thinking and planning *on paper* as those just getting established. But don't allow this advantage to lull you into a false sense of security. The most successful agri salespeople are those who consistently keep good records, think and plan ahead, and give high priority prospects the attention they deserve.

It is unrealistic to expect the full amount of preparation implied in this chapter to occur for each and every prospect and sales call. But remember we have suggested singling out high-priority prospects — prospects who potentially can increase a salesperson's success markedly. A customer who can singlehandedly give you 30 thousand dollars worth of hybrid seed corn sales, 90 thousand dollars worth of new feed business, or can move half a million dollars worth of chemicals for you next year is certainly worth a few minutes — or even a few hours of preparation time and pencil and paper thinking.

Figure 7.4 **Steps of Preparation**

1. Prospecting

2. Qualifying

3. Planning or Pie approach

4. Gathering Information

5. Forming a Sales Strategy

6. Defining a Sales Call Objective

7. Making Contact and Appointments

8. Making the most of your selling tools and yourself.

SUMMARY

* Preparation is the process that readies a salesperson for a call, and includes understanding the product, identifying prospects and their needs and pinpointing reasons why they should purchase.

* An effective salesperson understands his market area in order to spot potential customers and utilizes other tools such as: mapping present accounts to discover holes, being an active member of the community, keeping current through media, and taking advantage of other informational sources like fellow salespeople, customers and potential clients.

* One additional effective method of getting new prospects is making calls. Cold calling means stopping at every farm; cool calling means targeting farms that exhibit characteristics that will make them likely to purchase; following leads is an even more targeted approach.

* Targeting potential buyers may be made easier by rating them to determine their Prospect Priority Index, a one-to-ten rating that takes into account factors like account size, credit, need for product or service and loyalty, among others.

* A salesperson needs to develop an overall strategy to ensure sales to a client over a period of time as well as an individual strategy for each sales call. The overall strategy begins with assembling information, formulating a sales objective and working out individual call strategies.

* Information about prospects should be assembled that may include details about the farming operation, financial health, credit rating, and long-and short-term goals, as well as personal information about family and interests. Care should be taken to not appear "Nosy" which is a strong negative for many farm people.

* The sales call objective may be defined as a measurable goal which will clearly direct how the person handles a call and also as a yardstick by which the success of the call can be measured.

* Selling aids help to convince a prospect that the salesperson is a competent professional and may take the form of reports, samples, demonstration kits etc.

* Making contact with the prospect may be hampered by "roadblocks," — persons who must be dealt with before seeing the prospect.

Review Questions Chapter 7

1. What role does knowledge play in agri selling? What kinds of knowledge are important?

2. What is prospecting? Name three ways to find new prospects.

3. What are the differences among cold calling, cool calling, following up on leads, and targeting prospects?

4. Does "qualifying" prospects make sense? Why? When should a prospect be qualified?

5. What is a Prospect Priority Index?

6. What is the point of designing an overall selling strategy?

7. What are the components of a selling strategy?

8. How can a salesperson get information about a prospect without appearing to be "snoopy"?

9. Discuss the use of selling aids.

10. Should appointments be made in agri selling? Why?

Chapter Eight
The Opening

"The Opening is the starting gate for the face-to-face encounter with a prospect."

As Mike Adams pulled into the drive, he visually surveyed the farmstead. It was much as the vo-ag teacher had described: modern, neat and well-organized. The crops looked exceptionally good and he could tell at a glance that the hog setup incorporated some of the latest technology. The operation was just what he'd expected — except a bit larger. As he got out of the car, he was met by a seemingly ferocious German Shephard which he also expected. He'd been told the dog wouldn't bother him as long as he didn't hesitate. Mike was glad he'd done his homework and hoped his information was accurate, especially about the dog.

A woman Mike thought must be Mrs. Bradley met him at the door...

"Hi, I'm Mike Adams with Fast-Grow Feeds," Mike shouted above the barking. As the woman came out, the dog began to calm down and Mike relaxed a little.

"Good morning," she responded, friendly but with a question in her voice.

Mike jumped in quickly, "Is Paul around? I think he is expecting me. We spoke on the phone yesterday and..."

"Oh, that's right. Paul mentioned you this morning. He should be back shortly. He just ran up to the other place to check on a new boar we just got," Mrs. Bradley said.

Mike made a mental note about the new boar and complimented Mrs. Bradley on her garden. "The kids do a lot of the work — when I can corral them," she responded with obvious pride. Mike was about to ask her about the rose bushes by the house when a pickup pulled up in the drive. "There's Paul now," she interrupted.

Mike saw a large man in his late 40s emerge from his truck along with a boy around 20. "Must be his son — the one taking animal science at the university," he thought quickly to himself. As Paul walked over, he leaned down to scratch the German Shephard's head.

"I'm Mike Adams with Fast-Grow Feeds," Mike offered, extending his hand in greeting.

Paul responded a bit shyly but returned Mike's gesture with a weak but friendly handshake and slight smile. "This your son?" Mike questioned, extending his hand to the young man. "Yep, that's Ted," Paul replied with obvious pride. "I'm trying to get some work from him this summer before he goes back to college!"

Through some well-placed questions, Mike learned his prospect's son would be a senior this fall and would be joining his dad fulltime next year. "That makes their recent expansion of facilities make sense," thought Mike to himself. "Maybe I'd better make sure to include Ted in the conversation as much as I can. He may be a key."

After bantering a bit about the college's chances on the football field this fall, Mike decided it was time to turn the conversation to business. At an appropriate point, he interjected, "Say, I've been hearing about your new feeding system. Buzz Warren, the extension man, was telling me that it's got some new wrinkles in it. How's it working out?"

"Pretty good, so far at least," Paul replied. "Had a few bugs to work out at first but it's okay now."

While it was already clear that Paul was a man who didn't waste many words, Mike thought he could see Paul's eyes brighten as he discussed his hog operation. Mike was genuinely interested in Paul's new facility. So it was not hard to come up with some pretty good questions.

"What brand of feed mixer did you install, Paul?" Mike queried, trying to steer the conversation to his primary interest. As Paul described the system, Mike decided to take a gamble. "Would you mind if we took a closer look?" he asked. "I've got some boots and disinfectant in my car." He held his breath momentarily. He knew a lot of producers were sensitive about disease problems and didn't want to overstep his bounds.

"Okay," Paul said as he turned toward the new facility. "As long as we stay outside the farrowing house there shouldn't be a problem."

"Whew!" thought Mike as they continued their conversation. Through an open door he could see some of his competitor's premix bags stacked. At least he now was sure who he was up against.

"How's your new mixer and automatic feeding system work?" asked Mike, pointing toward the control panel and tanks. As Paul described how the system worked, it was pretty clear how it cut his labor costs and allowed him to mix precisely what each pen of hogs needed.

"But right now we've got to get our weaning weights up. With this system we ought to be able to average 12 pounds at 21 days weaning. But, we've got a ways to go."

Mike's ears perked up now. Perhaps this could be the "in" he'd been looking for. At the meeting last week, he'd heard a lot of talk about weaning weight research based on their new pig starter feeds. Now, if he could just get Paul interested in what his company had found. . .

****

As we have seen, the preparation phase of the selling process lays important groundwork for the selling relationship. The opening, on the other hand, is the starting gate for the actual face-to-face encounter with the prospect and is crucial to the success of the two steps that follow it: the presentation and the close. Having watched Mike Adams open his call with Paul Bradley, we are now ready to jump in and dissect the processes, objectives and methods involved in the opening.

GAINING ATTENTION

Everyone can easily remember television or radio commercial jingles which have made a lasting impression on the public's memory even though the jingle may have been aired years ago. The catchy nature of the commercial attracted and held the attention of listeners long enough for the corporate message to be conveyed. Although dated, we still remember that message. Commercials highlight key selling points of course, much like those offered in any sales situation. But they differ in one respect: they are a mere 30 seconds long. With only 30 seconds in which to compress their presentation, these commercials would never have been successful and remembered years after they were broadcast had they not almost instantly grabbed your attention and sparked enough interest for you to listen and absorb the whole message. That is the essence of any sales call opening. You must do the same thing to successfully launch your presentation. Luckily, you have more than a few seconds in which to open, but you still have a lot to accomplish in that important, relatively short time frame.

ANATOMY OF AN OPENING

The opening must do five things:

1) Create a favorable impression of you in the prospect's mind
2) Get and keep the prospect's attention
3) Build rapport between customer and salesperson
4) Probe for and dig out the needs and values of the prospect
5) Arouse customer interest in you, your company and your product or service

**Creating the
Right Impression**
The impression you create in the first several minutes of the call is crucial. Creating a favorable one will not necessarily make a sale; however, allowing a negative impression to form in a prospect's mind is enough to scuttle many a sale. As mentioned, a large number of potential customers may have a built-in prejudice against salespeople, so you may need to pay extra attention to create the right impression. It is entirely up to the salesperson to dispel at once any negative preconceptions, and to replace them with more positive impressions. That does not happen by accident.

How You Look
Creating the right impression begins with your conscious attention to grooming. You should be neatly and appropriately dressed using your discretion to choose the appropriate apparel. A formal sales call at an agribusiness headquarters obviously requires different dress than that worn in a field day booth at the farm show. Some companies specify a certain dress code for salespeople as part of the overall company marketing image. While dress codes or another person's values may force you to make adjustments against your tastes, the unfortunate fact is that since a customer's taste affects your sales relationship, you must try to accommodate that taste. Generally, that means reasonably conservative dress and grooming. Evaluate yourself carefully. Seldom do we perceive ourselves as sloppy or unacceptable, but others might. It's what the prospect thinks that counts.

How You Arrive
Many salespeople consider the sales call to be already in progress when they drive onto the prospect's farm or into the company parking lot. This means it's probably not a good idea to roar up to the place and screech to a halt in a cloud of dust just 3 feet shy of the front porch. You'll want to be driving a vehicle that looks nice but not too flashy. And it should be washed regularly to bolster the neat appearance you want to project. All these things create a favorable impression before a word or a look is exchanged.

Commonsense courtesy must be applied. Don't cut off access to the garage or barn by parking in an inappropriate place. Likewise, when you get out of your car — with confidence — *always* check at the house first rather than snoop around the barn to avoid arousing suspicion and distrust. Plus, stopping at the house may develop positive feelings in someone very influential in making purchases. And you should never enter the barn unless first asked to do so. Once you've developed a good relationship with a prospect, some of these rules may not apply. But at first, it's better to be cautious than sorry.

How You Greet
Your greeting with a prospect is more than just a "hello, how are you?" ritual. Try to greet your prospect with friendly confidence. This means developing the right frame of mind before the initial contact. Shaking hands is of course the traditional way of greeting, but remember that people read a lot into handshakes. Some customers actually express a feeling of discomfort as that outstretched hand aggressively reaches towards them. This is particularly true when the customer is a man and the salesperson is a woman. So be sensitive to those who may not want to shake hands. Should

you, as a male salesperson, offer to shake hands with a woman? While there are no hard-and-fast rules, many salespeople feel more comfortable waiting for the woman to offer the handshake especially when the woman is substantially older than the male salesperson. Other messages can be broadcast by the handshake too: the overly vigorous handshake and the weak, limp handshake all convey certain messages that build an impression of the person.

Because people sometimes have a hard time understanding (and, more importantly, remembering) a name the first time they hear it, when you announce yourself to the prospect, speak slowly and clearly. A good measure of exactly how slowly is to count quickly to yourself, "1, 2, 3," between your first and last name: "Mike... (1, 2, 3) ...Adams." Then slowly and clearly announce the company you're with. While a business card is a valuable tool, never use it as a substitute for speaking your name clearly. Try to avoid saying you're a salesperson. Instead it is more professional to say ... "I'm with Fast-Grow Feeds" or "I work for Fast-Grow Feeds." After all, the purpose of your visit should already be clear from your earlier telephone call to set up an appointment.

You will also want to pronounce the prospect's name correctly. Checking with a secretary about the pronunciation or directly asking the prospect is a good idea. This is a sign of respect and shows that you are interested enough to find out exactly how to pronounce the name.

How You Converse

Getting the conversation started is one of the most difficult parts of a sales call, particularly on a new prospect. You convey a weak impression if you awkwardly fumble around for the right words or seem to lack purpose. On the other hand, an overly pushy start could evoke one of many of the salesperson stereotype impressions . . . "fast-talker here, I'd better be careful!" You certainly don't need the barrier which either extreme might build. Thus, the salesperson must tread a delicate middle ground.

It is generally a good idea to use some kind of icebreaker. A non-threatening humorous comment tends to work well and puts the prospect at ease. Making reference to the prospect's hobby or interests; something mentioned at the last meeting; a gift related to the sale; and the mention of an acquaintance who suggested your visit are all acceptable ways to get into the call. Which is best depends purely on the personalities of the salesperson and prospect and the circumstances surrounding the call. Planning your opening line is a good idea, as long as you remember the need to be flexible. To step from your pickup truck into a mudhole with the prospect watching just cannot be ignored, no matter how well-planned your opening statement was.

Maintain good eye contact from the beginning to the end of a call. Good eye contact doesn't mean an unmoving stare nor does it mean excessive shiftiness. Simply showing your interest and openness are the standards by which eye contact is measured. The eyes are said to be windows to the soul, and the saying "Never trust a man who won't look you straight in the eye" has merit.

**The First
Impression**   The minute the prospect and salesperson set eyes on each other, literally hundreds of signals are being broadcast back and forth. The state of your attire — freshly ironed, dirty, rumpled or whatever — communicates an impression about whether you are responsible, rebellious, disinterested etc. Facial expressions, actions and your demeanor state loudly and clearly whether you're actually glad to see the prospect, nervous and unsure, judgmental or wishing the day were over.

At the same time, *you* will be receiving hundreds of messages from the prospect as you size up his/her personality and value system, mentally adjust the precall information you've gathered, search for areas of mutual interest and make last second judgments about the best opening line to use. In just the first few seconds of Mike Adams' sales call, Mike was able to tell that Paul Bradley was a reasonably quiet, conservative fellow with a great deal of pride in his operation. Mike, of course, didn't know specifics about Paul's likes and dislikes, but he had quickly gathered enough impressions to give him a pretty good idea about how to approach Paul. In fact, based upon Paul's willingness to talk about his operation, Mike made a calculated judgment about Paul's willingness to show him the feed mixing equipment. Fortunately, Mike called it well, for it turned out that Paul enjoyed talking with someone genuinely interested in his business. What better way to create a good first impression.

**Maintaining a
Positive Image**   But just as Mike Adams knows, the process of creating and maintaining an impression is not a task which is finished with the initial contact. That's only the beginning. You must continue to create a favorable impression of yourself in the eyes of the prospect and *maintain* that view continually throughout the sales call. In fact, you will have to continue creating favorable impressions of yourself as long as you deal with that customer.

**BUILDING
RAPPORT**   The first several minutes of any call are generally spent on building rapport between prospect and salesperson. It is sort of a get-acquainted period which provides you with the opportunity to find out just what type of person you're dealing with. First impressions create a thumbnail sketch of the prospect's personality. Rapport building adds depth and details to your understanding of the customer. It is the time in which you try to learn more about his values, beliefs and problems — problems you can solve, hopefully.

For example, during Mike and Paul's first few minutes of conversation, Mike gained some insight into Paul's situation, values and problems. Mike learned of Paul's satisfaction with the feeding system in general, and found that this producer was very concerned about performance. The fact that Paul is a good manager and interested in getting weaning weights up is a valuable starting point for Mike. He also discovered the potential role Paul's son will play in making operating decisions, and wisely chose to involve Ted in the discussions.

Another important function of rapport building is the development of mutual trust. As you are sizing up the prospect to confirm that he is indeed the person with the buying power, you are coming to trust him to some extent by getting to know him. More importantly, the prospect should be learning to trust you because of your sincere interest and approach. While you will continue to create a sense of trust throughout your selling relationship, psychologically the prospect needs to immediately feel that you are not just appearing trustworthy to sell him a product. The development of trust during the rapport-building stage shows in some small way that you are interested in your prospect's well-being regardless of the sales factor.

Trust is built casually. Empathizing with the prospect when he speaks of a problem or concern is one prime way. Showing that you share common interests is another, as Mike Adams did in his conversation with Paul about hog feeding equipment. The development of trust and mutual respect is the direct and planned result of your normal flow of conversation with a prospect as you meet the social expectations of the call.

Above all, remember that the prospect should do most of the talking, not you. Many salespeople believe that they must continually fill in the awkward transitional moments with statements. Many of these same salespeople one day suddenly find out enough about the prospect to read him well. If they would listen instead of just talking, they would learn more. It is possible to maintain control of the conversation without dominating it. And to do that you must draw out the information from the prospect by questioning him.

Although socializing can be enjoyable for the salesperson and/or prospect, remember that neither party has all day to fritter away. If the prospect is especially busy, he may become annoyed with what seems to be beating around the bush and a waste of his time. From your point of view, *too much* rapport building is wasteful too. You don't have unlimited time either. A delicate balance must be struck. As the minutes of rapport building wear on, the alert salesperson will begin looking for a bridge over which he can direct the conversation toward the main purpose of the call.

SALES CALL OPENERS

Another key aspect of the opening is to quickly grab the full attention of the prospect. Psychologists tell us that the brain can absorb information virtually two to three times as fast as a person can speak. You have only a short amount of time to capture one's attention before the mind strays. Even if you obtain the attention of your prospect at the beginning of a call, it's possible to lose it during the call. In fact, prospect attention fade-in fade-out is a quite common and devastating problem. If you've ever just finished what you considered to be a key selling point, and the prospect has a blank glassy-eyed stare on his face, it's a sure bet that you've been victimized by attention fade. You haven't kept his attention! The use of a carefully chosen call "opener" can help you get and maintain the prospect's attention past the initial rapport-building stage.

An opener is the way you begin to stimulate the prospect's interest and channel the call toward your objective. Obviously, Mike Adams needs to know more about Paul Bradley's operation and feeding program before he can suggest ways to improve it. Yet he can't just begin to discover needed information immediately as if the prospect were the subject of an interrogation. To do so would send up red flags to the prospect and inhibit communication. So Mike must gradually work his way into his questioning with the aid of an appropriate opener.

There are several openers, or attention getters, at Mike's disposal. Each of them can be effective when used in the proper circumstances with the proper person. The value of good precall preparation is clear when the time comes to select an opening strategy for calling on a new prospect.

Standard Approach

The most common opener in agri selling is virtually indistinguishable from rapport building. In fact, the standard approach, as it's called, clearly is a method by which initial rapport building is made easier. This approach involves the salesperson introducing himself and then conversing in smalltalk for a few minutes before moving on to the business at hand. While not a dramatic attention getter, the standard approach has its advantages. First, it's very effective in most rural settings, where a casual start is preferable. Secondly, the standard approach is designed to help meet social expections in a call setting, particularly when you are somewhat acquainted with the prospect. In other words, showing interest in the prospect as an individual is a prerequisite to selling success. Done properly, the standard approach treats your prospect as something more than an entity to sell to.

Mike Adams used the standard approach in his opening call on Paul Bradley. He was careful to avoid the prime pitfall of the method though...spending too much time in undirected chit-chat. While the standard approach looks highly undisciplined and easy to do, it is in fact one of the more difficult openers to use well, due to those very reasons. The professional salesperson can be conversing in casual tones about what seems to be trivia, when in reality he's subtly steering his questions toward increasingly more call-objective-oriented subjects. Had Paul been extremely busy, or had he forgotten about the appointment, Mike would have needed a different opener. In fact, a salesperson must be prepared to move quickly into the reason for a call, should a planned standard approach appear unwise at the onset.

Direct Approach

Should you suspect that your prospect is extremely businesslike, you may choose to immediately tell him exactly why you're there. This direct approach wastes very little time and doesn't keep the prospect wondering what you're up to. The most effective way to tell someone why you're there isn't to state your purpose in terms of buying or selling, but rather in terms of a benefit to the prospect. For example, when a prospect hears a salesperson say, "I'm here to sell you a tractor!" a different message is received than if the salesperson had opened by offering, "I stopped in to talk with you about our new tractor line and how the new transmission design will save you downtime and repair dollars." The difference is the focus of the call and the attention the prospect will give as a result. Common sense tells us that if we see personal benefit in an opportunity, we'll be more interested. Remember that in using the direct approach.

The major problems with using the direct approach is that it's more difficult to probe for necessary information. Consequently, it might be a good idea to use the direct approach in situations where you've already gotten some feel for the prospect's problem areas.

There are a number of other ways to open the call, get attention and keep it throughout your visit. But as with the direct approach, they tend to lead directly to discussion of your product or service...you may not probe for new information or clarification as much as you should. As a result, these attention getters may be most appropriate with established prospects or customers.

More Openers

* Give the prospect a small, but useful gift. This gesture may build some goodwill and serve as a reminder of your visit when you're gone. "Here's a barn chart to help you keep track of the breeding cycle."

* Have a product sample or physical object available to show the prospect. "This ear of corn is our new number. Notice the ear length and kernel fullness."

* Say something designed to be startling to your prospect. A comment like "We've noticed a serious magnesium deficiency in the area!" may shock the prospect into wanting more information.

* Ask the prospect about a problem you can solve. Your sincerity and naturalness are keys to this one. "Have you seen more broadleaf control problems this year?"

* Suggest that a mutual business acquaintance or friend referred you. "Ken Stone, who's been using our center pivot system for the last three years, suggested you might be interested in it, too."

All openers must be worked smoothly into the flow of the call or else they look manipulative and aren't effective. A new or different attention getter may seem strange to use until you get accustomed to it, yet any of these ideas can be implemented with great success. The professional salesperson recognizes the value in variety, plus it helps keep the job fun! The key is to select the right approach for the situation.

PROBING FOR NEEDS AND VALUES

Agri selling is, primarily, problem solving. Helping prospects find solutions to better meet needs is one of the most valuable and satisfying dimensions of the agri selling profession. So logically one can ask, "How can you solve problems you don't know about?" Though a rhetorical question, it points to the need for probing as a tool in the problem-solving process.

The objective of probing is actually twofold, first to discover the prospect's primary needs and second, to isolate his dominant buying urge. The dominant buying urge is the major internal force that compels your prospect to want your product, the real reason behind his purchase. For example, a farmer may need a new set of metric sockets, but the reason he may choose one brand from among many — and a higher priced brand at that —

is the reputation and reliability that comes with the brand name. In this situation, the need for ''a proven thing'' formed the dominant buying urge. Obviously there are many dominant buying urges. Prestige and status is a big one. Many thousands of dollars are expended each year on farm equipment based upon the prestige associated with a color of paint. Acceptance is another dominant buying urge for some. ''If Joe Schmidley does it, then it must have something going for it.'' Many are motivated for material possessions and buy those products or services which satisfy that need. Of course, showing that you have ''made it'' motivates many. A new farm home, the second high flotation applicator or the latest gadget may be trappings of that urge.

While it is apparent that probing plays a critical role in successful selling, it is often times glossed over, ignored or slighted in many a salesperson's haste to tell about his product. This makes it virtually impossible to zero in on a prospect's unique needs and dominant buying urge, thus minimizing one's chances for a sale. Some salespeople argue that their precall preparation gave them all the information they need about the prospect's problems and buying urges. Even if you have done your homework well (and it's highly unlikely that enough specifics will be found in advance), information must be uncovered during the call or else it looks like you've been snooping...not a good impression, to be sure! Equally dangerous, should you fail to confirm precall information about the prospect during a call, you may base your presentation on inaccuracies. So probing is the only way to find out what your prospect wants and why he wants it.

Probing serves a dual function. It helps the salesperson learn what the prospect desires. It also suggests ways to tell your customer how the product will fit his needs. It underlines the selling points the salesperson should emphasize later. There's no sense in emphasizing features in which the prospect has little or no interest.

The salesperson must discover from the prospect what he is looking for, what kind of experiences or problems he has had with similar products, where the product will be used and what kind of technical information is desired. Every customer differs in attitude, desire, organizational methods and priorities. Uncover the uniqueness of each prospect if you want to sell effectively. By probing for the particular needs of a specific customer, you also avoid unnecessary objections as you cover each and every important selling point. You'll also be less prone to tell the prospect about *your* favorite selling points, and more likely to talk about those which directly concern and affect the prospect.

An interesting effect of probing is that sometimes it reveals that a prospect isn't aware of his problems or needs. In many cases, this occurs when the prospect doesn't know there are any ways to be better off, until you show him. In effect, the probing process can result in a prospect gaining awareness of a need he had never verbalized, even though it was there all along. It's only when we see we can be better off that we become dissatisfied with our present situation.

Probing is not a difficult skill to hone. It involves the effective use of questions in a casual, logical sequence. The key to probing is to get the pros-

pect talking and to listen carefully to responses. By asking questions skillfully, the salesperson can direct the conversation and help the prospect actually
form his/her own conclusion. It is a much better idea to encourage the prospect to "sell himself" than for you to tell him what to do. So long as you
center on a prospect's needs and maintain a comfortable, natural tone,
probing is *not* a threatening activity. It must not be high-pressure interrogation, or your prospect will assume the stance of a tight-lipped defendant in a
trial.

Prospects love to talk about their operation, problems and achievements
once you get them started and they trust you. Encourage the prospect to tell
you more about his feelings, problems and needs and file this information
away in your memory for later reference. Generally note taking is a taboo
for it tends to stop communication and may even place the prospect in a
defensive polarized position.

METHODS OF PROBING

There are several methods of probing. Using them correctly requires that
you have an idea of what information you need before you begin probing.
As part of your precall preparation, you profiled information about the
prospect. Review that profile and ask, "What else do I need to know to
make an intelligent sale?" Using your answer as a quide, the following probing techniques will help you get what you need.

Open Probing

Open probing is a very open-ended questioning method. In general, this
technique is built around the asking of questions which encourage more
than a "yes" or "no" answer. Very little value is gained if your prospect
only agrees or disagrees with your questions.

Open probing is most frequently used in the beginning portion of a call,
or when calling on prospects you aren't acquainted with. There are several
reasons for this. First, the name implies that you want to "open up" your
prospect. In order to do that, you must give your prospect lots of room to
answer in a nonthreatened way, to keep the communication process open.
Another important reason to open probe on an initial call is to help you get
a feel for the mood and style of the prospect, increasing the likelihood the
prospect will share feelings and values, both of which are important in
discovering the dominant buying urge. Finally, since open probes are
generally very nonthreatening, they help the salesperson develop trust with a
prospect quickly.

An example of an open probe Mike Adams might use in talking with Paul
Bradley might be, "Tell me about your hog operation?" or "How did you
decide on this feeding program?" Recognize that in most cases, you'll get
general information from open probing.

Directed Probing

As the need to get more specific becomes evident, directed probing will be
most successful in obtaining specific information. Directed probing gets at
those facts needed to accomplish the call objective. Since this questioning
method asks for more pinpoint information, the salesperson must be ready
to assume greater control over the pace of the call. That doesn't mean talk-

ing all the time; rather control over direction and topics are the central issues.

Directed probing is most commonly used after the salesperson and prospect have gotten into the essence of the call, or when the salesperson makes a call on an established customer for routine business. Why? Primarily because trust has been somewhat established and the salesperson knows what he needs to discover, or because previous encounters may dictate a more time conscious, down-to-business approach. In either case, questions like "What kind of supplement or mineral additives do you use?" or "Do you have trouble with milk fever?" get at specific information Mike Adams may need to present the right selling points to Paul Bradley. And done at the proper time in a call, they are very acceptable and don't alarm or close the prospect's mind to new ideas.

Satisfied Customer Survey

Another method of probing helps a salesperson get at the needs *behind* the needs; those *real reasons* for buying. It is a simple, two-step process:

1. Before you approach your new prospect, take an informal survey of a few of your most satisfied current accounts. By approaching your key accounts and asking them what they like best about your product or service and *why* they like it, you can compile a list of dominant buying urges. Show your latest prospect this list and explain that these are some of the reasons your many happy customers like your product. Ask the new prospect which of the reasons most coincides with what *he* is looking for, or whether he has a need that should be added to the list.

2. Once the customer has chosen one, two, three or more reasons, you should ask why he has chosen those. Be sure you listen to the answer because this gives you more of an indication of his dominant buying urge — what he really wants from buying your product.

EXAMPLE:

"Bob, we recently surveyed some of our best customers to determine why they do business with us. Here are some of the reasons they gave:

— equipment was in good shape
— able to get product to them when promised
— soil tests and recommendations were complete
— prices were fair
— less trips across the field reduced compaction problems

"Which of these factors is most important to you? Prospect response. . . I'm sure you have good reason for choosing that one. Would you mind sharing why?"

Probing is an easy skill to learn and implement. We've established how critical it is. So keep the discussion channeled toward things of interest to the prospect so that probing will be viewed as natural and friendly (not nosey or negative). And the prospect will give you the information you need. Avoid sharing your experiences or philosophies except as necessary to prime the conversation. Remember, you can't learn while you're talking.

As the opening progresses, the salesperson must gradually move through rapport building, attention getting and initial probing, and toward the presentation portion of the call. This is accomplished by previewing the solution to the problem(s) you have uncovered (or confirmed) during probing, which in turn will arouse interest in your product or service.

THE TRANSITION TO YOUR PRESENTATION

Arouse Interest

In this phase of the opening, you are showing the prospect that you understand his problem and that you are concerned. You are striving to gain enough prospect interest in what you have to offer to allow you to present your product or service. There is no magic point at which you begin to arouse interest. Once you feel you have a handle on what your prospect needs and why he needs it, you, can show how you can meet those needs. Obviously, judgment is the key! It's at this point, however, that you begin to assume a knowledgeable role and in many cases, the prospect may actually ask for your help in finding a solution to his problem. It is essential, then, for the prospect to recognize the problem and the need for a solution. Without a prospect's perception of a need, you don't really have a prospect. Effectively arousing interest must be contingent on the prospect's recognition of a problem.

How do you arouse that much-needed interest? The key is to build on information gained during probing; information which conveys what's important to the prospect. Assuming you've done your job when probing and uncovered potential problem areas or needs, you can lead quite naturally and conversationally to the presentation and arouse interest at the same time with a solution preview.

Since the salesperson has gained a better idea of the prospect's concerns through probing, an excellent way to gain immediate interest is to state a benefit the prospect is interested in. When talking to a dealer about agricultural chemicals, a benefit statement like "Our credit and payment terms will help you minimize your seasonal cash-flow problem" will get the salesperson plenty of interest — if the dealer is concerned about cash flow. Make sure the spoken benefit can be provided!

State The Benefit

Many prospects are greatly attuned to products, services and salespeople who can help them overcome business or personal apprehension and insecurity. Consequently, arousing interest with a benefit statement which addresses this quasi-fear motive is a wise idea. Emphasizing the avoidance of financial loss, social acceptance resulting from the use of a "quality" product or actual physical safety are all appropriate ways to generate interest, with the proper prospect.

Another method of arousing prospect interest is to subtly encourage the prospect to revaluate his relationship with a current supplier. Clearly, this does not mean slandering your competition. Rather, the salesperson must create a new standard of excellence by which the prospect measures "good" performance...a standard which is created by emphasizing the positive features of your product or service, not by putting down the other product. By letting the prospect come to his own conclusion, "My current supplier doesn't do that," you maintain your credibility and eliminate the chance

FIND A NEW STANDARD OF EXCELLENCE

that you might insult the prospect by downgrading a supplier that he chose. Mike Adams will have the opportunity to do this very thing as he emphasizes Fast-Grow Feed's positive weaning weight performance record, rather than his competitor's failings.

It is imperative that you help your prospect see that the new standard — your product — is superior to the old. But that burden of proof makes agri selling a challenge. Consider introducing your product's strengths and benefits at several appropriate points during and after the probing process to help prime the prospect for more thorough explanations during the presentation. It's a way to prove your new standard of excellence.

Use Testimonials

Testimonials from satisfied customers, either in writing or recounted by you as anecdotes, also arouse interest in what you have to sell. They have the advantage of being more credible because they come from a *third party* who has already used and is satisfied with the product or service. You can build even more credibility into these testimonials by not making grandiose promises. Saying, "Of course, I'm not guaranteeing you will get entirely the same results, but you can get a pretty good idea..." helps a prospect know that this is an example, not a guarantee. Being specific also adds believability to what you are saying. Which would you be more moved by: "One customer got a better yield using our program," or "Phil Grishaw says he got 10 to 12 bushels per acre more with our program last year." Specific information also allows your prospect to figure for himself what his own benefit might be, based on his situation. And just to make sure he's figured it out correctly, be certain to tell him just how much he might be able to save according to your calculations.

When using testimonials, check with the source for approval before using his name and check his credentials!

Use Personal Analysis

Personal analysis is an outstanding way to capture one's interest. Based upon information from previous visits or generally accepted assumptions for an area, prepare an illustration that has been specifically designed for the prospect. Most commonly, personal analyses are numbers oriented, yet photos or written scenarios work too. People enjoy seeing how something applies to them, so long as you don't take too many liberties or appear to know too much in preparing the materials. That's why it's generally a good idea to base a personal analysis on information garnered from a previous call. It's safer and more effective that way. Mike Adams may well find this method quite effective in arousing Paul Bradley's interest on the second call when he shows Paul the improvement in weaning weight and profit dollars which can come from using Fast-Grow Feeds.

Utilize Prescription

A way to organize the attempt to arouse interest and build a bridge to the presentation is essential if the salesperson is to appear professional. Some experts suggest combining several of the methods of arousing interest in the following manner. First, review the prospect's needs or problems as you see them. Ask if those are correct. Next, state the benefit you think your prospect is looking for. Check to see if the prospect agrees with the importance of that benefit. Let the prospect know you can help, offer a testimonial to support your contention, and last, ask to detail your solution. This procedure lets the prospect know you understand the problem and the benefit he's interested in, but more importantly, it allows *you* to doublecheck their importance. It's easy for a salesperson to misread a problem area, or the value of a benefit to the prospect. Or sometimes, prospects are purposefully vague about their problems until they trust the salesperson. It's wise to check for accuracy before a whole presentation is based on misperceptions. This "prescription" procedure helps in doing just that!

Arousing interest in your products is one of the major intersections the salesperson crosses while enroute to a sale. If the road signs tell him there is no customer ahead, the salesperson has two alternatives. First, determine a way to change the signs. Does the prospect see his need? Do I have the right information? These and other questions must be answered positively! The second choice is to switch destinations completely and head for another, more viable prospect. Sometimes it's obvious that we aren't going to do business with that prospect that day, so it's better to move on for the time being.

SUMMARY

* The sales call opening has five major goals: create a good impression; get and keep prospect attention; build rapport; probe for needs and values; and arouse customer interest.

* A good impression stems from creating an appropriate appearance, both physically and with possessions. A well-mannered, tactful and articulate salesperson will make, and probably maintain, a suitable impression.

* A salesperson may build rapport by meeting social expectations to become acquainted with the prospect and build trust.

* Gaining and keeping attention may be accomplished by using an opener. The opener may be standard: introduction, small talk, sales presentation; or direct: skip the small talk and get straight to business. Additional openers may be gifts or informational statements.

* The purpose of probing is two-fold. It is to discover prospect's primary needs and isolate his dominant buying urge.

* Open probing is an open-ended probing method which utilizes questions that encourage more than a yes/no answer. Direct probing gets answers to specific questions that will help fulfill the sales objective.

* The satisifed customer survey includes two steps: Showing the prospect a list of the reasons why others buy the product and asking the prospect why he chose the reasons important to him.

* The salesperson must make a gradual transition toward the presentation. This may be accomplished by arousing and maintaining interest, stating the benefit, helping form a new standard of excellence and using testimony, personal analysis and description.

**Review Questions
Chapter 8**

1. What are some objectives of the opening of a sales call?
2. How does a salesperson build and maintain a good impression?
3. Is rapport building important? (Why or why not?)
4. Who should do more talking, the salesperson or the prospect? Why?
5. What is the direct approach when opening a sales call? When should it be used?
6. What function does probing serve?
7. Discuss methods to probe for needs and values.
8. Name several ways to arouse a prospect's interest in a product. Why is it important to arouse a prospect's interest?

Chapter Nine
The Presentation

"...the main component of the selling process shows the prospect how the product works and how it provides benefits."

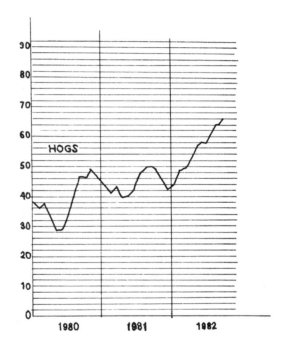

T oday would be Mike Adam's third call on Paul Bradley in a little over a month. Mike was more uptight today than ever because he was going to propose a feeding program for Paul's reaction. If he did it well, he could walk away with a sizable order — or at least a trial order that could lead to steady business. He'd really made a good impression last week when he'd taken his boss and the company nutritionist to visit about Paul's weaning weight problem. Both his boss and the nutritionist were pretty sharp and they'd been very helpful.

During the last two calls, Mike had learned a great deal about Paul's operation: numbers, breeding cycle, facilities, health problems, management ability, feeding philosophies and equipment. He really felt that part of the problem was Paul's choice of early medication programs and pig starter feed. His nutritionist had agreed with his theory. But he would have to convince Paul to try his ideas. "If I can just get him to try my program," thought Mike, "and show some good results, then I'll pick up a lot of pig starter feed business *and* get a crack at his premix business for his feeders. That's where the big bucks are in this operation,'' he reasoned.

Mike was ready. He had mapped out a total handling and feeding program based on Paul's facilities. He had even developed some simple visuals to show what he had in mind and how the numbers might work.

"Well, this is it," thought Mike as he pulled in the lane and spotted his friend, the German Shepherd, as it came tearing around the house. Paul was waiting at the kitchen door to calm the dog and Mike made his way into the house. "Boy, that dog sure could discourage someone up to no good!" Mike commented as he greeted Paul with a handshake.

"That's why he's here — to discourage salesmen and other pests," grinned Paul. Mike hoped he was joking and got the feeling that Paul might be on the offensive. "Well, if I can do my job well enough, maybe he'll wag his tail for me," Mike laughed.

Paul led the way to the kitchen table where Mrs. Bradley had coffee poured for them. In the small talk that followed, Mike learned that their oldest daughter had just been elected president of the county 4-H junior leaders. The easy flow of the conversation gave Mike a new sense of acceptance, but he knew he had a real job ahead of him. "These farmers are pretty cautious about switching feeds," he reminded himself.

"Paul, I've been doing a lot of thinking about that weaning weight problem," he began after Paul had refilled his cup. But first, let me check out a couple of things to make sure I understand, OK?"

"Sure," replied Paul, "shoot."

"As I understand it from our visit a couple of weeks ago, you're concerned about your average weaning weight, right?" asked Paul.

"Right."

"And what you'd really like to do is to increase that weight by 3 to 5 pounds in the same length of time without increasing your feed costs, right?" asked Paul.

"Exactly," Paul responded, "when those pigs go on the feeding floor, I want them ready for a faster start and I'd like to reduce disease problems if I can."

"I understand, Paul. I think you've got your finger on a critical production point. And that's exactly what I've been working on — some ideas that might help you. In fact, I've taken the liberty of having our computer prepare an analysis of your system and have asked it to suggest a few alternative plans for your reaction. May I show you what we did and what it suggested?"

"That's why I poured you a second cup of free coffee! Let's see what crazy ideas you've come up with," Paul said as he gestured toward the coffee. Mike hoped he was kidding but it was impossible to be sure.

Mike launched into his personalized analysis, being sure to check each assumption in his analysis and secure agreement before proceeding. He knew if Paul did not accept his assumption about the number of hogs, litter size, feeding rations and medications, that much of his analysis would break-down. While he wasn't sure Paul really accepted the computer, he certainly seemed interested in his personal analysis.

The analysis was a series of "what if" situations designed to show the impact of each additional pound of weaning weight, its probable cost and its probable impact on the profit of that year's production. It was designed to show the producer the economic importance of each factor. While Paul was aware of the problem, the economic impact on the total operation of each production variable was impressive and often helped generate interest in fine tuning management procedures. It was hoped too that it set the stage for the salesman by building credibility and interest. And it seemed to be working well in this case. Paul's interest was clearly peaked. "Now I've really got to go to work," thought Mike as Paul interrupted with a question.

"Well, what changes in my program would you suggest, Mike?" Paul asked with interest.

"I'm suggesting we alter the pig starter to include a slightly higher protein content and trace elements. I also suggest that we treat them in the first 10 days to prevent scouring. Our "pro starter 21" was designed especially for situations just like this. Its higher protein content is in a more digestible form than anything on the market. This means that it works more effectively in the young pig's delicate stomach and increases the rate of gain. At the same time, its organic form reduces the tendency for scours to develop in the critical first days. In fact, our field research shows 20 percent less scours and a 15 percent increase in rate of gain in the first four weeks over groups using conventional feeding programs."

Paul's interest was obvious as he nodded while Mike moved through his prepared visuals. Yet he knew that it would take more than words to help Paul make such an important decision.

"How long have you had this out?" asked Paul.

"We've been on the market about 15 months in various tests, but we've just introduced it in this region. Would you be interested in seeing some of our research?"

****

Until now, Mike has been handling several tasks at once in an informal, relaxed manner. He has been building trust and credibility with his prospect; qualifying the prospect as a buyer while projecting himself in a favorable light as a competent salesperson; and probing to find the prospect's "problem" as well as preparing him to accept the solution. He has also been gaining insight into how the prospect thinks, what makes him buy and what he values. And Mike has been arousing his interest in what he has to offer as he helps Paul clarify his problem.

Having worked his way through all these elements, a good salesperson will now want to pull his ideas together into a solution that will have mutual benefits for both the prospect and himself. He must present his solution in such a way that the prospect understands its merits and wants them. The process of communicating the solution and convincing the prospect of its value is called "the presentation."

THE
PRESENTA-
TION
PROCESS

The presentation is the main component of the selling process. Its goal is to show the prospect how the product works and how the prospect can benefit from that product. This is usually accomplished by highlighting the features that are important to the prospect. Don't forget, you should already have a good idea from your preparation work and the questions you have asked in the opening, what your prospect desires most in your product. Throughout the presentation, you will also be receiving signals and asking more questions. The answers will add to your understanding of what is important to the prospect. While your methods may be subtle, the ultimate goal of the presentation is to excite the prospect so much that he must have your product.

The basic approach of *Agri Selling* is to consider it a problem-solving process. The greatest long-term selling success comes when the salesperson can identify a farmer or dealer's problem and suggest a mutually beneficial solution. That's exactly what Mike was doing when he suggested "Pro Starter 21" to Paul. His probing and analysis told him his product would serve Paul's needs.

The presentation portion of the sales call is the time when you explain your solution; showing your prospect how your product or service can solve his problem and meet his needs. It capitalizes on all the preparation done before the sales call, the product knowledge you have and what you have learned about the prospect's special needs and values. The presentation lays out your solution or plan step-by-step so the prospect will understand how it can solve his problem and benefit him. Whether the identified problem is a difficult situation or simply an area where he can make improvements, an effective presentation will convince the prospect that your plan is a good one, and worth what it costs to adopt it.

**The Importance
of Organization**

When the United States decided to land a man on the moon, NASA did not put someone into a rocket ship, light the fuse and hope for the best. First they had to find out how to send a rocket into orbit and bring it back safely. Then they had to see whether living things — plants, insects and monkeys — could survive the gravitational forces of liftoff and the weightlessness of space. Next they had to prove that humans could also survive the ordeal. Then they had to see whether a spacecraft could journey to the moon and orbit it, whether the orbiting capsule could dock with the lunar lander as well as detach and whether the lunar lander was a maneuverable, flyable spaceship itself. Finally, all the individually-tested steps were put together into one production of sending three men into orbit, having them fly to and orbit the moon, board the lunar landing, drop down to the moon, perform experiments, take-off from the moon, reconnect with the orbiter, fly back to earth and land safely in the ocean.

Similarly, a sales presentation is a series of tasks that must be executed in a logical fashion. Each step must be designed, prepared and rehearsed to ultimately fit into the presentation process. Just as every space shot presents its own set of problems, every presentation will be different because each prospect has a unique set of problems, personality and set of values. Yet the same tasks must ultimately be accomplished to complete the mission successfully. You must outline your solution to your prospect, explain those features of your product or service that will benefit your prospect, prove the existence of those features and convince the prospect that your solution will benefit him directly. Finally, you must obtain some sort of "agreement" from the prospect which demonstrates and solidifies his understanding of the benefits and ultimately his acceptance of your solution. Beyond that, you must monitor the prospect's reactions to make sure the points of interest are being satisfied and to anticipate possible objections. The successful accomplishment of all these things demands good communications skills, organization and self-discipline. (See Figure 9.1.)

Figure 9.1 **Organization — the Key to Making an Effectively Communicated Presentation**

Know your customer's needs and desires so you can focus your presentation.

Speak clearly and in an orderly manner like a motion picture film.

Don't forget the S.O.S. — The significance of simplicity in explanations.

Know your product and how it relates to your customer's needs.

COMMUNICATION

Clarity

Effective communication starts with clear thinking. Your ideas should be organized in an orderly manner before you utter one word. When you start talking, be sure to choose concise, easy-to-understand words that perfectly convey your meaning. Visual aids, such as charts, graphs, photographs and brochures can aid your effort. But don't lean too heavily on them. And don't depend on verbal shortcuts like, "Oh, you know what I mean," or on technical language that the prospect may not understand. Start out by assuming the person does not understand and before you use "shorthand" ask whether the prospect knows the term. This should be done tactfully, so as not to embarrass the prospect. You can always pause to explain the technical process or jargon to him if he says he does not understand. If you place the momentum of the sales call higher on your list of priorities than clarity, you may win the battle but lose the war. Only when you have clearly transmitted your message to the other person do you have a successful meeting of the minds that could result in a sale.

Simplicity

Simplicity is another important element of effective communication. After all, it's not what you say that counts, it's whether the customer understands what you say. Though you do want him to know you are authoritative, your purpose is not to impress him with how clever you are. Your main objective is to teach him about your product and how it can help him. In any teaching process, that means starting from scratch with the "basics" and putting those blocks together to make an easily understandable structure. Examples help the person understand, as do actual case histories, comparisons, and analogies. Feel free to let these verbal aids draw vivid pictures for your prospect.

Overkill   It is important to limit your presentation to the most significant points. Overkill can discourage prospects. Don't give a prospect more than they need to know to make a positive decision. Time is often limited. If the presentation is too long you may lose the prospect before you get to the close. And there is also danger of confusing the prospect with too much data. Often highly knowledgeable agri salespeople are so enthralled by the technology of what they are selling that they bombard prospects with technical information. Some prospects might feel overwhelmed and need to "think it over" a while longer which may destroy your opportunity to solve their problem and make the sale.

Product Limitations   There may be drawbacks or limitations of your product that need to be part of your presentation. Your presentation may need to include adequate descriptions of what not to expect or what not to do. If done carefully, this part of a presentation can build additional credibility and trust — and more importantly, it can help avoid customer dissatisfaction and awkward confrontations later on. (Usually, product limitations should come near the end of your presentation.)

Satisfaction and Expectation   You should be cautious not to "oversell" the product, meaning don't promise more than the product can deliver. A customer's expectations about the product's performance may rise to such exhilarating heights that he will buy or use it for the wrong purpose. With such great expectations, however, he is in for a disappointment when he actually owns the product and finds out it's not a wonder buy. That can spell only trouble for you, the salesperson: customer discontent, callbacks, and potential badmouthing of you and the product. You may make one sale or ten by stretching the truth, but you will damage your reputation and drive far more customers away.

Product Knowledge   Product knowledge is, of course, crucial to your presentation. You must understand and know your product before you can explain it to someone else, answer questions about it and be able to choose features which will fulfill the needs and desires of your prospect. But product knowledge also requires a skill for relating the product features to consumer desires. The technical manual will tell you — or the customer — that lever "X" releases the hydraulic locking mechanism on the tractor, but you must know the product well enough to explain that lever "X" also does the job quickly and with minimum effort: two primary selling features. A combination of feature and benefit can only be utilized with a thorough knowledge of product.

Customer Signals   As mentioned in the previous chapter, the salesperson must direct the flow of conversation, however subtle, throughout the sales call. You must keep in touch with your prospect's thinking as you proceed. Encouraging questions will help because a prospect's questions or comments coupled with non-verbal signals are important clues about where they stand with the buying decision. For example, questions about whether a ridge planter "will work equally as well for soybeans as corn" is a positive clue that the farmer is visualizing how the equipment would fit into his own operation.

Other clues may indicate obvious interest when certain product features and benefits are mentioned. When a dealer asks more specifically where the warehouse is located in Minneapolis, it may be a clue that regular trips he makes to the Twin Cities could include a stop by the warehouse if convenient for him. Or when a farmer counts the rows of corn on an ear, he may be telling you of a special interest in ear size.

Clues to the prospect's thinking are abundant but may not be obvious. The experienced agri salesperson can frequently sense how the prospect is responding and adjust the presentation accordingly. A good salesperson knows his product so well he can concentrate heavily on his prospect's reaction and adjust constantly as the need arises. Always they are toward a firm objective — convincing the prospect that a product will best meet his needs.

Hot Buttons

Hand-in-hand with your encouragement of dialogue throughout the presentation goes your ability to recognize and capitalize on "hot buttons." Hot buttons are the customer's areas of strong interest in your product. If a prospect suddenly leans closer to you or displays interest via raised eyebrows and pursed lips, he is clearly giving nonverbal clues to you that he wants to hear more. Verbal clues, such as a string of questions about one of the features, should also send up flags to you that more information is required because the customer is interested. You should learn to recognize and use hot buttons to their advantage.

Hot buttons also offer an opportunity late in the sales call when you are summarizing positive reasons for buying. Make a mental note to include obvious hot buttons in your summary, so you can remind your prospect of benefits that are important to him.

ORGANIZA-TION

The presentation should begin when you feel you have a good understanding of the prospect's problem or needs, his values and circumstances. And you must have a firm solution well-in-mind along with a plan for laying out that solution in a logical manner.

In many types of agri selling, a presentation cannot be made on the first visit because the product or services must be designed to the specification of the prospect's situation. The building must be designed or a plan formulated that requires a great deal of work. In these situations it is usually necessary to collect a great deal of information from the prospect that will enable you to design your specific solution. The willingness of the prospect to give you detailed information should be considered a sign of good progress. It is important not to create false expectations of what you can deliver at what price until an adequate analysis can be made.

Length   How long should the presentation be? That depends on how complicated your product is and to whom you're selling it. Some presentations will take only minutes before the prospect is persuaded to buy; other sales will close only after time is spent dealing with a list of customer fears, doubts, questions and problems, perhaps over several different sales calls. Complex technical explanations, when they are called for, complete with cost breakdowns and specific "bottom line" calculations could take several hours. Remember though, that in most cases you will know more about the technical aspects than the customer needs — or cares — to know. You should not flood the prospect with more information than he needs to reach a buying decision.

Personalized Service   Every presentation should be designed to meet the unique needs of that specific prospect. There may be many facts about your product that are potentially important to users. The preparation process should provide long lists of reasons why various customers have been satisfied with the product or service you are selling. Some of these may be highly technical while others may be more esthetic or psychological. In dealing with one specific prospect, only those selling points that fit the situation should be included. If the farmer has teenagers who may be operating the equipment, then safety shut-off features may take on extra importance. But if the farmer has only one brand of tractor, the fact that your equipment can adapt to any type hitch with no alterations is not important. You should select selling points that fit each prospect.

Logic   The key to a strong and successful presentation is effective communication: creating understanding in your prospect. Customers seldom buy what they do not understand. Assuming you have accurately identified your prospect's problem or needs and that you do have a beneficial solution, *your* problem is to convince the prospect that you do have an answer worthy of his acceptance.

Even the most complex selling message can be communicated more clearly when it is reduced to a logical communication process. (1) You have a problem; (2) this product or service is a good solution to that problem; (3) it has these features that will solve the problem; and (4) the result will be that you'll receive these benefits from accepting this solution.

If the prospect is convinced of the benefits he will gain and believes they are worth the cost, he logically should decide to make the purchase. (See Figure 9.2.)

Figure 9.2 **Logical Sequence of Presentation**

The sales presentation involves three basic steps: first, a statement of the problem to be solved; next a solution needs to be presented; and finally, a series of selling points pointing out features and benefits of the product must be made to support the logic of the proposed solution and convince the prospect to proceed with the purchase.

Three Steps of the Presentation

Begin your presentation with a brief statement of what you believe the problem to be. This will reconfirm the validity of your solution when you present it. "Bob, it seems to me that getting a quality application job on your corn ground when you want it is pretty important to you, right?"

Step 1 Summarize the Problem

If your prospect gives you a signal that you have summarized his problem accurately, you'll know it's appropriate to proceed. If the prospect corrects you, take a step backward to identify the problem to the satisfaction of the customer. Begin probing again. Using questions, try to get a better picture of your prospect's needs. Clearly you can't solve a problem until you understand it.

Very often, when you summarize the problem into a concise statement, your prospect will agree with a tone that conveys relief that, "at long last, I've finally found someone who understands my problem — and cares." In such cases, a prospect will often volunteer additional important data at that point. "That's exactly what I need. And it's getting so bad that I doubt if I can get through the season!" the prospect might add. This kind of response is great encouragement for your presentation.

When you have clearly defined your prospect's problem, briefly outline your solution. Be sure to include a key benefit as part of the solution you suggest. "I've got an idea about your corn fertility program that I'd like you to consider for a minute. My idea is based on a flotation type applicator that can weed and feed your corn at the same time — and keep you on that planter where you belong. How does that sound to you?"

Step 2 Outline Solution

The reason for starting with a benefit is to arouse the prospect's interest and to direct your prospect's attention in the direction you choose. Select a benefit that you believe will have great appeal. Any sign of interest should be viewed as an invitation to move ahead with selling points. If your prospect doesn't stop you, it usually means it's okay to proceed.

To reiterate: this logic should proceed in a conversational tone. Each agri salesperson will handle it in their own way. On the first try it may seem awkward, but in the context of a salesperson/prospect conversation it will sound very normal — and it will accomplish the objective.

Through selling, you pinpoint things your prospect should know about your product or service. They are ideas that will help increase their understanding of your solution. Selling points are reasons why a prospect may want to buy from you.

Step 3 Present Selling Points

Potentially, there are many reasons a prospect might choose you and your product. It makes sense to select the ones you believe are most likely to be important to your prospect. They should flow logically and help him understand how your solution will benefit him. If your prospect accepts each logical selling point, it should lead to the desired conclusion - a sale!

Units of Conviction

As the sales call progresses, it is a good idea for the salesperson to treat each major selling point in the presentation as something called a "unit of conviction." A unit of conviction is an agreement from the customer that "Yes, that feature is a good one that will benefit me, and yes, that's a good reason to buy." You have *convinced* him to "buy" that one point. It is for this purpose that the salesperson should try to secure agreement from the prospect as each point is presented. By doing so, you get the customer to say, "Yes, that is a valid point and it is important to me. It is another reason why I should accept your solution to my problem."

Thus the sales call becomes something like a building, with each brick equivalent to one unit of conviction or valid selling point. Although the number of bricks needed to complete a sale varies from situation to situation, ideally once the structure is complete and has enough valid selling points to support itself, the sale should be closed.

Procedure for Making Selling Points

Making an effective selling point and creating one unit of conviction is a simple four-step procedure:

1. Highlight the feature that you expect your prospect to be interested in and explain why the feature is important.
2. Explain the benefit the prospect will gain from the particular feature.
3. Support what you say with evidence.
4. Secure agreement from the customer that he indeed understands the importance of the feature, believes what you are telling him and sees how it will benefit him.

Getting conviction on a selling point using these four steps makes sense. Stating the feature clearly at the outset focuses the prospect's attention on the point you want to make. Some explanation of its importance will help give additional significance to the point you are about to make.

Step two — explaining how the prospect will benefit from the feature — is the most important step because customers don't buy features, they buy benefits. That benefit must be explained in terms that the prospect understands and how it will benefit him.

Step three is a tool for ensuring the benefit is accepted. Give just enough evidence to support your claim and make it believable. The amount of evidence needed varies with each situation. (More on using evidence later on.)

Finally, it's important to gage the acceptance of your point. Sometimes an indication of acceptance comes from a simple nod of the prospect's head. In other cases, it may be necessary to ask a question, "How does that sound to you, Bob?" It's important that the prospect accept your point. If not, you should deal with it immediately or it may result in a lost sale.

Making selling points and building units of conviction requires a clear distinction between product features and benefits. Features are facts about your product, service or organization. Features are tangible things and are undeniable facts that can be proven. Products have weights, dimensions, horsepower, turning radius, capacity, genetic parentage, chemistry etc. Features can be seen, photographed, felt, measured, counted, tasted or smelled. No one can argue with product features because they are hard facts.

FEATURES AND BENEFITS

Salespeople who are technically oriented get excited about a product's features. Since they are highly interested in their industry and perhaps have seen the product gradually evolve to its present state, they may be impressed with its design, content and specifications. They are proud of what they sell, and are anxious to share their excitement with others who will listen.

While it's important for a salesperson to have a good understanding of their product's features and have pride in it, customers don't buy features— they buy benefits. They purchase what a product can do for them. A farmer doesn't buy fertilizer — he buys a better yield. A dairyman doesn't buy semen — he buys a more productive herd. A wheat farmer doesn't buy a negative pressure ventilation system for the cab of his combine — he buys comfort.

A product benefit is the end result of a product feature. In short, a feature should be translated into a benefit.

Another problem arises when salespeople believe that benefits are obvious. "Why, anyone would know that chemically combined fertilizer prills that are uniformally sized will give a more accurate spread pattern and improve yield. I'll sound dumb or I'll make my prospect feel dumb if I make a big point out of it," they argue. To the salesperson who concentrates on fertilizer technology 365 days a year, it may be a simple conclusion. But it may not be so obvious to a farmer who shops for fertilizer twice a year. Besides, the point is so important you cannot afford to assume the prospect understands it.

As part of the presentation of a selling point, you should strive to bring that feature to life for the prospect. By far the best way to do that is to have a sample or floor model of the product which the prospect can actually see, touch, kick, sit in or feel. Never limit yourself to telling a customer about something if you can *show* him. If you want to demonstrate the quietness of an engine, you need only turn the machine on. Mike Adams was prepared to show Paul Bradley a sample of his pig starter as part of his presentation. Such samples are powerful selling tools because they appeal to the senses and the prospect can actually "experience" the product. They create strong images that the prospect will remember. Don't forget, however, that samples are only tools — aids to the salesperson. They will not sell themselves. A salesperson is required to do the real selling.

Making Features Stand Out

In lieu of actually showing the prospect a sample, visual aids, such as brochures, pictures and charts, are helpful tools for the presentation. These too are most useful when they come with a salesperson who can draw vivid verbal images and put the picture that's in the booklet into the customer's environment: for example, if you are trying to demonstrate the turning radius of a tractor when you do not *have* a tractor, you might ask the prospect what the narrow distance is between the house and the barn; then you could explain that the tractor would easily be able to turn completely around between those two buildings "with 7 feet to spare," if that were indeed the case. (More selling aids in Section IV.)

Showing Benefits

The next step in the process of developing a single selling point is to explain how the customer will benefit from the feature. As already mentioned, customers buy *benefits,* not features. Many salespeople make the mistake of selling the features because they are truly excited about them, but fail to sell the product itself because the customer can't come up with a satisfactory answer to the question, "What's in it for me?" It is up to you to make the connection between feature and benefit. Never take it for granted that the customer will naturally see an obvious benefit. Show him.

The salesperson should clearly and simply explain how the customer will personally benefit from the product's features. It is not coincidence that many television commercials will show one scene of someone using their time-saving product followed by a second scene of the person relaxing by the swimming pool sipping a drink. Pretty rudimentary perhaps, but it makes a definite connection between feature and benefit. You, of course, cannot show the prospect the benefit of buying your product; that can only be accomplished once he *buys* the product. But you can explain by verbally connecting the feature and benefit.

How do you find benefits for the customer? Many times, such information will be described in the sales literature that accompanies the product. But a good part of the task is carried out by the salesperson, who has a clear understanding of the customer's needs, problems or desires and has an intimate knowledge of the product, what it can do and what it cannot do. This takes a bit of creativity and thinking, but the professional salesperson knows what the job is and does it. Many an alert salesperson will take note of a prospect's complaints or comments early in the sales call, then explain off-handedly how the product can eliminate that problem. For example, to the customer who complains about always getting his deliveries late because "You just can't depend on some companies," your firm's ability to make deliveries on time with a minimum of foulups would be a clear advantage, and the benefit to the customer would be increased efficiency, less out-of stocks and happier customers.

It is also helpful to develop a list of your product's features and the possible benefits that a prospect might gain. While you will never cover all of them with a specific prospect, having a catalogue of features and benefits readily available can be a gold mine. (See Figure 9.3.)

Translating Features Into Benefits

Translating a feature into a benefit is an art that good salespeople work at until they become very proficient. The secret is to use "linkage phrases" that connect the benefit to the feature. A linkage phrase shows how the feature leads directly to a benefit. "Because of this *feature,* you will be able to gain this *benefit.*" Because our new pig starter has a more digestible

Figure 9.3 **Examples of Product Features & Benefits**

.5 mm Mechanical Lead Pencil

Feature	Benefit
(Because of...)	(You will be able to...)
	(Which means...)
1. .5 mm lead	— Maintain fine point
	— Have sharper writing
2. Retractable lead	— Avoid holes in shirt pocket
	— Make better impression
	— Keep wife happier
3. Automatic lead feed	— Save time
	— Avoid dirty fingers
4. Easy to disassemble	— Easy to maintain
	— Less "downtime"
5. Lead type indicator	— Remember type lead used
6. Stainless steel parts	— Will last long time
	— Attractive — looks good

Liquid Nitrogen Solution

Feature	Benefit
(Because of...)	(You will be able to...)
	(Which means...)
1. Liquid form	— Handle it easier
	— Less effort
	— Cleaner
2. Low pressure storage	— Safer
	— Less fear of injury
3. Can be applied prior to planting	— No change of not getting nitrogen on
4. Can serve as carrier for pesticides	— Single application cheaper
	— More effective coverage
5. Chemical properties	— Less loss
	— Quicker plant response
	— Higher yield

source of protein (feature) you will get your pigs off to a faster start (benefit 1), reach a higher average weaning weight (benefit 2) and reduce your pig's tendency toward scours (benefit 3)." Or, "With our new planter that lets you plant on ridges (feature), you'll be able to plant earlier (benefit 1) and give your corn a warmer seed bed (benefit 2) and get it off to a faster start (benefit 3)."

Use of Linkage Phrases for
Translating Features into Benefits

Because of this _____(feature)_____
   you will be able to _____ .
This _____(feature)_____
   means that you will _____(benefit)_____ .

As with many selling techniques, this language may seem awkward and strange at first. To become familiar with the idea of translating features into benefits, it's helpful to actually practice verbally. You will gradually become more comfortable.

Supporting Claims   Many times, however, the prospect will either not believe your claims or have serious doubts. The customer suffering from the late deliveries mentioned previously, may be so cynical because of the bad service he has been receiving that he already may have it in his mind that, *"No* company can be trusted to deliver on time."

If you have correctly stuck only to facts, you will be able to *make* your prospect believe you by producing evidence, which is step three of our construction of a unit of conviction.

Proving Benefits   The salesperson should be ready to back up all his features and benefits with evidence, even though the evidence is not specifically requested by the prospect. After all, people don't always say what they're thinking. Making the presentation of evidence a regular step in your presentation will prevent you from making a wild claim that cannot be substantiated. When that happens, you lose credibility with the prospect, and even if everything else you say is absolutely correct, the prospect will always suspect otherwise.

Providing evidence not only makes what you say believable and builds trust; it also serves as a good selling device that drives home a point in a way that will make the customer remember. Seeing is believing, but seeing also sets the features and benefits in the prospect's mind.

Features are easiest to deal with because they are tangible and measurable: quick reference to the specifications chart of the customer's firsthand inspection of the feature can be evidence enough. Advantages that result from features are also easy to deal with — use logical deduction or, again, personal observation. Benefits, however, are another story. Because they are often not tangible things — something the prospect can hold in his hand or see with his eyes — it is tougher to support benefits. But there *are* ways to do so:

   * Demonstrating the product is one of the best methods. Allowing the farmer to actually operate the farm machinery and get the feel of it may be costly, but it is one of the most convincing things you can do. Detailed proposals which demonstrate with the prospect's own operating figures how a cost saving can be realized by ordering in bulk is another demonstration. They are almost as powerful. But demonstrations that *do not* work are equally powerful in stopping a sale dead in its tracks. Live demonstrations should be well planned.

* Testimonials from satisfied customers are very popular in agri selling, especially when the prospect knows the customer giving the testimonial. They are also very credible because the touting of the product comes not from you — who obviously has an interest in making a sale — but from people who have already put their money down and believe that money was well-spent.

* Pictures of the product in action or charts and tables showing the cost-saving benefits over time also give your prospect something he can hold in his hand and thus relate to.

* Comparisons are yet another good form of demonstration. If you can show how your product does one particular task that the competing product cannot do, you have given your customer something he can "point to." Comparisons are most effective when they closely relate to the customer's situation.

* Test results or surveys are also very popular in agribusiness selling. But although tests run by the company are useful, many customers still suspect their truthfulness. Thus tests done by an independent researcher are a better form of evidence.

* Company-supplied literature, films, videotapes or other audiovisual aids bring the demonstration to the customer when it is not feasible or possible to perform a live demonstration. And through the "magic of film," hard-to-show facts, such as how quickly two different sorghum hybrids will grow, can be easily demonstrated through time-lapse photography.

Tangible Agreement

Once you have mentioned the features, shown the prospect the benefit to him and given evidence that what you say is true, it is then important to complete the unit of conviction with some tangible form of agreement from him, which lets you know he understands and believes what you have said. As mentioned previously, this agreement also helps the prospect internalize the idea; the fact of the benefit becomes a part of him. It also commits the prospect to your point of view and presentation, and leads toward a successful close.

Many times the prospect will send nonverbal clues to show he agrees with you: the smiling face or the understanding nod of his head. If you see positive signals, it's okay to move ahead, but if you are unsure, it is a good idea to get the prospect to verbally express his agreement. This is usually accomplished by the salesperson asking a wrap-up question: "That's an important factor to you, isn't it?" Note that the wrap-up question is put forward more forcefully by making it a statement followed by a question: "You can see how our vaccine dramatically reduces the flock mortality rate (statement), can't you, Mr. Long (question)?"

Sometimes it helps to actually write out a brief scenerio for key selling points you'd like to make, highlighting each of the steps. By becoming familiar with the thought process and flow of the logic, the technique becomes much more comfortable. Once the scenerio is thought through and written, try reading it aloud until the words and ideas come easily. Avoid memorizing the scenerio. Anything that sounds memorized in a professional sales call is a big red flag. Instead, after you are quite familiar with the words and your voice sounds comfortable, try talking through the scenerio in a more conversational manner. Just make sure you maintain the key ideas. Go over it until all of the ideas flow logically and sound natural to you, and if the concept and logic are sound, it works.

Figure 9.4 **Selling Point Scenario:**
Custom Application of Fertilizer

Step 1

(statement) "Bob, we use a fertilizer applicator equipped with flotation tires and operated by a professional driver."

(evidence) "Quality application has become particularly critical in weed and feed programs where chemicals play an important role."

Step 2

(show benefit) "Using our customer application means you get a quality job without having to give up valuable time when you need to be planting."

Step 3

(give evidence) "In fact, last year we custom applied over 25 thousand acres in this county for farmers just like you who understand the value of their time in planting season."

Step 4

(secure agreement) Does time seem to be a critical factor in your spring workload?"

Handling Objections

Every salesperson must expect objections. An objection is a reason for not buying or not accepting a selling point. It may be a form of disagreement or misunderstanding between you and your prospect. When a prospect gives you an objection, he is really saying, "I don't accept that," or "I object to that point."

Obviously, every salesperson would rather not encounter any objections. But that is unrealistic. Salespeople must anticipate and be prepared for statements like: "I don't think it's got enough power"; "I just like to do business close to home"; "It costs too much"; "I'm concerned about how it will perform in a dry year"; or "I've always been satisfied with my present supplier."

The inexperienced salesperson dreads objections, usually because they don't understand them or aren't ready to deal with them properly. But preparation and experience can make a big difference. Any salesperson who has been around for any time at all has heard most objections, at least once. While it is forgivable to be "thrown" the first time you encounter an objection, there is no excuse for being tripped up repeatedly by the one which reoccurs. Successful salespeople have a plan for dealing with common objections.

In fact, many experienced salespeople view objections as an opportunity, not a stumbling block. They know that objections let them know exactly where the prospect's concerns lie and offer him the opportunity to allay those worries and objections alert the salesman that the presentation hasn't convinced the prospect yet. Objections also signal areas of prospect interest. Some objections that sound threatening are actually requests by the prospect for more information to help him understand, and once you've cleared up his objection, he/she might be ready to buy.

Not all objections are valid. Some are just excuses to hide the prospect's real reason for not buying from you. Perhaps he is embarrassed because he realizes he does not have enough money to buy. A young prospect may not want to admit that his father makes all final decisions in the operation. Or a dealer may not want you to know that his operation is too small to allow installing bulk storage equipment. So instead of letting you know straightforwardly, he puts up a barrier: "Your price is too high"; "I need more time to think it over"; or "I don't think it will do the job." **Excuses or Valid Objections**

Sometimes it's difficult to tell the difference between an excuse or stall and a valid objection. Body language can be a clue. Is he uneasy? Does he have difficulty looking you in the eye? Is he trying to change the subject? If you feel you are not getting accurate information about what your prospect is really feeling, go back to your probing skills. Try to uncover, as tactfully as possible, what is really bothering your prospect. Unless you uncover their real objection, you very likely will not be able to accomplish your sales call objective.

A good salesperson must also know when to quit. Occasionally you will encounter a situation where there are problems about which the prospect feels very strongly, but does not want to reveal. If you push too hard into a sensitive area, you may build animosity that may do long-term damage to the relationship and can endanger other potential relationships.

When your prospect gives you an excuse, you may choose to ignore it. If it was a valid objection, it will come up again. On the other hand, if it was just an excuse, it may simply fade away.

Another technique to test the validity of an objection is to ask your prospect whether satisfying the objection will lead to a sale. "If I can prove to you that my equipment will do the job for you, Bob, will you buy it?" This approach can be most effective. If the prospect says "no," the stage is immediately set for probing into other factors of concern and the real objections are often clarified. On the other hand, if the prospect says "yes," then you know exactly what problem you have to solve in order to close the sale. In actuality, the customer has told you that you have his business if you can satisfy this objection.

It is important to recognize that all valid objections are important to your prospect, no matter how small or unimportant they may seem to you. The prospect's fears, values, experience or level of understanding may make major obstacles out of issues that to you are unfounded. But to the prospect they are real, and you must deal with them sensitively. Remember, feelings **Feelings are Facts** and fears are "facts" no matter how illogical they may seem to you. So take all valid objections seriously.

Genuine objections can generally be overcome. They are honest statements characterized by strong supporting opinions. Broadly speaking, genuine objections are among the following:

* **The prospect just doesn't need your product — or, perhaps, thinks he doesn't.** This means you have not done an adequate job of making him understand the problem and the solution and you had better do some fast catching up. Of course, there is the likelihood that he really does *not* need your product. In that case you have fallen down again, in the prospecting, qualifying and determination of your customer's primary needs. This will generally result in a no-sale.

* **The prospect might indeed need your product, but he doesn't need it right now.** This might boil down to a lack of a sense of urgency in buying. You must instill this urgency by pointing out the lost benefits as well as the possible added costs of price increase from delaying purchase.

* **The prospect may need the product and may agree with all the benefits you have pointed out, but he may simply not want it.** The problem is lack of emotion. A lot of buying is done because the person desires a product. If this urge is missing, the sale may run into trouble. To avoid this objection before it happens, you should uncover the prospect's dominant buying urge early on in the sales call so that you can pitch the product directly at his desires.

* **No money.** If your prospect indeed does not have the available capital to buy your product and does not expect to have the required money for a long time, or if he is so far in debt that it would be unwise for him to take on more debt by buying your product, there is nothing you can do about his objection. Remember, the sale is not complete until the money is collected, and you should sell only to those from whom you can collect. But before giving up, be sure that there is indeed no money. A prospect may simply not have the money *at this time,* or may not want to spend it on your product. If that is the case, you must again make him understand the benefits of the product and create a desire for it. If someone wants a product and can get the money — even though he may not have the money in hand — he will get it.

Benefits Outweigh Objections

Some objections *are* valid reasons for not buying from you. But hopefully, there are enough positive reasons to buy from you to outweigh the prospect's objections. The challenge is to overcome all obstacles possible and then show how your benefits outweigh any remaining objections. If you cannot, then perhaps the prospect should not buy from you.

Strategies

When objections arise there is a tendency for some salespeople to become defensive — especially when the prospect is outspoken or lacks tact. In fact, sometimes a prospect may even seem to attack the salesperson. You can even be drawn into an argument as you struggle to defend a point you have made and feel strongly about. But seldom is anyone convinced of anything in an argument. Even if you win the argument, you are likely to lose the sale. The basic rule is: *Never* argue with a prospect. Control your emotions no matter what the prospect says. Instead of arguing, suggest or induce ideas tactfully.

It is also good strategy to provide a way for a prospect to save face when you are handling objections. If you think about it, dealing with a prospect's objection is really saying, "No, you're wrong," or "You don't understand." No matter how subtle or tactful you might be, the essence of the message is that the prospect's present thinking is incorrect or incomplete. The goal of handling an objection is to convince the prospect that your point of view is more correct or better. It is very easy for the prospect to feel trapped, become defensive or feel put-down. Therefore objections need to be handled very delicately, allowing the prospect to accept your point of view without having to feel or admit, "I'm wrong" or "Gee, I feel stupid" — or worse, "No, you don't! You're not going to make me admit I'm wrong."

Many salespeople have found that using the word "however" instead of the word "but" in handling objections is a way to reduce conflict with a prospect. A salesperson's comment, "Your point is important, but..." says to a prospect that the concern really isn't that important. It is certainly more harsh than offering, "Your point is a good one, however, there are some other considerations." The prime difference is in the active nature of the two words "but" and "however." "But" is more active and harsh than "however"; so consider choosing the word "however" as you deal with objections. You may antagonize a prospect less as a result.

Allow your prospect a respectable way out of an objection. One technique is to accept the blame yourself. "I'm sorry. I didn't cover that point very well. Sometimes it tends to confuse people. Let me review it again." Don't let your ego get in the way of accepting responsibility for a misunderstanding or disagreement on a point you feel you have already covered well. It costs little to accept the fault even when you don't believe you are wrong. And you could gain a lot.

Or let your prospect know he has company. "A lot of people feel that way until they learn about our repair records. When you consider that our model 170 has a five-year warranty on parts and labor, it makes the slightly higher price seem insignificant."

Still another technique is to blame the misunderstanding on the complexity of the situation. "I sure understand why you might feel that way. This new technology is pretty complex." This approach can help put your prospect more ate ease and less defensive.

When do you answer an objection? There are four different time frames in which it might be done. The most important of these is *immediately.* If the objection is a valid one, you should not try to sidestep it, sweep it under the rug or put it off hoping the prospect will forget about it. Deal with the **Timing** question as soon as it is raised so suspicion or resentment does not build up with the prospect.

The second time to answer the objection is *before* it is raised. Experienced salespeople, as mentioned before, often encounter the same objection over and over. In order to maintain a position of strength, many successful salespeople anticipate the objection themselves and deal with it as a selling point earlier in the presentation. This has an added benefit psychologically. Because the customer's objection has been headed off, the customer will not internalize the negative feelings about the product. Since he did not raise the question, it is in a sense removed from his possession and therefore becomes easier for the salesperson to deal with.

From time to time, you will want to answer an objection *later*. This usually is called for when the material you are explaining is extremely complicated. The prospect may have jumped ahead of you, raising a question that will be handled in the normal course of the presentation.

Explain that to the customer and ask his permission to delay answering. If you let the customer understand that the objection will be more easily answered in that way, he will usually yield to your request. But always be sure to request permission and always be sure to answer the question later.

Finally, you might decide to *never* answer the objection. This is only done, of course, when the objection is clearly not intended to be serious. "I don't know, man," a prospect might joke, "I'm going to have to go home and break open the piggy bank to pay for this." You should smile, if the objection is intended for humorous purposes, joke with them or just ignore it. However, if after having done that you suddenly see the prospect's objection was seriously stated, you should proceed to handle it on the spot.

Objection Procedure

Experienced salespeople have found many ways to handle objections. But all methods are based upon an effective, yet simple, three-step procedure:

1. Listen carefully to the objection.
2. Restate the objection in your own words.
3. Deal with the objection.

The first thing you must do in handling an objection is to *listen* to what the prospect has to say. Don't interrupt him. Let him say his piece, and in fact encourage him to express his doubts or problems. You might even want to probe to draw out the objections. Unless you understand what the concern is, you can't possibly deal with it. You might even answer the wrong objection if you only listen halfway. And you will surely anger the prospect if you keep cutting him off in midsentence with too many "buts."

Second, restate the objection as you heard it but in your own words. This tells your prospect that you indeed have heard what he is saying and understand it. If you did not understand correctly, it offers the prospect an opportunity to straighten you out, saving you time in dealing with the wrong issue. And restating your prospect's objection makes him feel like you care about his concerns.

Often you want to cushion the objection when you restate it. Objections are a challenge. Many prospects view salespeople as adversaries and like to position their objections as "Ah-ha! Now I've got you. Let's see you try to answer this one!'' In these cases, it is helpful to soften the negative tone of the objection and turn it into something that can be dealt with more constructively.

Prospect: "You guys are all alike — you set up delivery schedules that are for your convenience rather than the customers."

Salesperson: "Getting delivery at the right time is pretty important, so I can understand your concern, Bob. How often do you need delivery with your setup?"

The cushioning in the restatement can be crucial because, when done correctly, it instantly dissolves the adversary relationship created by the "challenge," and moves you onto the prospect's side. You are then working together, not against each other.

Note that in restating the objection, you are agreeing with your prospect rather than disagreeing. You are not agreeing with their objection per se because your agreement centers on your understanding of and appreciation for his concern.

Your old friend, empathy, comes in handy at this point. Empathizing with the prospect puts you in the right frame of mind to deal with the problem as if it were *your* problem. You understand. It also puts the prospect in the right frame of mind and helps him trust you. Don't forget, many prospects worry that they do not know as much as the salesperson or that the salesperson is out to take them. Empathizing makes you "safer" to the customer.

Third, handle the objection. There are a variety of ways to handle objections. Which method is best depends on the salesperson, the prospect, the situation and the type of objection. What to do when is a matter of judgment that comes with experience. But there are some proven methods that many agri salespeople feel are quite effective.

The Boomerang

As the name suggests, the prospect's objection is sent back to him. After first agreeing with the prospect on the point he raises, the salesperson "turns the tables" and creates a positive selling point. The boomerang is generally employed when the customer has simply misunderstood a benefit:

"Yes, Bill, our 12-row planter does the same thing the less-expensive six-row planter does, however for a 35 percent higher price, the 12-row model does the work of the six-row model 50 percent faster. I'm sure that will be important to you when you're trying to get your crops in."

The Explanation

When your prospect's objection questions what you have said, he does not fully believe what you're saying, most likely because he does not understand. The salesperson should pause and restate the evidence or explanation in a clear way.

"Are you sure that number will give me higher yields and profits?"

"Let's work it out on paper. This variety has about a 5 percent higher yield average and last year you produced..."

The Admission From time to time a prospect will raise an objection that is indeed valid. When this happens, it is best to admit the point, then quickly attempt to put the objection into its proper perspective. Remember, prospects will often buy a product despite minor objections as long as the good (benefits) outweigh the bad (objections). When was the last time you accepted a product of a different size or color than the one you really wanted, because you had an immediate need for the product or believed the product had a lot more advantages than disadvantages?

The Denial Sometimes a prospect will raise an objection that is simply not true. Rumors or misinformation are usually the sources of these objections. You should, of course, *deny* the negative point and be ready to back your denial with evidence immediately. It is also a good idea to help the prospect save face for his incorrect charge by coming up with a possible reason for the misinformation or perhaps by explaining that the misimpression is common.

"Several people have been asking about that. The fact is that there was no product recall at any time. However, you are not alone. That rumor seems to be going around. Where did you hear that? We'd like to check its source out."

The Question Search for the reason behind an objection by asking questions. This will give you insight into the reasoning behind the objection, and it may make the prospect realize the objection is really of little importance. Not only will this technique often yield additional information about the prospect's needs, but it may also get the prospect to answer his own questions.

"When you consider the price, convenience and quality, what is it you're looking for that you don't see here?"

The Counter-Question This technique takes advantage of the powerful psychological power of the question. The salesperson counters the prospect's objection by either highlighting the benefit of the product or pointing out negative aspects of not having use of the benefits available from the product if he doesn't buy it. Such questions may shake the prospect up, especially if he has not realized the consequences of not buying from you. You must position the counter-question in a nonmanipulative or nonthreatening way.

"I can understand your wanting to cut expenses this year by delaying new equipment purchases, however, have you realized how expensive your 10-year-old forage harvester's downtime will be during the peak season? How much longer it will take to get replacement parts when you need them?"

If you've been handling all the aspects of the presentation well, chances are it's about time you thought about closing, which will be the topic of the next chapter.

SUMMARY * The presentation is composed of solution, explanation and demonstration of how a product or service can meet prospect needs.

* The presentation is a series of steps which must be presented in logical order: outlining the solution, explaining product features, proving existence of those features and convincing the prospect of the solution's benefits.

* Important aspects of the presentation are simplicity, effective communication, acknowlegement of the product's limitations, extensive knowledge of the product and smooth conversation.

* The presentation should be designed for the specific needs of each customer and with simplicity.

* Making a selling point is a four-step procedure: highlight the feature, explain the benefit the prospect will gain from the feature, support the point with evidence and secure agreement from the customer that the aforementioned is understood. A distinct difference exists between features and benefits. Features are facts and benefits are what the features can do for the prospect. The most effective way to sell a benefit is to demonstrate or let the prospect actually try the product.

* Objections are to be expected periodically and the salesperson should "use" them to gage the prospect's concerns and offer solutions. Valid objections may include: no need, not a need at the present, need for product but no desire, lack of funds. The most effective way to handle an objection is to acknowledge the prospect's concern and counter it.

**Chapter 9
Review Questions**

1. Discuss the importance of each of the following in organizing a presentation: A) simplicity B) product limitations and C) product knowledge.
2. How long should a presentation be?
3. What are the three steps of a sales presentation? Discuss the four-step selling points process.
4. Define features and benefits and discuss the relationship between the two.
5. How can a salesperson prove benefits to a prospect?
6. When a prospect objects to a product because he doesn't need it, what should the salesperson's reaction be?
7. What is the general process for handling an objection?
8. What are examples of methods to handle objections. When should each be used?

Chapter Ten
The Close

"Ultimately, closing the sale is what really counts."

That research looks good," Paul admitted, "but research findings and what happens on the farm are two different things."

Mike grinned and leaned forward slightly. "Paul, you're right! For many feed companies, research on new feeding programs occurs in situations which aren't at all like those you have in your operation. That's one of the things that makes Fast-Grow Feeds different. Our research farm is just that — a farm. Our tests are run under conditions like yours. We feel that the trial data is more accurate that way. Do you agree?"

"Well, if what you're telling me is right, sure. Actual farm conditions in tests give this research more weight."

"Good. Paul, let me review what we've talked about this morning. We discussed altering your pig starter program to get the baby pigs started faster and healthier at weaning. Our "Pro Starter 21" seemed to fit that bill, didn't it?"

"Yes, if it tastes as good as it smells, those pigs should get eating quick," Paul offered. "Plus the medication seems right to me."

Nodding, Mike continued, "We also talked about your total feeding program incorporating our premixes with your grain and bean meal. That way, you can take advantage of your own storage and mixing capabilities, plus ensure that you tie into a balanced ration at all stages of the hog's life cycle beginning with our starter feeds." Pausing slightly, Mike decided to test the water. "Paul, would you prefer to take premix in bulk, or in bags like you've been doing?"

"Well, since I've got that extra tank, I suppose bulk would be the way to go. 'Course, I've heard stories about how feed premixes hang up in the tank."

Mike was encouraged. Paul had been reasonably positive so far, even though he'd asked for additional information and voiced some objections along the way.

"Well, Paul, our premix has good flowability characteristics, which keep it from hanging up in the bulk tank. In fact, that hasn't been much of a problem in our tests or in the field." Noting Paul's nonverbal acceptance of that point, Mike's confidence continued to rise. He decided it was time to get Paul's commitment to the feeding program.

"Paul, when can we get started on this program?"

"Just a minute, Mike," Paul began — Mike sensed that this wasn't going to occur as easily as he had hoped — "I'm not one to change total feeding programs just because someone tells me theirs is better. You start playing around with your program all the time and those hogs are going to pay the price — which means I lose! Granted, seems like your program has some advantages over what I'm doing now, but ... well, I'm just concerned about changing."

Mike considered Paul's reaction and took a deep breath. Paul seemed concerned about proven performance and a consistency in his feeding program. "Maybe there is a way to convince Paul to give us a try," Mike thought to himself.

"I can understand your desire to have a feeding program which gets hogs to market quicker, not hold them back. That's just good sense, Paul. If we can figure out a way to give you firsthand experience with Fast-Grow Feeds without creating problems in your operation, can we do business?"

For what seemed like an hour to Mike, Paul Bradley thought to himself. "Sure, I'm anxious to find better ways to do things. I just need to feel like they're really better." Paul almost seemed relieved.

"Great," Mike said. "I think I've got a solution to the problem. You said your next weaning will be..."

****

At this point in the selling process you may find that you've been progressing nicely, getting some positive feedback from the prospective customer, answering questions, presenting your product or service in the best possible light. Now you want to do some serious "reality testing:" Is the prospect as impressed as he seems? Is he ready to buy? After all, verbal compliments on the product are important, but ultimately, closing the sale is what really counts.

CLOSING — ACCOMPLISHING YOUR OBJECTIVE

The close in the selling process is the point when you can accomplish your call objective. Many assume a close occurs when you have a firm sales commitment from your prospect — who then becomes your *customer*. However, the objective of every sales call is not necessarily to secure an order from the prospect. Sales call objectives range from dropping off a few pamphlets to keeping the lines of communication open by checking the customer's inventory status. But this does not detract from the importance of closing. No sales call can be totally successful without a successful close; defined as meeting your sales call objective. Mike Adams' objective on his last call on Paul Bradley was to sell a trial order and, if possible, obtain a larger portion of his feed business. So Mike will consider himself successful with some type of sale, greatly different than when his first call was successful in its attempt to gather information.

The close is not some inevitable point along a track; it does not occur without the salesperson's directions. It is a vehicle that requires a skilled salesperson behind the wheel, and frequently involves a good deal of work. Even many seasoned salespeople find it extremely difficult to close at times. One of the hardest hurdles to overcome is motivating the prospect into buying.

THE DIFFICULTIES OF CLOSING

Even experienced salespeople tell us that despite years of work in this area, they still find completing the sale the most difficult step in the process. One possible reason is that we live in a society where we are trained from birth not to ask for things, particularly for money. We are taught to have more "pride." But salespeople who find this kind of false pride a stumbling block should stop to consider the true nature of the selling process. All things considered, a sale is designed to be mutually beneficial: something of value for something of equal value. You are not "begging" for money when you complete such an exchange. As long as you deal honestly and fairly with the prospect, you are performing a *service* which enables the prospect to enhance his business. If you believe in the benefits your product or service offers, help your prospect gain those benefits by closing the sale.

There is another prime reason why closing is a difficult process. The fear of rejection, a natural human phenomenon, is a leading reason why salespeople may be unable to close a sale. Since successful closing represents results in a selling environment, many are fearful of the "failure" which is conveyed when a prospect says "no." Obviously, a "no" dampens enthusiasm and could affect one's drive to approach the next prospect. Generally, the best way to deal with the rejection in selling is to recognize that it is common. It goes with the profession. Separate business rejection from personal rejection. The fact that prospects don't do business with your organization is not necessarily a personal condemnation. The professional maintains confidence by being competent in all areas of the sales process.

Motivating the Prospect

Let's assume that in a given sales call your objective is to actually sell the product. We have now reached the moment of truth. The question is: Will he buy or won't he? Unfortunately, the prospect is hedging, telling you that he would like to think about it before making any decisions. Fulfillment of your sales objective is in danger. You must act quickly to motivate the prospect into becoming a customer. What do you do?

Primary Motives

As we discussed in Chapter 5, science tells us that there are two different kinds of motivational forces within all human beings. The first of these is primary motives. Hunger, thirst and safety are just three examples of universally experienced biological motives among humans. These are the things people need in order to survive and, pushed to the limits of endurance, they will do almost anything to fulfill them. Food and water may be important enough to you in everyday life, but how much more important would they be after you spent several days in the desert with no food and no water? Indeed, when primary needs have already been met, as they are under normal conditions in agri selling, they may seem meaningless, but in fact are extremely powerful drives that should not be underestimated.

Acquired Motives

The second kind of motives, the so-called acquired ones, are learned from culture and society. Examples are the importance of money, need for recognition, prestige, organization and dependability. Because acquired motives have been a part of our lives since childhood, they are often as important to us as primary motives. And it is these motives that aid the salesperson in reaching his ultimate goal of closing the sale. The astute salesperson will tap into these drives as a normal part of the selling process.

Obviously, the salesperson must first know which motives are most important before he can try to utilize them.

Motivating With the Dominant Buying Urge

Remember the *dominant buying urge?* During the opening you began to discover the prospect's dominant buying urges. With that you were able to tailor your selling strategy in the direction of the prospect's needs and desires. Having done so throughout the sales process, you can now relate to those needs in the closing process. This will increase the likelihood that a sale will be made.

The prospect's primary need may be easy enough to pinpoint: perhaps he's looking for ways to cut costs so that he can increase profits. But what's behind that desire to increase profits? Does he hope to buy a new tractor with the money? Put one or more of his children through college? Expand his operation? Take a nice vacation? These are all possible hidden motives behind a prospect's stated objective.

If you're comfortable with the prospect's dominant buying urge, use it as you move toward the close of a sale. Some sales experts recommend the following procedure as a way to harness and use the prospect's dominant buying urge in closing:

1. **Review the "problem."**
   The dominant buying urge must be clearly reflected in the problem review.

2. **Review the solution to the "problem."**
   Ask the prospect to assume that his dominant buying urge is met.
3. **Project the prospect as a satisfied customer.**
   Help the prospect see the dominant buying urge being met. Create in the prospect's mind a picture of the benefits of his use of your product.
4. **Ask for the order.**
   The application of an appropriate closing technique will allow the dominant buying urge to be fulfilled.

ATTITUDES AND ACTIONS

Closing is a time to show confidence and a positive attitude. Generally, the salesperson must maintain active control in the closing process. Tone of voice should be strong. The prospect should be involved throughout. You are selling to a person; one who will be more likely to agree to a purchase if he feels involved. The more interactive the closing process, the easier it is for the salesperson to become a sales counselor.

Your body language becomes extremely critical during the closing portion of the call. Lean forward slightly to indicate interest. Use gestures when appropriate and maintain eye contact. Don't hesitate to move closer to the prospect if possible, yet be careful. Your body language should enhance, not inhibit, your closing posture. Consequently, be careful to avoid looking pushy or manipulative. It is wise to be alert to any resistance which may become obvious during closing, as it is likely that objections or unanswered questions will surface. The salesperson must be perceptive to these and other potential barriers to a sale.

When to Close

There is one best time to close — whenever it's appropriate. At varying times throughout the selling process, opportunities to close a sale may present themselves. Consequently, the professional agri salesperson must be ready — and willing — to close anytime the prospect is ready to buy.

Many salespeople tell the prospect more than he wants to know about the product or service, actually to the point of persuading him not to buy. Granted, as problem solvers, agri salespeople have responsibility to dispense information and share solutions. Yet, a fine line exists between solving problems and proving that one is an "expert." The difference is significant: the true problem solver will never bore a buying buyer. Even if the salesperson hasn't said all that was planned, when the prospect is satisfied, close!

Attempting a close at a less than ideal time is worse than not asking for the order. The number of salespeople who never attempt to close is amazing. These people attempt to drag the selling process into the "Do you have any more questions?" quagmire time and again. Perhaps the fear of rejection, lack of expertise or forgetting are reasons for the lack of "closing" effort! For whatever the reason, many dollars in agricultural sales are lost daily because the salesperson doesn't ask for the order.

While it's up to the salesperson to watch for the proper moment to close, there are some situations which are especially noted as closing opportunities.

Sending Out Signals

These situations occur when prospects send *buying signals*. Buying signals are verbal or nonverbal clues a prospect drops to say he is ready to buy. For example, if he begins asking questions that imply by their choice of wording or tone that he has already accepted the product in his mind, close! If he asks, "Do you have a volume or cash discount?" he may be indicating that he will buy and is now figuring out how to pay or asking if he can get a bargain. If the prospect has been agreeing with the points you raised and starts offering the confidential information you need to offer a tailor-made proposal, close! If he says "You'll have to be dealing with our three branch managers who each are set up on a profit center basis." And if you notice your prospect becoming more friendly and open toward you as he eagerly picks up your proposal to give it a closer look, close!

The time to act is right after the buying signal, when he is most receptive psychologically to buying. In all likelihood you will have more than a split second to recognize the customer's purchase readiness. But don't drag it out; think of the best way to close and then act on it!

Another opportune time to close may be after successfully handling an important objection or making a strong selling point. If the objection or selling point is very important, it may provide an immediate entry to the close. Obviously judgment is the key. Don't make it difficult to go back to the presentation if you judged incorrectly.

The Trial Close

Once you have spotted a buying signal, or covered a strong point in the presentation, doublecheck to see whether the prospect is really prepared to buy. This doublechecking is accomplished by means of a *trial close*.

The trial close is a verbal technique phrased to determine the extent or degree of the prospect's willingness to buy at a given moment. It differs from the true close since you are not specifically asking for a sale; just determining the customer's mental preparedness for buying. If you determine all systems are go, you proceed directly to the close. If you detect hesitation — and depending upon the reasons for it — you may attempt to draw out the customer's objections and deal with them, or you may want to return to the presentation. There is great psychological value to a trial close. A trial close gradually leads the prospect from the realm of impartiality to a personal decision and action — without causing the customer undue stress. It's a transitional stage, or a moment of passage from theory to commitment.

Trial closes generally take the form of questions, and are most effective when they appear naturally. For example, "How would you like to handle the financing?" "Would the 1410, or 1540 model fit your needs best?" "What days are best for you to take delivery?" An enthusiastic response to these or similar questions suggests that the customer is on the brink of an internal commitment to buying, and the next logical step is for you to finalize the details of the sale. A halfhearted answer, or an objection, means that your work is cut out for you and it may be a while before you can safely attempt another trial close or succeed at a final close. Remember, the trial close must be low-keyed so that you can have the opportunity to continue.

If your trial close has indicated the prospect may be ready to buy, you are ready to close by one of several methods.

METHODS OF CLOSING

The first is the *direct close,* in which you ask the prospect whether it is all right to go ahead and submit the order for him. This is appropriately used when the sales visit has been open and positive throughout. If that has been the case, there is no sense beating around the bush at closing time. The direct approach is also used when there is already an ongoing customer/salesperson relationship and all that is really required of the close is to reconfirm that the relationship is continuing. "I'd like to do more business with you. May we go ahead?"

A second closing method is the *summary close.* In the summary close, the salesperson quickly and briefly recaps all of the major points made during the presentation, highlighting the benefits of the product to the customer. This technique is especially helpful when the subject has been complex. It refreshes the whole presentation for the customer who may have forgotten some key points. Finally, at the tail end of summarizing the major points, the salesperson follows the logical progression and asks for the order or other commitment. But be sure to summarize everything in sequence so that the outcome points toward a purchase. This method is particularly effective when done on paper. Listing the positives and negatives in almost balance sheet format may graphically show the prospect why he should do business with you.

Summary Close

A third effective technique is the *choice close.* This close differs from the others in that it does not give the person a choice between buying or not buying. Rather, it recognizes that the prospect intends to buy and offers him a choice of one thing vs. something else. For example, "Will you want me to set it up as a single account, or keep the landlord portion separate?" gives the prospect a choice of buying or buying. The choice close is a very strong one in its expression of confidence, and it is best used after you have successfully dealt with sales resistance. Although some young salespeople may view this style of close as overly aggressive, when the presentation has gone well and objections have been successfully dealt with, it almost becomes a matter of logic that the sale *will* take place, and you should not worry about appearing presumptuous.

Choice Close

A fourth way of winding up a sale is the *assumption close.* In this type of close you do not ask whether the person wants to buy, you assume that this is the case and proceed from there to finalize the sale. However, you must say something that clearly implies you believe he has expressed his willingness to buy. "OK, I'll talk to our credit people and come back tomorrow with all the forms ready for you to sign," is a *routine assumption* close. Actually telling the customer that he will need attachment X or accessory Y is a *command assumption.* And a *dramatized assumption* is one in which you express how "you're going to appreciate keeping your planter rolling without having to worry about seed spacing."

Assumption Close

Once you have given the customer this signal of your assumptions, you must immediately formalize the transaction by filling out the order. If you suddenly realize the customer has become uneasy, he is not clear that you have assumed he's going to buy. You must get the message across to him by dealing with this lack of communication as another objection. Most often, an assumed close is used with established customers or when little resistance is encountered.

Special Features   Finally, there is the *special feature close.* This close gets its name from the fact that you bring up a special feature about the product or service (not previously mentioned) that will be available to the person if he orders. It is especially effective when there have been a number of objections and perhaps giving the customer "something extra" will push him to buy. Special feature closes are most effective when the buyer agrees with the seller's assessment of the feature. Recognize, however, that special "favors" may become addictive, so be cautious about an overreliance on "something extra."

Another special feature can be the "limited-time offer." You may tell your prospect that if he orders now he will be able to take advantage of the current prices because next week semi-annual adjustments will add 7 percent more onto the price. One must be careful with this approach, however. Prospect's often feel that the limited-time or availablility approach is merely a ploy to get a quick sale. Sincerity and honesty are critical here.

Concluding the Sale   Once the close has been completed and your objective has been accomplished, it is best to leave quickly. There is little advantage to your sticking around because the customer can always change his mind. Most likely, however, your continued presence may reflect presumptive behavior about your customer's — time which could be damaging.

In the event the prospect rejects making any commitments, do not press the issue. It may just not be his day for buying, and you will only antagonize him if you persist against his wishes. Graciously thank him for his time and ask whether you may return at some later date to discuss the subject again. Many a sale refused on the first go-around has been successfully completed on the second or third try when more evidence of a problem is available to the prospect, or other pressing factors are playing less heavily on his mind. It would be a wise idea, however, to evaluate the reason for failure to make a sale on this call. Many mistakes or areas for improvement can be recognized and honed before the next call as a result.

FOLLOWUP   Perhaps one of the most neglected aspects of the selling process is the *real* last step: following up on an account. The followup encompasses everything that occurs after the sale is made: ordering, delivery, billing, service, use, collecting payments and maintenance of the product. It is crucial to the long-term relationship between your company and the customer.

In some cases followup is taken care of by other people, not by the salesperson. However, you are the most visible and most available representative of the company, and that means the customer is going to make his way to you should there be any problems. The professional salesperson recognizes his responsibility in followup and fulfills the customer's needs.

Your first followup tasks will take place while you are still at the sales call. Once the close is completed, you should apprise the customer of what will happen next: when delivery can be expected, when he can expect a bill, what the payment terms are and, above all, that you are willingly available to answer any questions or correct any problems.

Next, of course, you will want to make sure your orders get processed promptly and correctly. If any problems crop up, be ready to solve them quickly.

It is a good idea to contact the customer on, or shortly after the delivery date or use of your product. Numerous foulups can occur, such as delays, sending of the wrong product, damage, or billing errors. Checking yourself, rather than having to be chased down by an angry customer, builds goodwill and gives the customer a sense that you are concerned about him and that you have not forgotten him once the order is placed.

Followup work may also involve a call just after the product's peak use period. The customer will be glad to know you are interested in how the product performed and will probably tell you whether he is pleased or displeased. You will be especially interested to learn whether he is displeased. Many problems can crop up because a customer does not understand how the product works or has misunderstood some technical procedure. Better for him to tell you the problem so you can correct it, rather than for him to tell other potential customers that he bought a lemon — from *you*. Further, many customers expect followup field checks as a part of doing business with you. Frequently, supplier changes are made as a result of less-than-expected followup work.

Occasionally it becomes necessary for you to assist in collections. As the saying goes, "The sale is not complete until the money has been collected" and many companies expect the salesperson to deal with problem accounts. This puts you in an uncomfortable, uneasy situation. The best way to handle these rare cases is delicately. You must walk a thin line of making the collection without losing a customer. However, many such uneasy situations can be headed off at the pass by making the collection and credit policies of the company absolutely clear to the customer at the time of sale, and by working closely with the credit department in your company when the customer is first being considered for an extension of credit.

SUMMARY

* The close is the most difficult part of a sales call for many salespeople. One reason is that asking a prospect to buy is viewed as a favor or unreasonable request, rather than as an exchange mutually beneficial to buyer and seller. Another reason may be fear of rejection and its effect on a salesperson's self-confidence.

* Closing a sales call means meeting the call objective, which may or may not be making a sale.

* One important aspect of closing the sale is motivating the prospect. Peo-

ple are motivated by two different kinds of urges: primary and acquired. Primary motives are those needed for survival, while acquired motives are learned from culture and are many times as important as primary ones.

* The salesperson should also use knowledge of a prospect's dominant buying urge to move toward the close. Steps in that process are: reviewing the problem, revealing the problem's solution and previewing the results of solution acceptance with the prospect.

* The salesperson should be confident in attitude, personable to the prospect and infer both through his nonverbal and verbal signals.

* Clues to a prospect's readiness are buying signals. The signals may imply the prospect is ready to buy if he asks a question or makes a statement showing he is ready to buy. A salesperson should try to close immediately after he senses a buying signal.

* One doublecheck of a prospect's buying readiness is the trial close, a verbal technique to gage the willingness of a prospect to purchase at a given moment.

* There are several methods used to actually close a sale: the direct, summary, choice, assumption or special feature close. All utilize a salesperson's ability to sense the most appropriate given the prospect and conditions.

* Followup is a crucial element in any sale. While others may have responsibility for delivery, service etc., it is still the salesperson's duty to make sure any problems or questions are handled.

Review Questions Chapter 10

1. Name and explain the two major reasons why salespeople encounter difficulty in closing a sales call. What can a salesperson do to overcome these feelings?

2. Is the purpose of closing a sales call always to make a sale? Why or why not?

3. Human beings are motivated by two types of factors. What are they and why should a salesperson make the effort to understand a prospect's motives?

4. How can a salesperson use the prospect's "dominant buying urge"to close the sale?

5. How might a salesperson intimidate a prospect with incorrect body language?

6. When is a prospect most receptive to making a purchase? How can salespeople use the "trial close" to gage a prospect's willingness?

7. What is a "command assumption"? Why might it make a prospect feel uncomfortable?

8. Why is followup so important?

Selected Agri Selling Readings

The problems encountered in the process of selling and servicing the agricultural marketplace do not have to serve as a daily reminder of the inevitable consequences of doing business.

Taken as a whole, the following selected condensed readings serve as a step-by-step guide to everything from how to avoid pitfalls associated with farmer meetings to selling a foot-weary farm show visitor on your product, to pleasing a dissatisfied customer, and more...

So use this guide wisely. And treat its suggestions as you would those of a trusted friend — one well-seasoned and knee-deep in common sense knowledge about the minute details that can make or break a sale.

Reading One
Planning Meetings

Every winter the average agribusiness salesperson arranges or rushes to and from farmer meetings, dealer meetings, sales meetings, customer appreciation dinners and technical meetings. Each is heralded as a potential boon to sales. And each meeting may enhance or tarnish the firm's reputation. The key to an interesting, productive customer meeting is proper planning and attention to detail — combined, ideally, with a wealth of experience.

Conducting Farmer Meetings

Developing objectives is the single most important factor in planning customer meetings, yet many firms virtually ignore this factor when formulating their plans.

Developing Objectives

Customer meetings, like good sales calls, require well-defined goals. What do you hope to accomplish with the customers who attend? How will you measure your degree of success in reaching these goals? Even an intangible goal such as ''building goodwill' requires some standard of measurement. It might be the percentage of attendees who mention the meeting favorably during subsequent sales calls. What about the number of requests for new product presentations? The choice is yours, based on the objectives you have chosen.

Once you have decided on your objectives, commit them to paper along with the yardstick you have chosen for measuring results. This helps to solidify the objectives in the minds of everyone involved and avoid potential misunderstandings.

The Written Plan

Never assume key employees know about the meeting. Such people can contribute significant key input and support to the effort if they are included in the planning. So talk to them about the meeting and solicit their ideas.

The set of written objectives need not be formal. It might read as follows:

1. To establish or maintain contact with key customers.

2. To provide farmers with the most recent findings concerning use of a key product.

3. To enhance an image of professionalism among customers.

Your measurement of the first objective's success could be the number of customers who attend. The second objective would be met through an informative presentation. The third and least tangible objective might involve oral and written customer evaluations.

Tying a Theme to Objectives   Your meeting will be more cohesive if you tie a theme to one of your main objectives. If the theme is "Acme Fertilizer — Safety First for the Eighties," you might consider focusing customer attention on the objective of safety through tasteful banners, table decorations and gifts (e.g. safety goggles). This lends visual impact to your verbal message.

Handling Details   Once overall objectives have been established, shift your attention to the many details that make a meeting work. This may mean keeping a checklist that outlines the steps to finalizing the meeting. Several of the checklist items are of special importance and should be considered separately.

Location Counts   One particular aspect of the meeting communicates a great deal about your firm — the location you have chosen. The key word here is *appropriate*. Fried chicken at the local community hall may work if the meeting is intended to communicate technical information but it will not create the same impression as steak at a first-rate hotel. On the other hand, if the firm goes overboard and sponsors an elaborate affair, the customer may worry that he has paid for such excesses in higher-than-necessary prices for the firm's products.

Meetings for key customers are usually first class, befitting the customer's status with the firm. Everything else is a matter of judgment and taste.

Basic Checklist   No matter what kind of accomodations you choose, check that all the basics are in order. The place should be clean, well-equipped, roomy and comfortable with adequate lighting and ventilation. Confirm your reservation *in writing* and check that every item you need is available before committing yourself to rent the facility.

Room Size   The chances of a room being precisely the right size for the number of people you intend to host are slim. It's better to have too much space than not enough. You can always eliminate unnecessary chairs and direct your audience into one small area. Never overcrowd people; they should feel comfortable enough to be receptive to your message. Never allow them to scatter over a large space. This tends to make individuals feel isolated which hampers communication.

Seating Arrangements   People are sometimes intimidated by the "schoolroom" style of seating in which they wind up looking at the back of each other's heads while someone in the front of the room speaks. A roundtable seating plan enhances the group feeling even when meals are not being served. Since the traditional "breaking of bread" together has connotations of sharing in rural America, coffee at the beginning or middle of the programs often serves as a harmonious icebreaker. To further personalize the meeting room, consider lining the walls with five-by-seven inch photos of your customers. Modesty doesn't often preclude the enjoyment of seeing a picture of oneself prominently displayed.

To avoid the pall that cliques can bring to a well-planned meeting, conduct an activity to break the ice and encourage mixing at the meeting's onset. Provide explicit instructions as most people are more comfortable when they know precisely what they are to accomplish. For example: Ask each group to total the number of children at the table, the number of people who prefer beef or pork, or total acres of corn or cotton etc. To avoid the impression that such activities are contrived or juvenile, link them somehow to the objectives of the meeting. The psychological strategy of early participant involvement will pay off with a more cohesive meeting.

The Emcee's Role

The chairman or emcee has a critical role in the success of a meeting because he sets the tone and keeps the proverbial ball rolling. Customers will feel more important if the person chosen for the job is perceived as having an important position. The emcee need not be the top person in the organization , although the VIP should be heard from at some point if it's only to welcome the participants to the meeting and introduce the emcee.

Strive to keep the program fast-paced. When it comes to joke telling, the best idea is to avoid it unless the emcee is capable of a top-notch professional delivery. Humor is appropriate but avoid inside jokes understood by only part of the audience as well as any ethnic or vulgar jokes that may be offensive.

Focus on Personnel

Customers often like to see the person with whom they've been doing business ''all cleaned up'' and on display, so introduce company personnel along with brief bits of information about each. Don't embarrass anyone and in the interest of keeping the program moving, be sure to request that applause be held until all the introductions have been completed.

The Beverage Question

The question of whether to serve alcoholic beverages can best be answered by consulting local traditions and customs. In some areas customers may find it offensive, particularly at husband/wife dinners, while in others it will be expected. If you decide to serve such beverages, see that customers are not given enough to cause embarrassment to themselves, their peers or the sponsors of the meeting.

Choosing Speakers

Entertainment is appropriate in some instances, such as appreciation dinners, but can be a very tricky thing to coordinate. Scout the entertainment personally before you contract for it. Be on the lookout for possibilities months in advance of an anticipated meeting. Seldom is a meeting made successful by entertainment alone but it definitely can be hurt by entertainment that is poor.

Speakers — such as extension personnel, supplier representatives or outside experts — are usually a welcome addition to a meeting but they *must* be carefully selected. The speaker's contribution is as much the responsibility of the sponsor as the meal arrangements since both reflect on the sponsor. Work closely with the speaker on content, length and style of presentation, particularly if he or she is not a professional.

Time Considerations

You will do yourself a favor — not to mention the speaker — if you set a time limit, anticipate any problems with visual aids and leave ample time after the meeting for questions.

To ensure the time limit is followed, particularly when there is a series of speakers, have a member of your staff stand in the back of the room and signal each speaker when their time is up. This is a tactful way to accomplish the objective of keeping the program moving while not embarassing anyone.

Emcees have been known to resort to the use of an oven timer to "police" several speakers. This device sounds off impartially with each passing of scheduled time. All are treated equally. The more firmly and consistently you treat time limitations, the happier your audience will be.

Even a poor speaker can make a good impression if you plan carefully. If such a person can field questions well, allot 10 minutes for the formal speech and 20 minutes for the question-and-answer period afterwards. For added assurance, plant a few questions in the audience in case the discussion does not begin immediately.

When a large group is anticipated, meet with the speaker in advance and plan 10 questions for participants to ask that will coincide with the speaker's major points. Directing the talk will often make an otherwise dry subject more appealing since the question-and-answer format focuses attention on the issues being discussed.

Length of Program

The best way to ensure that the customer is enjoying the program is to look at it from the customer's point of view. How long should each part run? What if something starts to go wrong? Allow time for the mechanical things — like the clearing of the dishes after the meal — and add a few minutes onto each time estimate in case things start to go wrong. Make contingency plans, including a determination of which things can be best shortened, cutout or lengthened if other parts of the program don't go as scheduled. Give the customer a starting and ending time for the entire program only. This way you and only you will worry if the program starts to lag behind schedule.

Since audience discontent is fired primarily by expectations, wrap the program up five minutes early rather than five minutes late. As they say in show business, "Leave 'em wanting more."

It's natural for some parts of your program to be more interesting than others. All this means is you will have to pace it so that everything flows smoothly. Don't start with a speaker who brings down the house and end with one who puts them to sleep. Not only will you make the latter look bad, but you'll leave a bad image of the meeting in customers' minds.

Remember, too, that the mind can only absorb what the seat can endure, so a stretch break before an important speaker will pay off in dividends of attentiveness. Restroom breaks are often in order, particularly if liquor has been served and the audience has been shifting in their seats for a couple of hours.

Followup

It's bad enough to make a host of mistakes but there is no excuse for repeating the same ones year after year. Try to step back and see your meeting objectively after it's all over and above all, learn from your mistakes.

A short evaluation on the back of the program may help you to see things the customer's way. Or invite a representative panel of customers to lunch — perhaps a week after the meeting — and invite their ideas, suggestions, complaints. But be sure to get response *promptly,* as time has a way of coloring people's memories. Not only will the customers' responses help you to plan future meetings more effectively but they will demonstrate to the customer in a concrete way that you care what he thinks.

* Developing objectives and proper advance planning are keys to successful farmer meetings. Meticulous attention to details results in a smooth meeting and lasting professional image.

* An important planning factor is the time element. The audience shouldn't be forced to sit through a tedious program. Boredom can be prevented by a strict schedule and quick-moving agenda.

* Speakers should be chosen with care. A less-polished speaker may appear more at ease and be more enjoyable if the time is spent answering audience questions instead of straight speaking.

* The audience can give vital input on the success of the meeting through either a written evaluation or during a followup meeting.

**SUMMARY
Planning
Meetings**

Reading Two

Exhibiting At Farm Shows

Farm shows can be viewed as the opportunity to enhance, or tarnish, an agribusiness' reputation. For it is at the farm show, whether it be a giant national exhibition or a local fair, that images are on display.

Opinions are varied whether or not the money and time spent at farm shows is worth the expense. Most will agree, however, that to remain competitive they must participate. Even if they do not see a tangible increase in sales, exhibiting keeps the company's name and employees in the public eye and establishes a company's credibility as a member of the agricultural community. Once the decision is made to participate, many hours of work lie ahead to ensure the time spent is profitable. If it is worth doing, it is worth doing well. Two lounge chairs sunk in the mud behind a poorly constructed display with a few old brochures and matchbooks convey a clear message. On the other hand, a sparkling booth with friendly staffers and sufficient information says: "We want to be here and we'll make good use of your time and ours."

That kind of successful attitude will result only if proper planning takes place. The following tips will help prepare you for participation in most farm show situations.

Companies spend money on everything from tables with standup displays to carpeted areas with country western bands. More expensive

**Physical
Arrangements**

does not always mean more effective, however, and you will do well to have an exhibit that represents your company accurately.

Unless someone within your firm has the creative ability to put together an attractive display, it may benefit you to enlist the help of professionals. Firms that deal in displays may be able to construct a plan that will stress company philosophy and portray the appropriate image.

Keep in mind that some shows are held in buildings and some are outside. The location will make a difference in what kind of display you utilize. Obviously, intricate audio-visual or electronic equipment may not be appropriate for an outside show while tractor demonstrations may not be practical with an indoor exhibition. Knowing the physical details and limitations as you do advance planning will make the difference between success and failure.

Even if the main reason for exhibiting is to display products, have written literature on hand. You can refer to it as you demonstrate products and send it home to serve as a reminder of your company. While much of your literature may be tossed once the day is over, some of it will be ready by the intended audience.

Attention-grabbing

To be recognized as a "company with something more" you'll have to grab the attention of passersby. Countless gimmicks have been used — giveaways, pretty girls and games. Gimmicks can also detract. The trick is to use them as means to an end, namely, drawing the customer's interest to the product itself. For example, a prize for identifying weed types that can be eliminated by your company's new chemical will put the focus right where you want it.

Enticing people into your display area is not an easy task. If you have too many staffers, passersby may feel overwhelmed. In the same vein, staffers may spend their time talking among themselves, consequently alienating would-be visitors to the area. Too few company representatives pose an equally serious problem. Overworked and harried greeters will not be able to devote adequate time to each visitor.

The key, then, is moderation. Realize that there will be peak times during the show and increase the staff assigned to work during those periods. Put workers on a schedule — two-hours-on/two-hours-off works well. Such a schedule gives them time to see the show and present a refreshed image to visitors.

Visitor Relations

Don't sit sipping lemonade in the shade and wondering why people are passing you by. You'll have to draw people out with a friendly handshake and smile. Initiate discussions that will lead to your product or service and, if necessary, prepare a short presentation that highlights product benefits.

Make the customer feel at home. Go out of your way to see that regular customers feel recognized and valued and potential ones get a positive first impression. Whether this means sitting down for refreshments or giving small gifts, making people feel special will go a long way toward maintaining a good image for the company.

Designate a "special situation area." Whether you have a hot prospect or an irate customer on your hands, you'll need a spot away from the crowds in which to discuss business. The special situation area affords exhibit staffers a mechanism to separate "high potential" prospects from those with only casual interest. A table where information or complaint cards can be completed provides an additional means to gathering tangible valves from the exhibit. The area should be out of the main flow of traffic and tired salespeople should beware of taking over the area while on break.

Show Followup

After the show has ended and the truck is packed, the tendency is to wipe the show out of your mind. The most important work may still remain, however: following up on new leads and taking care of information requests and complaints. Without that followup, it is very difficult to justify presence at such a show.

In order for the followup contact to be most effective, pre-show planning and preparation should take its design and mechanics into account. An efficient system of obtaining, classifying and recording leads, particularly those with seemingly higher potential is essential. Prepare and mobilize dealers, distributors and the appropriate company salespeople to handle the process well in advance. Involvement on all fronts tends to encourage individual recognition of the value of the farm show and followup.

Make followup contact promptly, particularly with prospects who were more than just casually interested. Whether it's a phone call, sending information or a personal call from the local dealer or distributor, followup activities are most valuable when the prospect still has a recollection of the exhibit and company.

As noted before, if the farm show's worth doing, it's worth doing well. A well-planned and attractive exhibit staffed by courteous, knowledgeable personnel and backed with a systematic followup will accumulate in more than just another off-season activity. It can be an integral part of your organization's overall marketing strategy.

SUMMARY Exhibiting at Farm Shows

* Most companies exhibit at farm or trade shows because attendance gives them exposure as part of the competitive agricultural community.
* Expensive displays do not necessarily equate a successful exhibit; creating a positive, accurate portrayal of the company is more important.
* Making your presence valuable at a show means getting the attention of passersby. Only then will they be receptive to you and your product information. Most people have to be encouraged and making them feel special will payoff in good public relations.
* The work is not over at show closing time. Correct followup in disseminating further information and arranging for calls is crucial.

Reading Three

The Farm Wife's Influence

There is no doubt that decision-makers other than the farmer have an impact on a salesperson's success. Most notable is the farm wife, or spouse.

Farm wives have always played a vital role in running the farm, whether that role meant being supportive or actually driving the tractor and keeping production records.

With the elevation of farm management to such an integral aspect of overall farming, it is only natural that wives should assume the role of full-time business partner in this area as well. In many cases, the wife may be the most important decision-maker in the family and whether or not the family buys a new feed system may hinge on the household budget as much as the farm's need for more efficient equipment.

Along with the traditional chores of housewife, part-time farmhand and overseer of the kids' 4-H projects, many women keep the books, coordinate the farm labor and take charge of farrowing or calving. Husband wife teams attend extension meetings, farm management seminars and supplier-sponsored meetings together. More than likely, they make crucial buying decisions together as well.

According to many dealers, farm wives are taking more and more interest in technical information and market programs. Obviously, the woman's degree of involvement varies with the individual's personality, circumstances, education, cultural background and geographic region, but when in doubt, your best bet is to assume strong interest on the farm wife's part.

Poll Says She Decides

High involvement on the part of the farm wife is especially evident in the Midwest, where sales managers reported in a recent poll that as many as 30 to 40% of all farmers make supply decisions with some input from their wives. Of those cases, 15 to 20% revealed a wife who played a decidedly active role. (Informal polls show less active involvement on the part of farm wives in the Northwest and Southeast).

This active involvement is particularly true when considering large substansive purchases such as tractors and machinery. In such instances, wives are usually involved, at least, in the decision whether or not to buy. And according to some salespeople, the wife or spouse's role becomes more evident when problems arise, since this can force an otherwise reticent partner to voice complaints.

In any event, it is clear that the influence of the farm wife may have great bearing on the short-and long-term relationship between salesperson and farmer.

It is imperative then, for all salespeople, especially *salesmen,* to rethink their attitudes about farm women. If he understands the importance of the wife's role, fine. If not, the last thing a salesman needs is to come across as chauvinistic in tone or manner, or condescending in conversation. The salesman who thinks he is charming and ingratiating may actually be alienating the woman who considers herself a business partner. She may react negatively without realizing why. Even passive farm wives may be offended and cause a missed sale.

How to make the right impression? Know her name and use it respectfully. Welcome her participation in any business discussion. Make eye contact as you discuss your product or service, and invite her questions. Don't be fooled by a farm wife's disclaimer that she isn't "important," or that an issue is, "Too complicated for me!" Some women downplay their roles because they underestimate the value of their opinions or are simply modest.

Consider Her a Partner

When winter snows blow, much agri selling is transacted right in the home. This is your golden opportunity to include the wife in the selling process.

The kitchen table is an ideal place for the presentation of a product or service for many reasons, not the least of which is the convenience to the wife. Her interest provides you with the perfect opportunity to solicit her ideas and respond to her objections. This is by far more preferable than having her voice her objections after you've gone.

Despite the seeming contradiction, farm wives can be treated as ladies as well as business partners. Sincere compliments on her traditional skills as wife, mother or community leader are often appropriate, as are small gifts with domestic appeal.

On a more formal level, special recognition of farm wives is appropriate during the period of farm appreciation dinners.

Making Contact

Some salespeople feel a little awkward dealing with farm wives, particularly where the wife's role is not obvious. You may want to keep a couple of standard icebreakers in mind, such as references to the children or home.

When you first come into contact with the farmer's wife, show respect for her position by introducing yourself. Let her know the purpose of the call as briefly and positively as possible. This legitimizes the call, not necessarily to get permission to see her husband, but to elicit her cooperation and support.

An experienced salesperson can turn the involvement of the farm wife into a selling asset by enlisting her support to sell the product to her husband. Or if she is the more reluctant of the two, by enlisting the husband's support to sell the wife.

Get the couple to sit together whenever possible in order to maintain eye contact with both of them and keep control of the interview. If they sit apart, your attention will be split and theirs may drift too.

When the wife's support is critical to the success of your sales call, be sure to hear and answer her objections accurately and promptly. Even if she is not interested in the technical aspects per se, she may be sold on the more tangible benefits such as safety, security and convenience. Or she may simply intuitively like and trust the salesperson. In either case, her support may clinch the deal.

Problems of Saleswomen

You might think that saleswomen would have a special edge in selling to the farm wife, since they are more apt to understand the special problems of a woman. But initially saleswomen may actually pose a threat to farm wives who are less accustomed to seeing women in agri selling than are their husbands.

Yet once the saleswoman develops a relationship of trust — through proper dress, businesslike manner, friendliness and a sense of camaraderie, and respond with tact and sensitivity to avert potentially awkward situations — the farm wife can become as active an ally of the saleswoman as of her male counterpart.

All these precautions may seem difficult at first, but as many agribusiness firms are discovering, the increasing involvement of the farm wife in buying decisions presents new opportunities for selling for the professional salesperson who is sharp and willing to be flexible.

SUMMARY The Farm Wife's Influence

* Farm wives are active participants in farming operations and therefore take part in buying decisions. The salesperson should view wives as an important audience in attempting a sale.

* A salesperson should always be respectful, never condescending, maintain eye contact and answer all questions.

* Take advantage of husband/wife meetings when you see both partners at once.

Reading Four
Peak-Season Selling

For many agribusinesses, peak-season selling responsibilities increase to where overburdened salespeople feel the situation is out of control. But since peak periods fall at nearly identical times each year — planting, harvesting, calving, farrowing, seasons etc. — there is no reason why planning can't relieve some of the time congestion.

The peak season can make or break a firm. While most sales may have been locked in beforehand, it's a fact of human nature that many customers will wait until the last minute to buy. Servicing so many people at once can present a big headache, especially when supplies become temporarily unavailable. Customers left dissatisfied in this season are highly vulnerable to next season's competition.

There is, however, an "up" side to all this. This is the only time of year when customers anxiously seek the salesperson, rather than vice versa. Last-minute needs, a temporary lack of product elsewhere and other factors, drive many customers into an active search during which price is seldom a primary consideration. So dealing effectively with business during this period offers an opportunity to build credibility and loyalty with regular customers as well as to establish a wider customer base.

The salesperson's peak-season selling responsibilities vary with the type of agribusiness, its size and the specific orientation of the immediate supervisor. In some of the smaller companies, for example, distribution may figure heavily in the salesperson's schedule. In other firms, the salesperson's role may consist entirely of coordination and service, exclusive of any assistance in physical product movement. Salespeople at the manufacturing, distribution, and retail levels are particularly prone to the seasonal rush.

Peak-Season Responsibilities

Organization and planning are the most effective weapons a salesperson has against these seasonal pressures. You need to know inventory availability as well as delivery potential in terms of previous commitments. You must fill customers' needs accurately, especially if the order requires technical specifications.

Customers who have placed early orders should not feel penalized for doing so, or next year's sales will be last minute! Hence it is important to maintain the maximum flexibility when customers request adjustments. Of course, what that maximum will be depends in part on the nature of the business involved. In many cases, climate and other unpredictable factors necessitate changes in quantities, delivery dates, varieties, blends etc. Making such adjustments within reasonable time periods increases customer satisfaction limits and strengthens business.

The Early Bird May Need an Adjustment

Service is always a priority, but in this case *good* service on key accounts is particularly important. Every agri salesperson knows that some accounts need a little extra care. This is not to imply that other accounts be ignored. However, larger or first-time customers should be thoroughly serviced and followed up on — as an aid to future business.

Service Basics

The salesperson serves as a middleman between customers and management, so it is advisable for him to exercise the best communication techniques. Most professionals know their customers well enough to predict where problems are likely to occur — because of the physical aspects of operation, management ability of the customer, or the buyer's personality. Calling or stopping by at the right moment can head off many potential problems. Even when specific problems do not occur, a simple "How's it comin?" or "Don't forget to..." reassures the customer of your continuing interest and involvement.

On the other side of the spectrum, the salesperson who sees a wide variety of operations and customers and who monitors his company's image among customers is the best person to provide management with constructive feedback about the effectiveness of the distribution system. This may have an immediate payoff for the salesperson as minor midseason adjustments improve the quality of service and keep his customer satisfied.

Some in-season complaints come early: germination problems, equipment breakdowns, the ever-present delivery foul ups etc. Many of these can be avoided by quick appropriate action by the salesperson. Simply because it *is* the rush season, prompt resolution of all complaints is more important than ever.

"Greasing the gears of the distribution system" means tactfully assisting service employees in the company. Only if they perform their jobs well will the salesperson look good in the customer's eyes. This job calls for tact because the salesperson is generally not the service personnel boss. A well-timed helping hand lent to drivers, plant workers, office employees, credit personnel and supervisors can be mutually beneficial. When the peak season rushes people off their feet, individuals performing specific jobs become part of a team effort more than ever. Adopting this attitude may mean that ultimately you will be the big winner.

Since true rush season business leaves little time for anything but reacting to whatever orders come your way, it stands to reason that the salesperson must do considerable pre-season planning to ensure that everything runs smoothly.

Planning to Avoid Problems

In planning, review the previous season and answer these questions:
1. What problems arose?
2. How could they have been avoided?
3. What changes in demand are anticipated this season?
4. Will the physical facilities hold up?
5. What changes in the system are planned?

Then carefully review operating procedures: the physical flow of materials and flow of paperwork.

Finally, review the organization and specific responsibilities of each person. Pay particular attention to items like the coverage of functions and supervision in the event of absenteeism or the policies to be followed if a major piece of equipment breaks down.

Peak periods are not the time for new and part time seasonal employees to become familiar with company routines and procedures. *Before* the season starts, walk through their responsibilities with them. Let them become acclimated to the people and facilities. The payoff will be in smoother, more professional service.

Under the circumstances, a certain amount of strain should be expected. After several hectic 15-hour days, the tempers of both suppliers and customers tend to grow short. By anticipating these reactions, you can control a potentially explosive situation and help defuse it.

Since the salesperson is the primary channel of communication between customer and company, it is up to you to make yourself available to customers in time of need. All too often customer service is delayed because the salesperson — who may be the only person with the information necessary to service the customer — is in some inaccessible place.

When problems do arise, a quick call to the customer goes a long way toward resolving any difficulties. For example, one good policy is to notify any customer whose delivery is expected to be delayed by more than 15 minutes. Since disappointment is relative to expectations, the customer will be more satisfied if his expectations have been modified to fit the situation and will view this as a highly responsible gesture on the part of salesperson and company.

Good agri salespeople normally spend a considerable amount of time phoning regular customers to anticipate when they will need various products and services. Because farmers and dealers often get too involved in their own hectic schedules to put in an order until the last minute, this kind of "staying in touch" will minimize some of the salesperson's headaches.

The peak season is tough not only on salespeople but on the families they "leave behind." Long hours, fatigue, frustration and even guilt are not the stuff a happy home life is made of. There's not much you can do to avoid this — it comes with the territory. You may elicit more understanding and cooperation from your family if you tell them what to expect in advance. Companies often sponsor employee family social functions just before and after the season to compensate for the stress — and you may just want to ease the stress yourself by giving the family some activities of your own to look forward to once the season is over.

Peak-season pressures may offer little time for formal selling — it's mostly last-minute service and order-taking — but by organizing and planning properly, you may sow the seeds of a brighter next season for you and the whole company.

* Peak-season selling can be coped with, through proper advance planning. Salespeople can be prepared for additional orders, order adjustment and emergency service by keeping in close contact with customers.

**SUMMARY
Peak-Season
Selling**

* Salespeople should be prepared for strain on relationships — with customers as well as family. Long hours and frustration may lead to problems which could be coped with in advance by preparing the family by telling them what to expect.

Reading Five

Handling Customer Complaints

The customer may not always be right, but if you lose a sale — present or future — or precipitate a messy lawsuit, you're the one who loses. To put the matter in a more positive light, there are worse things than a customer voicing complaints. Things such as complaints that are never heard only to show up later as the customer refuses to deal with your company. This is particularly damaging if the customer tells others about his unhappy experience.

We live in an age of consumer awareness spurred in part, by government regulation, court rulings and media attention to consumer issues. The average farmer has become more willing to exercise what he sees as his basic right to challenge or question a product or service. When the salesperson neglects to resolve a complaint, he risks losing the customer and, perhaps, winding up in court.

Agricultural supply and marketing firms are particularly susceptible to this kind of action. It therefore becomes critical for the salesperson to recognize the potential inherent in any complaint. While legal action against agricultural suppliers is not widespread, it is increasingly common and consequently a consideration in customer relations.

Because complaints are frequently unpleasant for a salesperson and because they have the potential for damaging future sales or spurring legal action, it's easy to see their negative side. But there's a brighter side as well. Successful salespeople always recognize the need to turn a disadvantage into a plus whenever possible — and complaints may offer just that opportunity.

Case Study   Jack Wilson was so steady and dependable that you could set your watch by him. And when Jack sold a farmer a particular combination of chemicals and fertilizer, that farmer was assured of quality both in the product and the services that went with it. After all, if you could trust Jack, you could trust what he sold.

But no matter how dependable Jack and his company were, it was inevitable that someone would end up with a product failure sometime. Jack received a call one day from Pat Emery, one of the most influential farmers in the county and a long-term customer of his. Pat was extremely upset because the chemical application that Jack had recommended was not working out at all. "We've got cockleburs worse than we've ever had them. That darned stuff did about as much good as distilled water!" Pat complained. "You really screwed up this time. I want you to get out here and take care of it!"

If Jack had been less experienced, he might have let Pat's abusive tone and uncomplimentary words rattle him. Complaints were always uncomfortable but Jack had worked this territory for years, and he knew his worst mistake would be to lose his professional objectivity when a customer was upset. He also knew Pat as a loyal, sensible customer, not one given to delivering wild, unsubstantiated accusations.

To further complicate matters, Pat was recognized as an influential member of the farming community, so Jack knew it was particularly important to handle this complaint well.

When Pat blamed the chemicals, Jack listened carefully to what Pat had to say. Never one to commit himself until he knew all the facts, Jack promised to investigate fully and come to a conclusion as quickly as possible. Clearly, quick action was necessary to salvage the crop — and his relationship with a valued customer.

Jack asked every question he could think of — what equipment had been used, application techniques, the soil type and conditions. Yet the questions yielded no good answer. Everything seemed to be in order. By the time the sun had risen the next morning, Jack had the regional technical service representative for the chemical manufacturer on the way to Pat's farm. Jack's company was one of the manufacturer's biggest dealer accounts so he expected to get prompt help with one of his most important customers.

He realized, of course, that the manufacturer also had a lot at stake. But good service from his supplier was one of the reasons he promoted this manufacturer's product.

Accustomed to dealing with a wide array of problems, the company's technical rep walked the field with Jack and Pat, looking for clues. A battery of tactful open-ended questions had revealed a unique set of weather conditions, cropping practices and soil type that, along with the application method used, had interacted to significantly reduce the effectiveness of the chemical.

Jack *had* made the correct recommendation and Pat *had* applied the product according to instructions. It was an unusual situation to be sure, but the representative admitted having seen the problem "at least a half dozen places this year."

Then, quite methodically, the representative, Jack and Pat sat down to determine the economic impact of the problem. There was no damage to the crop — only a large amount of cocklebur that would reduce yield or require additional treatment.

The representative recommended a post-emergent spray to correct the weed problem and agreed to cover the cost of the additional chemical. Pat agreed to handle the second application on the 20 acres himself and seemed pleased they'd found the answer.

In fact, Pat was more than satisfied. He was impressed with how rapidly and professionally Jack had handled the problem. As Jack left, he knew his customer's faith was restored. He also knew the relationship was more solid than before. Jack hoped Pat would share his experience at the local coffee shop where he could get more mileage out of the situation.

While Jack was never sure how vocal Pat had been with his praise, he did manage to get *all* of Pat's business the following spring — and that was no small reward.

Turning Problems Into Opportunities

Jack's experience illustrates how even problems can create opportunity. Whenever a salesperson helps the customer feel that the company is looking out for its customer's best interests, loyalty to the company and its products is sure to improve. This does not imply that all situations can be so easily resolved. Occasionally, a given customer may be unable or unwilling to recognize that a judgment *against* the customer's wishes can still be fair.

But when customer and company part as friends, both have much to gain, and the salesperson is assured of having turned a sticky problem into a golden opportunity.

When one is handling a customer relations problem of the magnitude that Pat's presented, it's invaluable to follow the maxim: "be prepared."

Jack was lucky enough to have background on Pat's personality and situation by virtue of his long-standing relationship within the community. A newer salesperson might have had to so some serious digging to uncover the same information. For example, Pat might have been the kind of person who registered the same complaint every year. The problem might even have been caused by an error on Pat's part — and what if Pat had been unwilling to admit any fault?

These are details the salesperson needs to know *before* handling a complaint.

Jack was well-acquainted with the procedures for making restitutions within his company. He knew the bounds of his authority and that if any restitution were to be made by his local dealership, it would need to be discussed and authorized by his boss.

This kind of knowledge is important if the salesperson is to avoid making promises to the customer that he cannot deliver. Again, being prepared is the answer.

Another aspect of preparation is note-taking. Jack jotted down significant bits of information Pat provided, not only to get a handle on the facts, but to assure Pat that his complaint was being taken seriously. This was one of the first steps taken showing Pat that the company cared about his problem and was determined to treat it fairly and professionally.

When dealing with customer complaints, keep in mind that the customer may not be expressing facts, but intense feelings. The salesperson who is prepared to listen empathetically to a seemingly endless tirade of complaints may find that when the customer finally runs out of steam, so do the negative feelings.

People sometimes bottle up real or imagined wrongs. Feelings become so intense that they must have a release.

Creating an outlet for their feelings can often alleviate much of the problem. If you can listen without sitting in judgment or becoming irate yourself, you may find that the problem will be much easier to deal with when the storm has blown over.

You don't have to agree — simply *hear* with both ears and occasionally repeat the gist of the customer's point to show that they have registered.

As the foregoing section may have implied, you should always keep your cool. It does not help to become involved in a heated argument with the customer, no matter what bait is being used. The purpose of the talk is to turn a problem into an opportunity, and you will never do that if your primary concern is to stifle your anger.

If the two of you become polarized, no compromise will occur. Keep in mind that the person who maintains self-control has the upper hand in any disagreement.

The Value of Questions

When Jack questioned Pat about equipment and techniques related to chemical application and cropping practices, he accomplished two things at once. By ferreting out valuable factual information that might have led to another diagnosis of the problem he enabled Pat to move from an emotional, accusatory state to a logical, exploratory one. In fact, Jack was calming Pat down and assuring him of his concern simply by asking such in-depth questions.

One problem is that customers with complaints are sometimes half-convinced they will not get a fair hearing before you even talk to them. Probing, to-the-point questions often help alleviate this fear.

As it happened, Pat Emery registered a complaint with merit. But what if he had leveled accusation in the strongest terms possible, threatening legal action and staking his reputation as a farmer on the chemical's ineffectiveness, only to find that he had caused the problem himself? Should Jack flaunt this development and walk away whistling "We Shall Overcome"? Obviously not.

The most productive response to such a situation is to offer a "face saver." Offer some explanation or suggestion that draws attention away from the customer's unfortunate error and attempts to characterize the whole episode as understandable confusion.

On occasion, when the problem is not serious and involves little or no economic harm, the salesperson may even want to accept part of the responsibility for the "confusion." Perhaps he should have explained some facet of the product more completely, or maybe his instructions were not clear enough.

Even if the salesperson is convinced that the instructions were clear enough for a chimpanzee to follow, he may find that the payoff for such face-saving suggestions is the customer's gratitude and an even more comfortable sales relationship in the future.

But be extremely careful in accepting blame for product failure when it is not warranted. You will likely end up making matters worse as the customer will expect restitution that you may not be able to give.

There are two pitfalls in relation to one's status as a representative of the company receiving the complaint: an unwarranted admission of error and a tendency to disclaim the company when the going gets tough. While there are some simple straightforward situations in which the best policy is to admit and correct an obvious mistake, most circumstances are not that easily resolved. Once the salesperson has admitted an error, the effect is irreversible. The customer will not consider any other possibility and an attempt to backtrack may be treated by the customer as an example of dishonesty.

Another related problem is attempting to placate the customer by talking about the company as "they" instead of "we." You may find that talking about another section of the company — billing, for example — as if they had nothing better to do than propagate mistakes and generate red tape, will get you off the hook. But it will do nothing for your company's image or future sales potential. Even worse, it creates a kind of false camaraderie between you and the customer; a state that may make it difficult to deal objectively with the customer when a billing question does come up.

You alone, without the company, cannot serve a customer adequately. Without your verbal support, the company risks losing the customer's goodwill. When you split the customer's identification of you with the company, you lose the most precious and useful allies a salesperson has — the total team.

A discussion of handling customer complaints is not complete without pointing out that many complaints can be headed off before they ever arise. Since many agriproducts and services are highly technical, the customer must be well-informed — educated on how to use the product and what to expect. A large number of complaints can be traced back to a customer's misunderstanding or misuse of the product. Then, either to save face or because they legitimately don't know they erred, they blame the product, the company and ultimately, you.

Head Off Complaints Before They Happen

These situations are often the most difficult to handle because the customer is in error and no restitution can or should be given. This occurrence calls for the greatest tact and skills a salesperson can muster. Often the customer cannot be convinced and will "get even" by dropping you as a supplier and/or telling everyone of his dissatisfaction.

The only good way of handling these situations is to recognize, through experience, the most likely areas of misunderstanding, confusion and customer error. Then develop a special program or make a special effort to educate your customer about potential problems. When you close the sale, or still better, at the time of delivery, caution the customer about areas of concern. Demonstrate what can go wrong when certain procedures are not followed. Use your selling skills to drive home your point.

Don't oversell the product. All discontent is relative to expectation. If the product performs better than the customer expects, you'll be a hero. If it's less than expected, you'll be a villain. Make sure, through careful presentation, that your customer's expectations are reasonable.

Just before or during the product's heavy use period, make a service call to see that your customer is using the product correctly. This is a great tool for building goodwill and can save a multitude of problems later on.

But no matter how well you point out possible pitfalls or how skillfully you handle complaints, you will not be able to handle them all successfully. Some people are just difficult to deal with. You will win some and you will lose some. Winning and losing are *both* part of the game, and even the best of players has to accept a setback occasionally.

But the salesperson who can fully listen, judge fairly, prepare on the basis of facts and retain control of the situation, has a decided edge. With such assets going for him, he can turn a majority of complaints into long-term repeat business — and that has to qualify as a happy ending.

**SUMMARY
Handling
Customer
Complaints**

* Most customers consider it their right to complain if a product or service does not deliver what they expected. Therefore complaints are sometimes a matter of emotion or unrealistic expectations rather than logic.

* It is the salesperson's responsibility to judge the validity of a complaint and choose appropriate action. Complaints may be viewed as opportunities because, if handled in a tactful, correct way, they may allow the salesperson to increase his credibility with his customers.

* Preparation is an important component of handling a complaint. A salesperson should have background information on the person who issued the complaint along with facts about the farming operation. Knowledge about company restitution policies prevents the promising of unrealistic compensation.

* Salespeople handling complaints need to maintain a calm, tactful appearance and react with interest and respect to a customer's charges. They must also properly maintain their status within the company so as not to shift blame from themselves to their firm.

* Many complaints can be prevented before they ever arise by carefully monitoring the customer and his operation. An alert salesperson will sense potential problems and help alleviate them before they occur.

Reading Six
Dealing With Price

"But how much does it cost?"

That question causes many experienced salespeople to feel a pang of fear. As one Midwestern farmer recently expressed during an opinion survey about salespeople, "I like to ask about the price right away! That really throws 'em 'cause it's the last question they want to hear."

This farmer has learned he can gain the upper hand by raising the price issue. If you do not have a plan for handling the question, your presentation may be in trouble, especially when your product is priced higher than that of the competition.

Any company can sell products on a low price basis. But cutting prices may bring disasterous results. While you may sell more product more easily, the reduced gross margin may not be enough to cover costs.
The profit equation:

$$\text{Price} \times \text{Volume} \star \text{Expenses} = \text{Profits}$$

reveals a delicate relationship. Price and volume are continually working against each other. Management must constantly monitor this relationship to insure that there is adequate revenue to cover the expenses and still field a profit.

In some agribusinesses, salespeople are not given authority to make price adjustments. Meeting a competitor's price or reducing price for a special customer is possible only with approval of management. In other companies, the salesperson has authority to adjust prices within an approved range. And in still other agribusinesses, the salesperson has authority to set the price.

But in every case, it's critical to remember that the ultimate objective is not just to make a sale — it's to make a profitable sale. A salesperson can easily become engrossed in the business of selling and lose sight of the necessity of generating a profit on the sale.

Negotiating Price

There is always the temptation to reduce the price to get a large order or a new customer. There is undeniable logic for doing so. As long as the negotiated price covers the direct or variable costs associated with making the sale (cost of the product, shipping, delivery etc.) and makes some additional contribution to the overhead costs of the business, it's wise to make the deal. Though the price might be less than normal, some larger-volume customers will undoubtedly argue their larger purchase justifies the discount and thus they demand the lower price.

But before the price concession is made, there are several other extremely important considerations. First, how will regular customers who paid a regular or high price react when they hear about the "deal you made?" (They will hear. You can count on the rural grapevine.) Second, by accepting additional volume customers will you be able to maintain the level of service to both the new account and regular customers? And third, next season will you have to once *again* lower your price to capture that larger customer?

Finally, and perhaps the most overwhelming consideration, is the probable reaction of your competition. Even the rumor of a special deal is enough to start a domino chain reaction in many commodity-like farm supply markets as competitors retaliate to protect their market share. As competition lowers price, the hopes for additional volume are shattered because the total demand for most farm supplies and services is fixed for any one season.

The end result of a round of retaliatory price cuts is essentially no change in the volume of business but significantly lower dollar sales. And everybody loses, except the customer.

The temptation to lower the price to capture additional business or keep an old account from slipping away is very strong, especially when a customer is threatening you. But the complications from negotiated pricing, especially in commodities like supplies and services, can have devastating effects if it is not well managed.

When price is commonly negotiated, as it is in farm equipment, buildings, livestock and a host of other supplies, the salesperson must have an accurate understanding of his cost structure and simultaneously consider the implication of the negotiations in the rest of the market.

Not having pricing authority may seem like going into battle with one arm tied behind your back. But separating the pricing from the selling function can help isolate the emotion that comes from being threatened by a large customer who must have a good deal, immediately. The time taken to check out how far you can go can greatly defuse the situation. It's amazing how often the threat of going someplace else is just that — an ideal threat by an aggressive customer who is trying to establish a bargaining position.

Overcoming the Price Obstacle

So how do you sell when your price is higher? The answer lies in this fundamental fact: people don't buy on the basis of price alone. They buy on the basis of *value*.

If there ever were a matter of subjective judgment, it's value. Quite simply, if the customer feels that the value offered is equal to or exceeds the price demanded, the price is perceived as a good one.

So it becomes the salesperson's job to convince the prospect that the total bundle of attributes is worth the asking price. If you can do so, price is no longer an obstacle. If you cannot, then the ethics of making the sale can be seriously questioned.

Perhaps that sale should not be made at all.

There is evidence that decisions are based on the best value rather than the lowest price. Were it not so, all products that are the same or similar would be reduced to the lowest price. But evidence abounds that prices vary widely in the marketplace. Even identical products of the same brand often vary a great deal in the market at the same time.

This is not because customers are stupid or unknowledgeable, but because they perceive the bundle of attributes to be different.

The "Bundle of Attributes" is a concept that represents all of the benefits that having the product or service can bring to the prospect. This includes not only the physical features and accompanying benefits but also the emotional and psychological benefits the prospect can expect.

Salespeople in the field of commodity-like products generally find that differentiation is even more difficult in cases where competitors are offering exactly the same product. These are the situations that more readily lend themselves to price buying. The salesperson must strive to establish a personal relationship that stresses service, integrity, dependability etc., in order to capture customer loyalty in these markets.

It is fundamental for the salesperson to remember while the physical product might be identical, the personal service can make his bundle of attributes greatly different.

One attribute your competitior can never duplicate is you as a unique personality and the services you might provide.

In fact, it's not uncommon for prospects to decide they "want" to buy a particular product from *you*. But they may need help in justifying the purchase on a more tangible basis. Customers are business people who like to think they are making sound, logical financial decisions. In these cases, it's your job to arm the customer with the logic, data and other evidence necessary to convince peers, superiors or family members of the wisdom of their choice. The fact that they were primarily attracted by a personality may never be made known to anyone.

It therefore becomes the salesperson's task to highlight the value of the product or service, differentiate it from similar competitive products and ensure that customers who are simply comparing prices realize that they may be comparing apples and oranges. Subtle differences in value in either the product or the service the company offers, may justify the price difference.

Value is a complex question, one on which the customer may already have a preconceived opinion. So without bragging or being cocky, point out how you can offer unique differences that add value.

There is no need to put the competition down. You can point out your unique strengths without saying anything about your competitor. It's fine to emphasize areas in which you have a clear superiority but it is seldom necessary to point out a specific competitor's weaknesses. Only when confronted by a direct question should you speak of a competitor's product, and then it should be factual.

Let your customer draw their own conclusions based on facts. You will appear far more professional.

Deal From Strength

Always deal with price from a position of strength. Defensivesness or wishy-washiness has no place in a sales call. Such traps can be avoided by knowing where you stand on price and why, particularly if you have a well-thought-out strategy for handling questions and objections on price.

Confidence is critical in dealing with price in the sales call. If *you* don't believe the price is justified by its value, there is little chance the prospect will be convinced. Nothing will kill a sale quicker than a salesperson who doesn't believe in his product. The prospect may sense the lack of confidence and react accordingly.

Resist Phone Price Quotes

It is usually bad judgment to quote a price by phone since the salesperson has no way of explaining what is included with the product or knowing if that product is right for the prospect. Often such a call means the prospect is merely price shopping, leaving open the distinct possibility of an unfair comparison.

Instead, ask to meet with the prospect and at his earliest convenience. If the caller persists, ask questions to clarify his needs, perhaps asking questions that cannot be answered except in person or point out some key benefits to hook his interest — anything to encourage face-to-face contact.

Some firms have established a strong policy against price quotes by phone. Phone price quotes are very prone to misinterpretations and confusion, especially in regards to complex products.

When Price Comes Up Early

When a prospect questions price before you've discussed benefits, you may wish to postpone your response. Sidestep the issue and ask if you can come back to it in a few minutes. Reply with "Price is always important to sharp farmers, John. But as in so many things, an exact price is difficult to quote until we have more information about your situation and what will work best. May I ask you a few more questions first?"

Direct Price Comparison

When confronted with competitive price quotes. It's seldom a good idea to allow the products to be directly compared. Remember the "Bundle of Attributes" concept. Whether your product is higher or lower priced, reinforce unique qualities to establish a value advantage. First review the tangible benefits you have already established. Then emphasize the intangible benefits such as service and your personal knowledge of the customer's situation.

Managing Expectations

High is a relative term that is based on some level of expectation. So when a prospect tells you the price is too high, he is saying the price is higher than expected. One method of dealing with the price obstacle is to establish a price expectation early in the sales call. When the actual price is discussed, it may be viewed in a more favorable light. This technique is particularly valuable when dealing with products or services that are high-ticket items that the prospect has little knowledge about.

A statement like "Some farmers are spending as much as $20,000 for planting equipment with electronic monitoring equipment," can help create an expectation level that avoids shock. Expectation level that is higher than your own price puts you into a more favorable position when they learn your price is a little lower.

When a prospect objects to price, it may be appropriate to ask to what they are comparing it. Often the prospect will simply be playing a complaining game about "price of things now a days." Empathize, reinforce the importance of getting the most value for his money, summarize the key benefits and attempt the close.

On the other hand, if the prospect has a specific comparison in mind, deal with it openly. Once it's identified you can point out the unique benefits of your product, making the prospect recognize that a direct comparison on price alone may not be a fair evaluation.

Another technique is to refer to a list of comparative advantages when you summarize to justify the higher price. "These are some of the extra benefits and services you get with our Model 8600, John. They are the reason I believe our product is worth the additional cost." **Summarize Benefits to Add Value**

Be prepared to present price on a per usage basis. This is a useful technique when dealing with higher-quality products that may have a longer life. The cost per acre, bushel, animal may dramatically illustrate how the higher initial price might provide a lower cost advantage to your prospect. Point out that not price, but the cost per usage and the profit it generates is the most important issue. **Break Price Down**

Another dimension of the price value concept is the time factor. Many higher-priced products are made to last longer or have lower service costs. Yet the life of the product or the repair record are much less tangible than comparing the outright purchase price. **More Value Over Time**

Although many salespeople think mentioning the quality advantages is sufficient, these benefits must be driven home by interpreting what they mean in cost per year, savings in repairs or dollars gained from less downtime in the busy season.

Word pictures of these benefits, reinforced by testimonials or records of satisfied users, can be helpful in reducing the initial impact of a higher-priced, quality product. The technique is more powerful whenever benefits can be demonstrated using numbers or circumstances from the prospect's situation. It's using the "You-get-what-you-pay-for" concept to justify your price.

The price objection is usually difficult for the inexperienced salesperson because he doesn't have a strategy for dealing with it. But experienced salespeople know that price need not be a reason for losing the sale. The secret is to be ready to deal with the price objection from a positive position. **Strategies for Handling Price Objections**

There are several ways to justify price when it comes up as a specific objection during the close. Some ideas:

1. **Quality of the product**
   Be ready to offer proof of various features and benefits.

2. **Value, not price, is the primary consideration for a smart buyer**
   Summarize the benefits the buyer gets for the price. Emphasize those points in which the customer has interest and in which are unique among the competition.

3. **You get what you pay for**
   This cliche sells product to quality/value-oriented customers. It appeals to the basic psychology of many buyers.

4. **Your company could produce cheaper products too**
   But it doesn't because your company knows what it takes to do the job correctly.

5. **Your competition knows what their product is worth**
   If the competition sells lower there must be a reason.

6. **You**
   You are providing unique personal services no one else can duplicate. This is a strong point but you *must* deliver.

SUMMARY
Dealing With
Price

* Quoting a price to a customer and coping with resulting comments may pose problems for salespeople. Especially challenging is the situation where the product is higher in price than that of the competition.

* Salespeople may or may not have the authority to adjust prices and the risks involved should be carefully weighed before making any concessions. The advantages of landing a big deal must exceed the disadvantages of alienating other customers, increasing the service load or causing a price war.

* Convincing prospects the higher price is worthwhile may be accomplished by stressing the product's value. The "Bundle of Attributes" includes the product's physical features and benefits along with its emotional and psychological benefits. If the competition is offering a nearly identical product, the salesperson should stress the personal service aspect.

* If a prospect perceives a price as too high, it's because the quote is high in relation to his expectations. It is up to the salesperson to make sure the prospect expects a high price so he will be pleased when the actual price is less.

* The value principle may be illustrated in several ways. One is by presenting price on a per usage basis. Another is showing value over time in long product life or a positive repair record.

Reading Seven
Collecting Accounts

"The sale isn't complete until the money is collected" is as accurate a rule today as ever. Collecting overdue accounts is one of the most unpleasant functions of sales for most any salesperson. It's discomforting and sometimes embarrassing to have to ask a customer for money.

Part of the problem is that there's a good deal of emotion tied to money. People learn early that money is not a subject for discussion with strangers and collection is associated with villains in black capes and handlebar mustaches who prey on honest, hardworking people. It seems such personal matters just aren't appropriate topics of discussion for moral agriculturalists — and that's where the problem starts.

Collecting money is an essential part of the selling process. And when problems arise, the logical candidate for making the collection call is the person who knows the account best — the one who made the sale. Still, most salespeople approach the collection call with fear and trepidation.

Having some responsibility for collection makes salespeople more cautious in dealing with accounts that have questionable payment records. Such salespeople are more understanding of credit department regulations, which aids the control of credit without diminishing the role of the credit department in the extension and management of financial matters.

Past due accounts are critical to agribusinesses. The older the account, the less it's worth to the business. A recent Iowa State University Extension publication, *Credit Management For Business Firms,* reports overdue accounts rapidly decline in value because of the increasing likelihood they will never be collected, as illustrated below:

Costly Credit

ACCOUNT STATUS	VALUE
Current	100¢ on the dollar
2 mos. past due	90¢ on the dollar
6 mos. past due	67¢ on the dollar
1 yr. past due	45¢ on the dollar
2 yrs. past due	23¢ on the dollar
3 yrs. past due	15¢ on the dollar
5 yrs. past due	1¢ on the dollar

Or, stated another way, if an agribusiness makes a profit of 5% on sales, a bad debt write-off requires about $100,000-worth of business to generate enough profit to offset the loss — not including the costs accumulated in attempting to collect the account.

There are many reasons why customers don't pay on time. Some are related to whether the customer's a farmer, dealer or distributor. While excuses are never acceptable reasons, understanding them offers a clue to dealing with them.

Why Customers Don't Pay

1. Some customers just don't understand credit terms. Credit terms can be complicated — especially on highly seasonal agricultural products. Manufacturers and distributors of fertilizer and chemicals, for example, offer early-order discounts and credit terms designed to spread their sales and shipments over a longer season. The result is complex credit terms that vary widely from company to company.

A farmer or dealer exposed to several different ''simple'' plans may easily get confused or just misunderstand.

2. Some customers are poor managers. They're habitually slow and often so busy with the physical operations that they let financial matters slide. They don't intend to pay late, it's just not a high priority.

3. Some customers have cash-flow problems. They just can't pay when the bill's due. It's not as bad if the customer at least notifies the salesperson or company that he can't pay on time. But when he just lets it go, it becomes a problem for everyone.

These customers are not intentionally dishonest, they just have a tendency to avoid reality — believing that if ignored, the problem will go away. A farmer or dealer in financial difficulty may not think logically.

4. Some customers will try to push the supplier to the limit. They know full well what they're doing. They pay late intentionally, banking on their importance to the supplier that nothing serious will come of it.

This customer operates on such a "float" regularly. Once he learns a supplier will not take action until a couple of weeks past the due date, he'll always pay late.

5. Some customers are dishonest. Fortunately, dishonest customers are few. But occasionally a customer will openly attempt to delay payment for a variety of "manufactured" reasons — designed as excuses to withhold payment as long as possible or even permanently.

Collecting Begins With Communication

The most critical part of collection begins before the sale is completed. The customer must thoroughly understand the total payment process — including any cash discounts that may be applicable to the purchase. A clear understanding is critical to smooth financial relationships with customers. This will draw upon the salesperson's communication expertise.

Question the farmer or dealer about his understanding of the terms of the sale — assume nothing. Remember, if a misunderstanding occurs, the customer almost always blames the salesperson. This is only reasonable, since it's the salesperson's job to create understanding.

If something does go wrong, there's a good chance it will affect the customer's perception of the product and the salesperson's competency — hurting future business.

Educate the Customer

The customer must be educated about the real cost of credit and the value of any discount policy. Help him analyze available credit plans and select the one best suited to his needs. Steer him to other sources of credit available from banks, PCAs etc., that offer a cheaper source of cash.

This not only builds credibility with the customers but saves the company unnecessary grief. Most manufacturers, suppliers, dealers and distributors do not want to be in the credit business. It's costly, even with annual interest rates of 12-18%. Carrying charges of 1-1½% a month cannot cover the cost of extending credit in most ag firms.

Maintain Sales/Credit Relationships

Salespeople should work closely with the credit manager in obtaining complete financial information and credit applications from customers. For many salespeople this is a real nuisance, because they do not see it as part of their jobs. Sometimes there's a tendency to be sloppy or the salesperson is so anxious to work with his customer he forgets who he's working for.

In the eyes of salespeople, the credit manager's primary objective is to prevent salespeople from meeting their quotas. Credit people tend to view salespeople as irresponsible extroverts who promise anything in order to make a sale. This conflict often leads to credit problems in the field.

Both departments should meet regularly to discuss each other's problems and keep the lines of communication open. Each has an important role to play in the successful use of credit as a marketing tool.

It's wise to help the customer obtain credit — somewhere else. In fact, some sharp salespeople work with their customer in preparing cash-flow projections and even accompany them to the local lender to assist in arranging financing and help them take advantages of cash discounts. After all, commercial lending institutions are in the business of lending money — they want the business. But if the local bank or PCA won't extend credit to the customer, watch out.

This effort is time-consuming, but pays off in present and future transactions. Salespeople should familiarize themselves with how credit can be arranged. Get to know local bank loan officers and PCA managers. Take them to lunch occasionally. Once they trust and respect you, they can be a source of good leads, as well as a help in arranging customer credit.

Provide Help With Credit

An account is usually considered overdue when it's due date has passed. Most companies have established policies and procedures to follow. Normally, the credit department issues several impersonal reminders to the customer — each a little stronger than the one before. It often only takes one reminder to complete the collection.

It's important the salesperson be kept advised of the collection process, as the subject may come up during routine sales calls. Or more embarrassing, he may continue to sell the customer — compounding an already sticky situation.

Sometime during this process, the salesperson may be called upon to visit the customer. The salesperson must be familiar with the situation and all applicable company policies. Take care not to make promises, threats or imply judgments to complicate the problem further.

The call should be handled tactfully, but firmly. If there has been a misunderstanding, it can be cleared up and some procedure for satisfying the account established.

If the problem persists, it is likely a company supervisor will accompany the salesperson on a call to the customer. It's up to the salesperson to arrange this if necessary.

Eventually, legal suit may be filed by company lawyers. But this is an expensive last resort.

The collection process need not be distasteful if approached fairly and firmly. In fact many ag customers report dissatisfaction with suppliers who do not enforce stated credit policies. Inconsistent treatment is unfair to those who manage their financial affairs well and they are well aware of their share of the cost of credit over-extended to others. Such inconsistent treatment has legal implications for the company as well.

Collecting Overdue Accounts

Credit can be an effective sales tool when used wisely and responsibly. Most ag companies would prefer not to provide credit, but do so because it's an accepted means of doing business.

It's up to the sales force — in tandem with credit personnel — to use it properly. By accepting this responsibility, salespeople can turn credit from a

Credit as a Tool

nightmare into a positive tool for working with customers.

SUMMARY
Collecting
Accounts

* Salespeople may share the responsibility for collecting overdue accounts because of their close ties to the customer.

* Customers don't pay bills for a variety of reasons: they misunderstand credit terms, are poor managers, have cash flow problems, know they can get away with late payment or may be dishonest.

* The salesperson can help alleviate some problems before they occur by communication, education, good sales/credit department relationships and by assisting the credit efforts of customers.

Reading Eight
Selling Introverts and Extroverts

Selling is a people business. And selling success depends on the development of mutually rewarding relationships between the salesperson and customer. While a close personal relationship is not necessary, or perhaps even desirable, the chemistry between buyer and seller must be at least acceptable for the business relationship to survive. When a hog producer finds a feed salesman irritating or a fertilizer dealer doesn't like the chemical company sales representative, and future business may be in spite of the salesperson rather than because of him or her.

Case Study

Jack Berne had just been hired as a sales rep for a young but rapidly growing feed company in central Illinois. Jack had an excellent background for his new job. Raised on a large and progressive Iowa hog farm he acquired a degree in animal husbandry while working part time on the university swine farm where he assisted in nutrition research projects. Jack also led a very active social life as a fraternity officer and member of the football team. His "B" grade average was especially good considering all of his activities.

Jack hadn't been interested in sales at first. He didn't like the idea of being a "fast-talking, pushy peddler" like those who used to call on his dad at home. But his new employer was working hard to establish itself as a high technology company in the rapidly growing low-inclusion base blend market, appealing primarily to large producers. Jack had been convinced he would really be using his interests in and experience with hogs to help producers solve problems. And besides, the idea of working with lots of people fit well into the leadership and social activities he was used to on campus.

But after six months on the job, Jack was having second thoughts. The realization of covering seven counties, holding numerous producer meetings and trying to call on large successful operators was overwhelming. Jack never was good at organization and some days he was meeting himself coming and going.

He was also having some problems with prospects. One nearly threw him off the place yesterday — said he was too "pushy." "And that caused me to be late at the next call," Jack lamented to his wife. "And then *he* was upset because I was late. I'm not sure if I'm going to make it in sales!"

While Jack has what many would call a "sales personality" and was considered a good catch by those firms who actively recruited him, he was off to a rocky start. He is bright, warm, aggressive, out-going and extroverted. And therein may lie the key to his current problem and future success or failure.

Jack must understand more about his personality and how he can use his strengths to build productive business relationships while he copes with some natural tendencies that pose problems for some customers.

There are many different dimensions to personality. Introversion-extroversion, sometimes referred to as temperament, is one personality/dimension that is particularly valuable to understanding and improve selling relationships. There are some basic principles about introversion and extroversion of which every salesperson should be aware. **Temperament**

First, Jack must understand that there is nothing inherently good or bad about being an extrovert — or an introvert, for that matter. A person's temperament is a fact of life. It can work for or against a person in any circumstance, depending on how it is accepted and used.

Second, the temperament personality characteristic is a continuum. People are not simply introverts or extroverts but a mixture of the two. The degree to which a person possesses introverted or extroverted characteristics determines how they may be classified. Probably there is no one who could be classified as purely introverted or extroverted. Even some strongly extroverted persons are likely to have some introverted tendencies — and vice versa.

Yet when a person possesses a strong tendency toward one end of the continuum, it's fair to classify that person as either an introvert or extrovert.

Actually, a majority of the population is classified as "ambiverts" because they exhibit a significant mixture of both introverted and extroverted tendencies. However, even ambiverts usually favor one side or the other. And recognizing these tendencies can be helpful to agri salespeople who are trying to develop productive relationships with customers.

Introverts tend to be quiet and not particularly outgoing. Some would rate them as aloof and unfriendly but this is not really the case. It's just that they are not usually aggressive in social situations and are slow to initiate or perhaps even respond to social interchange. They don't make friends quickly. But given time, their relationships develop considerable loyalty and depth, particularly when these relationships involve other introverts. **Introverts**

They generally prefer small quiet groups to large or loud social situations. In large groups, they will usually fade into the background and prefer to remain unnoticed.

Introverts are generally unemotional. They do not laugh easily and a smile or chuckle may be considered the equivalent of a belly laugh. Similarly, they generally show only hints of the displeasure or anger that they may actually feel — until they explode. It's easy to be misled by their stoic behavior since only the tip of the iceburg shows.

Introverts often seem moody. While they seldom seem bubbly, the often appear "down" and are quick to tell how bad things are. Their natural tendency toward pessimism sometimes turns to suspicion, particularly when regarding the competition.

It is particularly important to recognize that introverts tend to be thinking-type people who solve problems unemotionally with logic and data. They are analytical and curious by nature. Introverts continually try to figure out how and why things work as they do.

Consistent with their analytical nature is a strong drive for organization and punctuality in their lives. They plan ahead as far as possible and dislike surprises. Consequently, they often seem inflexible and distraught when the unexpected occurs — especially when they believe the situation could have been avoided. They are methodical and purposeful in their activities. They don't waste emotions or words in daily activities.

They are neat and orderly with personal possessions, usually taking great care in putting things away properly after they are done with them. "A place for everything and everything in its place" is the introverts' motto. They like to fine-tune and adjust until things are "just as they should be."

Introverts tend to be perfectionists about their work and often prefer to do things alone rather than work with others. "If you want a job done right, do it yourself."

Introverts also tend to be highly opinionated and even unspoken in their views. They say what they mean and mean what they say — and they don't expect to have to repeat it! Their views are usually well-thought-out and well-entrenched. Consequently, it is frequently difficult to influence introverts. They are often quite willing to argue their point rather than make concessions or changes.

In short, strong introverts tend to be conscientious people who think things through carefully before acting. They are quiet, sensitive and productive people who behave in a predictable manner.

Extroverts   Extroverts are out-going persons who thoroughly enjoy interacting with others. They are talkative and make new friends very quickly. They prefer many relationships to a few close friendships. They have a strong need to have people like them and frequently take positions of neutrality so they can get along with everyone. A frequent motto is "Don't make waves."

Extroverts trust others from the start. They are eternally optimistic and usually rebound quickly from difficult situations.

Extroverts are intuitive, feeling people and often make decisions based on what "seems like the best thing to do." This does not mean their decisions are necessarily poor, but often more subjective than objective. They usually make their decisions quickly.

Extroverts are often disorganized and inefficient. They generally can be found amid disarray, running behind schedule and in a hurry. The situation seems to control them — yet remarkably they nearly always come through somehow at the last minute. They have great difficulty with consistent punctuality and are often late for appointments. They dislike detail and finishing up jobs. They are highly flexible people and seem to thrive in situations where lots of things are happening at once.

In short, extroverts are likable people who respond quickly to changing circumstances. They are capable of handling difficult situations where human relationships and communications are critical to a successful outcome. Their intuitive judgment is an important key to their success.

Recognizing Introverts and Extroverts

Customers send out many signals that alert salespeople to their temperament. Care must be taken in making judgments too quickly (an easy trap for extroverts), since everyone has both introverted and extroverted characteristics. But when a customer exhibits a whole series of characteristics of an introvert or an extrovert, it may be safe to make some assumptions about their probable values and behavioral patterns. Your accuracy may prove critical to developing successful customer relationship.

SOME IDENTIFYING CHARACTERISTICS OF INTROVERTS

1. Quiet. Laughs privately or just smiles when amused. Rarely shows much emotion.
2. Well organized. Desk and office orderly, car clean and well-maintained, neat personal appearance etc.
3. Punctual and controls schedule.
4. Difficult to get to know. Keeps things to themselves.
5. Thinks things through. Knows where they are going.
6. Curious. Wants to know why often.
7. Opinionated. Difficult to convince.
8. Concientious. Follows through on whatever promised.

SOME IDENTIFYING CHARACTERISTICS OF EXTROVERTS

1. Friendly, out-going, talkative.
2. Runs behind schedule, always in a hurry.
3. Office in disarray. Can't find things, doesn't read mail thoroughly, late in paying bills, car dirty with dents, personal appearance slightly untidy etc.
4. Makes snap decisions. Bases decisions on personal factors and intuition.
5. More concerned with results than causes.
6. Concerned about image and being liked.
7. Shows emotion easily but can change quickly.
8. Trusts people, optimistic, asks for help easily.

As one might expect, salespeople in general tend to be extroverts. Some, like Jack, tend that way rather strongly. Of course, other salespeople, some very good ones, tend toward introversion.

While the nature of selling tends to attract extroverts, some characteristics of introversion are ideally suited to the selling environment. Except for those who might be too strongly introverted, there is no reason to believe that introverts cannot become excellent salespeople. Furthermore, strongly extroverted people might have equally difficult (if opposite) problems in relating to customers — especially when long-term repetitive relationships are the key to success as they are in most agribusinesses.

Farmers in general and many dealers tend to favor introversion — some rather strongly. While there are extroverted farmers, their general tendency toward introversion could set the stage for a classic temperamental conflict between buyer and seller.

Selling Strategies

Appropriate strategies for selling customers who are strongly introverted or extroverted are rather obvious. Yet they are not necessarily easy to implement since each salesperson has his or her own particular set of temperament traits which are natural and instinctive. The more difficult circumstances, or course, entail calling on and developing a relationship with customers who are quite opposite in temperament. But such relationships can and do develop — especially when salespeople are alert to the differences and compensate appropriately.

When a new prospect is approached, assume he or she is an introvert. If the initial approach is too aggressive, it will tend to turn off an introvert and cause distrust. Extroverts are not usually offended by a "laid-back" approach. And besides, extroverts will send dozens of signals quite early in the initial contact that will make their extroversion apparent. Then the approach can be adjusted. However, to approach an introvert rapidly with a fast "come-on" may build defensive barriers that are hard to break down later.

Strategies for Selling Introverts

Each contact with an introvert should be as carefully planned as possible. The salesperson should be particularly neat in appearance. Their car or truck should be clean. All materials should be well organized. The selling strategy should be a patient series of calls, allowing ample time to develop trust and credibility.

Every call should have a clear objective that is obvious and mutually valuable. Appointments are highly desirable and great care should be taken to show up precisely on time. The approach should generally focus on hard data, with painstaking explanations as to why certain conclusions are drawn. Do not assume benefits are obvious. Spell them out and have ample evidence available. Introverts are often hard to convince and tend to be defensive of their established patterns and relationships. They change only after much thought and analysis. So patience is the key.

Introverts are worth the effort. They tend to be loyal customers once they are converted. And if they are successful businessmen, others subtly watch their decisions as clues to their own choices.

Jack should take particular note of these tips on selling introverts. His natural tendencies as an extrovert mean that many of these strategies will come only with concentrated effort. Yet Jack's behavior is his own responsibility. His customers cannot be expected to adjust to his personality. That's just not the way it works.

While Jack may find the going easier with extroverted customers, he will not likely be successful in selling unless he learns to mirror many of the characteristics that are important to his introverted customers, especially when he is calling on introverts.

Jack Berne needs to carefully examine his own behavior in relationships with his customers. While there are many factors that will be important to his success, his personality and style will be critical. His extroverted personality can be highly beneficial if he recognizes that he must work hard to control some characteristics that are in direct conflict with those of some of his introverted farmers.

Strategies for Selling Extroverts

Extroverts tend to respond to more aggressive selling strategies. They are often quite open to new personalities and enjoy getting acquainted. They are more likely to find spontaneous sales calls acceptable and are even known to make spur-of-the-moment or impulsive decisions.

The sales call strategy should focus initially on the relationship. They enjoy chit-chat, gossip and war stories. It is not uncommon in an established relationship for business to seem almost incidental to the call.

Presentations should aim primarily toward end results and benefits. While detailed explanations may be necessary on some points, it is not necessary to bore extroverted customers with details. Their decisions often are intuitive and can come at any time in the presentation, so it is imperative to respond to buy signals with a prompt close. It is possible to oversell the extrovert and lose the sale.

Extroverts may be prone to switching suppliers without much warning. They often like to try new ideas, making it easier for a new salesperson to get a foot in the door — a phenomenon that can work for or against a salesperson.

Extroverts like to be entertained and taken care of. Their ego needs to be stroked frequently. They enjoy being taken out socially. Playing golf or hunting with their salesperson can sometimes seem to build as much loyalty as detailed business services.

This is not to suggest that extroverted customers do not demand quality products, good services, and reasonable prices, because no business relationship is safe without a sound business basis. But it is clear that the unique personality characteristics of extroverts demand decidedly different selling strategies.

Strategies for Selling Ambiverts

An alert salesperson can gain important insights into the behavior of ambiverts simply by recognizing the existence of both introversion and extroversion and taking these into account in the customer relationship. For example, Jack would profit greatly from simply realizing that the customer who is generally all business and highly methodical and analytical in seeking solutions to his nutrition problems would thoroughly enjoy talking at length about the exciting high school basketball game his daughter played last week.

People Buy From People They Like

The fact is that people buy from people they like. That is a prerequisite to most ongoing business relationships. It is not at all uncommon for a farmer or dealer to be swayed primarily by personality factors and *then rationalize* their decision by searching for facts and figures that support their choice. There may be several measurable differences between competitive alternatives, but each has its own unique list of pros and cons that can be used to justify an intuitive purchase.

As the customer subjectively weights the list to determine which is best, his judgment may be greatly influenced by a host of intangible factors that are closely associated with the chemistry of the relationship.

Of course, personality is seldom enough. Service, performance, profitability etc., must be in evidence before and after the sale or there will be no repeat business. As farmers and dealers become increasingly sophisticated in business decisions, personality may become a less significant factor. But it will *always* play an important role as a necessary prerequisite to a profitable ongoing business relationship. And temperament is an important dimension of this relationship.

SUMMARY Selling Introverts and Extroverts

* Salespeople need to understand personality types, their own as well as those of their customers, to maintain relationships conducive to selling.

* One way of categorizing temperament is by defining personality types as introverts and extroverts. Rarely is a person a pure example of either. Most people possess some characteristics of each and are termed ambiverts.

* Introverts are thoughtful, logical, neat and reserved. They tend to carefully think through buying decisions and, once having made the choice, usually stick to it.

* Extroverts are talkative, friendly people who base their decisions on how they feel. They are trusting and may seem disorganized. Since extroverts respond well to changing circumstances, they are not at all shy about changing a decision once it has been made.

* The best selling strategy assumes the customer is an introvert and adjusts easily if he is an extrovert. Extroverts tend to favor more aggressive selling while introverts prefer a well-organized, patient selling strategy.

Giving Customers A Performance Review

Performance planning is a powerful selling technique that's gaining popularity with professional agricultural salespeople.

It entails working closely with key customers to define their business objectives and develop a strategic plan for accomplishing them. Performance planning can result in a more productive and efficient salesperson-customer relationship.

Performance planning is much more than a sales projection for the product. Based on a management-by-objective philosophy, it concentrates on the customer's individual ambitions through a strategic plan and the supplier's contribution to that plan in terms of product and services provided to the customer.

But just as important, the strategic plan details the customer's commitment to activities that will help ensure successful results. Performance planning is a mutual commitment to mutual action with mutual benefits to both customer and supplier.

The psychological and operational advantages are numerous. Once objectives are established and a strategic plan is agreed upon, the salesperson can service the account far more efficiently. Because of performance planning, decisions regarding essential support services, physical distribution and even production scheduling can be made before the busy season even begins.

Perhaps the greatest benefit of performance planning as a sales tool is the relationship it builds between the customer and salesperson.

Its emphasis is on the customer and how the agribusiness can help him accomplish his objectives, rather than on the sales goals of the marketer.

Once this point is accepted by the customer, credibility and trust can lead to a close, mutually beneficial, cooperative relationship.

The purpose of performance planning is more than simply increasing sales. Customers who have developed a closer business relationship with their supplier and feel some sense of commitment to a plan are likely to be less vulnerable to competitors.

The basic procedure for customer performance planning is: 1. selecting accounts; 2. preparing for the performance planning interview; 3. performance review; 4. defining customer objectives; 5. developing a strategic plan; 6. commitment; 7. action; and 8. monitoring progress.

Preparation is essential to performance planning. And it begins with choosing customer candidates with which to work.

Selecting Accounts

Since the primary purpose of performance planning is not necessarily to generate new customers but to increase the volume and efficiency of sales with current customers, it makes sense to pick candidates with whom you already have a good relationship. Select good, sound businesspeople who are likely to recognize the benefits of forward planning.

Customers should be approached confidently but not so aggressively that they feel the salesperson is meddling in their affairs.

Agribusiness people at all levels tend to be very sensitive to maintaining their independence. Initially, for example, some managers are reluctant to share any financial information with the salesperson.

Yet after two or three years of performance planning, benefits become obvious and trust levels build. Only then do many agribusinesses readily share detailed financial statements and operating plans.

Preparing for the Performance Planning Interview

Before a performance planning session, the salesperson should thoroughly review all information about the account and its relationship to the company.

For example, how long has the customer been doing business with the firm? How much of each product has been purchased over the past few years? What kind of financial arrangements have been made? What problems have come up in ordering, inventory, distribution, pricing etc?

In short, it's important to be knowledgeable about the customer's relationship with the supplier, so that full advantage of opportunities can be taken.

The customer should also be asked to prepare for the performance review and planning session. Performance planning is a joint process and thus requires prior thinking by the customer as well. The customer's preparation should take the form of defining goals and basic plans for the future, especially, but not exclusively, as they relate to the product.

Some salespeople find it very useful to give the customer a brief worksheet to help him think through his goals before the planning session. Suggestions for the worksheet might include:

A. What are the goals of your business (volume, size, profits, community, personal)?

B. How will your operation be different a year from now?

C. How will it differ over the next five years?

D. How will personal changes likely affect your business in the next year?

E. How do you expect the local market to change in the next year?

F. Who is your most significant competition and why?

G. What are your most limiting factors (equipment, facilities, personnel, management, financial)?

Once candidates are selected they should be approached as in any sales call. The idea of performance planning as well as its benefits and costs must be conveyed.

Arrange for the performance planning session to be held in neutral territory if at all possible. Successful planning sessions often require several hours of discussion and must have the full attention of the customer.

The constant potential for interruption in the customer's place of business is just not conducive to performance planning. The salesperson's office also has potential for interruption and may put the customer on the defensive.

A neutral location such as a local motel with ample work space is often a good alternative for this special once-a-year session.

It is highly useful to summarize much of this information — particularly sales history — for review with the customer.

Performance Review

Simple charts and graphs reflecting product sales trends can be quite effective in evaluating past performance and planning the future. It may be difficult for an individual dealer or farmer to have an accurate perspective on how he is doing. Positioning relative to other customers can be beneficial so long as it is not done in any way that threatens or manipulates the customer.

Probably the most important part of performance planning is defining customer objectives. This may be the most difficult and time-consuming.

Defining Customer Objectives

Although some dealers, distributors and farmers are able to define their direction, most have not done so in a way that can be helpful for planning. Yet any plan must be built on the customer's specific goals.

Objectives are accomplishments desired by the business. They are represented by broad statements of what the business wants to become, what it wants to concentrate on and where it is headed.

Objectives suggest overall business philosophies and pinpoint what is really important to the customer. A key objective might be to become the dominant factor in providing agronomic services to farmers in the county.

Another customer's primary objective might be to provide a good source of family income and maintain the business for Junior, who graduates from state university next year.

These goals may be very different from a company store that is more interested in maximizing sales volume and minimizing costs in order to ensure a promotion for the resident manager. And each set of objectives likely suggests a different selling strategy.

Goals represent the specific measurable accomplishments to be obtained in a certain time frame. They must be consistent with broader objectives and provide well-defined targets that dictate what and how things will be done.

In football, for example, the objective is to win the game. The goal is to score a touchdown. The strategic plan calls for scoring touchdowns that in turn will win the game. Goals represent specific sales volume levels, cost factors and efficiency measures.

Through analysis, calculation and discussion, the professional salesperson works to develop a set of objectives and goals for the customer for the next year — or longer. It is highly important these be written and measurable in numbers. Otherwise the stage is set for misunderstanding and confusion.

These goals and objectives are not the goals and objectives of the salesperson for the customer. They are the goals and objectives of the customer. The salesperson simply serves as a catalyst to help the customer think them through.

It is appropriate for the salesperson to influence the customer — particularly as it directly affects his product — so long as it's done with integrity. But the resultant plan must be consistent with the customer's goals and objectives or it will likely meet with resistance and be doomed to failure.

Developing a Strategic Plan

A strategic plan is a time-phased action plan that will accomplish the established goals and objectives. It is a mutually agreeable written statement of how the customer will use the product and what support the salesperson will provide.

Note that it spells out what action both the buyer and seller will carry out. The time schedule helps avoid logistical problems and improves communication throughout the process. Everyone knows what is expected and when.

Hammering out the strategic plan depends totally on the product, company marketing plan and the customer's needs. It is common for the strategic plan to include: orders by date, subject to any change necessitated by later market conditions; services to be provided by the company and by the salespeople; distribution and shipping arrangements as appropriate; and detailed marketing, promotion and advertising plans in the case of dealers and retailers.

Commitment

Commitment to the plan is indicated by the total planning process. A formal commitment such as a signed contract is usually counter-productive since it implies distrust.

Additionally, it is impossible in most cases to force the customer to do anything and still maintain the relationship. Joint commitment is the essence of performance planning.

Commitment requires a thorough understanding of mutual expectations. It's a good idea to review the total performance plan and make sure both the customer and salesperson have a copy.

Action

The action step is carrying out the plan. This should be done according to plan but not with such rigor that it ignores changing market conditions. All strategic plans should maintain flexibility to capitalize on unique opportunities as they arise.

Monitoring Progress

Monitoring progress as the plan is executed is essential to successful performance planning. In fact, the salesperson should build monitoring points into the plan and be prepared to check them carefully throughout the season.

Monitoring points might include checking to see that orders are placed at the proper time, that co-op advertising programs are arranged, that dealer personnel receive proper training by a certain date etc. When performance does not meet the plan, corrective action should be initiated or the original plan altered to become appropriate.

Some form of performance planning is common to many agribusinesses. Roy Tuttle, district manager for the Ortho Division of the Chevron Chemical Company in Toledo, Ohio, pioneered the application of performance planning with fertilizer dealers in the Midwest. Roy and his sales force have used performance planning with their customers for several years and find it a useful tool.

But Roy suggests it's a sales tool that requires real professionalism on the part of salespeople.

"It takes a salesperson who can exert leadership and has the confidence and knowledge to work closely with his customers on a business level. And that takes lots of training," Roy says.

Several of Roy's salespeople have worked closely with their independent dealers for many years and regularly develop detailed plans for the total business. "This is a great help when it comes to forecasting sales," adds Roy. "We can service our customers better because each of us knows what to expect from the other."

Performance planning is not new but as agribusinesses become more sophisticated, the benefits of its application to distributors or national accounts should be obvious.

But it can also be used very effectively with dealers, retailers and even farmers. Larger customers appreciate the value of forward planning because it helps them accomplish their objectives. But most of all, performance planning is mutually beneficial to both customer and salesperson.

SUMMARY
Giving Customers
a Performance
Review

* Agri salespeople can play a vital role in the business success of their customers by developing a strategy for accomplishing their goals and reviewing performance to make changes for future growth. This can be viewed as a sales tool as well as a way to build relationships between sellers and customers.

* Planning comprises eight distinct steps: Selecting accounts, preparing for the performance planning interview, performance review, defining customer objectives, developing a strategic plan, commitment, action, and monitoring progress.

Reading Ten
Controlling The Sales Call

You've been doing business with Bill on-and-off for five years.
You'd like to have a lot more of his business but you haven't been very successful.
You've had trouble getting his attention because he's always in a hurry.
You've finally slowed him down long enough to talk business.
You've got him talking about his operation and he's mentioned a couple

of problem areas with which you know you could help.

You're in the middle of your presentation — the best part — where you give him your strongest points and show how you can solve his problems.

You're ready to shoot your big gun — give him the information that proves the superiority of your total program when...

...the phone rings...(You've never known a phone to be so loud!)

Your customer listens a moment and jabbers a few short bursts into the phone. He practically runs out, muttering about the way they make trucks nowadays and managing to mumble something about being sorry and getting together again sometime.

If you're like most people, you're probably sorely disappointed. But it would be more productive to examine what has just happened and how to avoid it.

It is impossible for a salesperson to avoid all disruptions of sales calls. Interruptions and disruptions are part of the game. While they can't be totally avoided, much can be done to reduce their frequency and impact.

The primary problem caused by disruptions is that the salesperson loses the attention of the prospect and, often, control of the sales call itself. When the salesperson does not have total attention, there is no way the customer can follow the internal logic or emotional appeal necessary to reach a favorable buying decision point. No matter how much preparation has gone into the call, the salesperson cannot be successful if he/she loses interest or control.

Control Strategy
There are many ways of controlling a sales call. Some deal with communication methods while others deal with the environment. All depend on the skill of the salesperson.

A cardinal rule of salesmanship is for the salesperson to maintain control of the sales call. Even when the best strategy is to allow the prospect to *think* they have control, the salesperson should maintain actual control of the content and pace of the call, sensing the prospect's needs and tactfully adjusting behavior to fit the situation.

Controlling the sales call does not necessarily mean being dictatorial or dominating the conversation. It does mean the salesperson should determine content, timing and procedures that are most effective in working with that particular prospect. In some cases it may mean leading the prospect through a logical thought process that reaches a favorable conclusion.

Tactics
Control tactics should be employed in the sales call itself. Experienced customers who are used to dealing with salespeople may act tough, especially with younger, less-experienced salespeople. This may be a natural tendency for some ego-oriented customers, or it may be a defensive ploy executed to maintain a competitive bargaining advantage. In either case, the salesperson who becomes intimidated quickly loses control and will be successful only by accident.

The most important control tactic is for the salesperson to know precisely what he or she wants to accomplish during the call. A feasible, well-thought-out objective does wonders for helping a salesperson maintain a sense of direction. The customer invariably senses when the salesperson has no specific objectives and either rambles along with the salesperson or takes charge of the vacuum situation. Neither response is likely to be productive.

A firm tone of voice and solid eye contact also helps create the perception that the salesperson has a purpose and is confident.

Maintain body posture that shows confidence. Stand or sit tall. Lean forward slightly when sitting. Offer to shake hands when greeting people. Initiate the greeting. Do not hide behind counters or desks if possible.

Directed questions are a useful tool for maintaining control and steering conversation into favorable directions.

Be firm and positive in summarizing progress or results of the sales call. Suggest action and specific steps that you and the customer will take next.

Then act decisively. Strong and timely follow-through also builds respect and makes the next sales call easier to set up and execute.

Directly ask the prospect to allot a specific period of time. Tell them you will stick with your mutually agreed time limit — *and then do it*. If appropriate, suggest or ask that the secretary hold all calls for that period and to let you both know when the period is up. The new alarm wrist watches, conspicuously set to go off in thirty minutes, can be very effective in building credibility.

Building credibility with customers is critical in maintaining control of the sales call. When the salesperson asks for time and gets it but delivers nothing that the prospect believes is important, the customer quickly learns not to waste time with this salesperson in the future.

But when a customer's repeated experience is that the salesperson asks for uninterrupted time only when it is important and then sticks to it, the customer usually is willing to meet.

If the sales call is relatively complex, consider preparing an agenda or checklist. All too often a salesperson must call back to bother the customer with one necessary item that was forgotten. This creates a bad image for the salesperson. The agenda or checklist also informs the customer what has to be done and that the salesperson is prepared.

The Environment

Location of the call is one of the most critical factors. Whenever a salesperson is in the customer's home, office or business, the customer has a strong control advantage. It's difficult and less appropriate for the salesperson to exhibit an aggressive behavior when on the prospect's turf. It's the customer's perogative to accept phone calls, messages and interruptions of almost any type when they are "at home."

So clearly, one key to maintaining control, especially when concentrated attention is needed, is to move to the salesperson's home base. When this is not feasible, the salesperson can suggest meeting in a neutral location such as a motel or restaurant. This is probably the most effective way of maintaining control and avoiding interruptions.

When the sales call is an important one, consider renting a motel studio for the presentation. When overnight travel is required, request early room cleanup and coffee or meal service to produce a very private environment away from phones, secretaries, hired hands, friends, family and other interruptions.

If you use a restaurant, choose a place where the atmosphere is conducive to discussion rather than entertainment and one where you are not likely to end up feeling pressured to invite other customers or your customer's friends to join you. Arrange ahead for a reserved table for only the number you expect and request the table in a corner or at the back (even if it costs extra). In any case, *plan* for this time.

These things can be done quite economically, especially considering the value of both party's time. Such treatment is often impressive to the prospect or customer. But most of all, the neutral environment controls interruptions and increases the ability of the salesperson to maintain control of the sales call.

Controlling the sales call is habitual with most agri salespeople. Patterns develop over time and habits become ingrained which may be hard to change. Gaining and maintaining control of the sales call is the sum total of many factors. But planning the sales call and its circumstances can be highly important to successful selling in agribusiness.

SUMMARY
Controlling
the Sales Call

* Disruptions frequently undermine even the best sales presentation. Salespeople must take steps to control the call to the extent that interruptions do not occur.

* Salespeople may maintain control by determining content, timing, location and procedures. A well-developed sales objective can help the salesperson steer the client through the call as well.

* Many interruptions occur because of the call environment. Sellers should take care to hold the meeting, if possible, in a place that minimizes distractions.

Reading Eleven
Selling Aids and Demonstrations

Selling is a demanding job. Arousing the prospect's interest, convincing him of your product's benefits, and motivating him to buy is a big job that requires more than just talking to a prospect. A good salesperson takes advantage of other forms of communication as well.

Consider that the average person speaks at the rate of 125-150 words per minute. Meanwhile the listener can think at a rate far greater than that — many times not even bothering to translate mental thoughts into words at all. The alert salesperson looks for ways of using his prospect's excess mental capacity by capturing the attention of their other senses along with their ears.

Visual contact makes a powerful impact and can greatly enhance communication. The old adage "A picture is worth a thousand words," is certainly valid for the salesperson. Every time an effective visual aid is used, the impact of words can be multiplied. In fact, some experienced salespeople believe that as much as 87% of all mental impact in a sales call may come from the visual contact alone. So relying solely on a verbal presentation greatly limits a salesperson's potential.

If doubting this statistic, stop and think. Psychologists remind us that we think in pictures, not in sounds. When a prospect wants to show understanding of your point, he usually says "I see," not "I hear." (This despite the fact that you are *speaking* to him.) It's his way of saying that your audio communication has gotten through to him on a level he can visualize.

There are other senses that can be brought into play as well. Touch and smell can reach deeply into a prospect's mind to communicate more effectively than words. Feeling the cool air flowing out of the cab's air-conditioner or smelling the aroma of a high protein dairy feed are powerful ways of convincing a prospect of the validity of a point. Every time another sense is brought into play, the chances of making the desired impact is greatly enhanced.

Imagine for a moment that a district manager for a seed company is making a sales call on a prospective farmer dealer. His presentation is entirely verbal — asking questions, giving information about hybrid performance, quoting commission schedules and very skillfully telling his prospect of his company's greatness.

Next consider a competitive company making a call on this same high priority prospect. But his district manager has come prepared to demonstrate his company's benefits.

First he has a notebook of information, well-organized and neat. The district manager shows photographs of key hybrids in local fields. He uses a brochure to point out important strengths of key hybrids, circling critical points with his pencil as he stresses each one. He happens to have a sample of his top-selling hybrid which he hands to the farmer to demonstrate the weight of the ear and the small diameter of the cob. Then, using a worksheet, the district manager works through an example showing the financial benefits that the farmer would realize simply from purchasing the hybrids for his own farm operation and then works through an estimate of his potential earnings as a dealer from reselling 500 units of seed to neighbors.

And to top it off, he makes arrangements to take his prospect along with two other top-producing dealers to a field day to examine this year's plots.

While none of the latter techniques would be considered exotic in any sense, they are very effective methods that should be an integral part of a salesperson's everyday tool kit. Selling aids of all types, when used in a professional manner, can greatly improve a salesperson's call/close ratio.

There are a wide variety of selling aids available to every salesperson. "Exhibit A" lists several different selling aids along with helpful suggestions. Don't be limited by this list. The possibilities are limited only by your imagination and well worth some creative thinking.

Develop selling aids that will evoke interest, illustrate points, show features, demonstrate benefits, offer evidence and convince the prospect. Selling aids should assist you in convincing the prospect that your product will meet his needs and encourage him to want your product.

Exhibit A

POSSIBLE SELLING AIDS

1. Company promotional brochures
2. Product literature
3. Objective and independently published information
4. Gifts, trinkets or other attention-getters related to product
5. Photographs of satisfied customers
6. Photographs of product in use
7. Testimonials from satisfied customers
8. Research results
9. Copies of product advertisements
10. Tables showing comparison with competition
11. Examples showing impact on typical customer
12. Worksheets for analysis of prospect's situation
13. Sample of the product (where possible)
14. Demonstration of actual product
15. Calling or business card

Effective selling aids just don't appear overnight or as a last minute gesture before a sales call. The best ones evolve over time as a salesperson finds what works best for him. Manufacturers often provide large amounts of sales literature, product manuals and elaborate materials to assist in the presentation. These materials should be professionally done and, if used properly, can be a big help.

In using company-prepared selling aids, you must be very familiar with the materials. You can quickly lose a prospect while you madly search a three-hundred page manual, looking for the details of a technical point. Product manuals are not substitutes for basic product knowledge. Detailed technical information should be referred to when that point has become critical to your prospect, and then should be looked up as efficiently as possible.

Also be careful of overkill. Too much data, or too heavy a reliance on prepared materials, makes it look like a crutch — as if you don't have your presentation well-in-mind. Remember, your presentation must be unique for the needs of each particular prospect. To walk through a professionally prepared notebook just as it is laid out may make your presentation look "canned." That doesn't mean you shouldn't have selling aids prepared and organized. It simply means that materials — particularly printed materials — should *supplement* your presentation, not *become* your presentation.

Professional agri salespeople are constantly on the lookout for examples that will vividly illustrate the benefits of their product. They make notes on how a satisfied customer has profited from their relationship and ask for permission to use that situation in their work with new prospects. Because agricultural products lend themselves so well to photography, many salespeople constantly keep a camera available to get effective shots. They try to capture satisfied customers using their product in such a way that it becomes a subtle testimonial in addition to illustrating a selling point.

Consider developing your own satisfied customer notebook complete with color shapshots (take plenty and use only good ones that flatter your customer) and a brief scenario that describes what you have done. Include worksheets and typed summary information you are likely to refer to often. Place frequently used materials in 8½'' x 11'' acetate sheets to keep them clean and neat.

One of the simplest selling aids, and the most underestimated, is the pencil. In keeping with the spirit of visual reinforcement, you can draw diagrams, graphs and rough sketches to clarify your sales points. John H. Patterson, considered by some to be the father of modern selling, always advised his salespeople to "Talk with pencils." Personalize important points for your prospect. Work through an example — especially when you're dealing with helping your prospect make more money.

Some good salespeople set up worksheets that provide a format they can tailor to each prospect's situation using *their* assumptions. Just know your product well enough to know in advance how it will turn out! And be careful not to oversell or overpromise in your example.

If your company has a brochure that contains data or pictures that you can use in your presentation, don't hesitate to hand it to your prospect. But maintain control over the brochure so that you can physically point out important things as you talk.

A brochure is also a good tool to get closer to your prospect. If you can physically move beside him to point out portions without him becoming uncomfortable, it may be a sign of added trust. Even across a table, you have an opportunity to move in closer.

Circling or checking key items on the individual's brochure as you make the points in the presentation is a good tactic, as the customer has something to refer back to later. The same general idea applies if you are using a notebook. Turn the pages so that you both can see it easily and again point out each important issue as you come to it.

If you just hand the brochure to the prospect, he may be distracted by points you have yet to make and by searching for what you have just referred to, miss your next point.

Using the brochure as a "leave-behind-piece," is fine but don't relinquish control of it too quickly in the call.

SUGGESTIONS FOR MAKING BETTER USE OF SELLING AIDS

Neatness: Make sure that each selling aid is clean and neatly laid out, so the impression it creates is positive.

Organization: Tab notebooks and use other markers so you will be able to refer to any section of the selling aid quickly and without fumbling.

Testimonials: Include statements or results from satisfied users, but make sure you get permission from the users first.

Photos: Use crisp, clear photographs that personalize whatever you are trying to show.

Numerical Examples: Demonstrate how the numbers add up with appropriate illustrations.

Worksheets: Develop step-by-step worksheets to calculate through each prospect's situation.

Brochures: Use manufacturer's literature to refer to, point out, markup, and leave behind.

Calling Card: At the very least, leave a business card. (Far better though, to staple it to a brochure ahead of time so that it is not misplaced and is easy to find.)

Evidence: Make sure you include enough data or information to prove any claim you are prepared to make.

Benefits: List key features and benefits the customer will receive and use this list in the summary and close. Leave that behind, too, for the customer's study.

Showmanship: Selling With a Flair

"You show me a showman and I'll show you a salesman.
You show me a salesman and I'll show you a showman!"
—The late Mike Todd

Mike Todd was popularly believed to be one of the greatest showmen of his time, perhaps of all time. Yet his feet were planted firmly enough on the ground to recognize that showmanship was nothing more or less than a first cousin to salesmanship, and vice versa. What the most successful salespeople accomplish throughout the world each day is but a smaller-scale version of what Todd accomplished with his spectaculars: presenting things in a vivid, emotional, dramatic and exciting manner. This is what *Webster's Collegiate Dictionary* defines as "Exhibiting things to advantage."

And why not? Why should a salesperson want to exhibit his merchandise to *dis*advantage? Yet many salespeople resist this sales technique in the mistaken belief that it is somehow "cornball" and laughable. If you're one of those people, find out what showmanship is all about before you write it off. If it is intelligently conceived, appropriately executed and creatively appealing, odds are you'll find it makes your sales presentations more effective, not more laughable.

Gordon Bethards, regional sales manager for DuPont Ag Chemicals, relates an excellent example of how showmanship can make the difference:

Many years ago, when polyethylene was a new plastic, somebody in our company conceived of the idea of coating kraft paper with a thick layer of it. Because of the properties of the plastic, it seemed that polyethylene-coated paper could offer numerous possibilities for use.

We introduced the idea to the paper industry with words and data sheets listing the physical and chemical properties of the various densities of polyethylene. I was one of the sales representatives making the introduction. The initial response from the research directors to whom we showed our data and explained the concept was polite disinterest.

On the second tour of the paper companies, we had the same data sheets, but this time we also had 3" × 5" × 1/8" molded pieces of three different polyethylene densities. The paper company research people felt the pieces, flexed them and calmly speculated on what uses might be found for paper coated with one of these plastics. But beyond this mild interest, we left with no commitments for positive action.

At about this time, one of our engineers constructed a laboratory-size melt extruder to coat a 6-inch web of paper. At the next gathering of our sales representatives, he demonstrated this extruder and gave each of us a few feet of the 6-inch web of polyethylene-coated kraft paper. We talked about the interest we could arouse among the paper companies by displaying this coated paper.

One of our sales representatives did one thing more. He took the coated paper home, cut a 12-inch length and folded it in half with the plastic coating on the inside. With a hot iron, he sealed two sides forming an open-ended pouch. He then poured water into the open end and sealed the last side. In so doing he formed a paper bag of water completely enclosed. The plastic was not visible; it appeared as though by some magic, water was contained in kraft paper (which anybody who has suffered with a wet grocery bag knows is impossible).

Polyethylene, as every man in the street knows today but didn't know then, is water impermeable. Paper companies at that time produced water-resistant papers, but none that could literally hold water. We all instantly recognized the potential drama of showing kraft paper pouches of water and rushed home to make our own pouches.

As expected, the display of the paper pouch of water on our next tour of the paper companies proved electrifying. I vividly remember walking into the office of one research director to whom I had talked on the two previous trips. Without saying anything else I almost shouted, "Did you ever see a paper bag full of water?" as I tossed the pouch on his desk directly in front of him.

The director leaped to his feet, grabbed the pouch and rushed out of the office. After about 10 minutes, he came back. "Come with me! Our president wants to see you!"

Never before nor since have I seen a man as excited as he was. This was the same director of research who had glanced at the data sheets on my first visit and had handled the molded plastic rectangles on the second visit with little interest either time.

The chemical and physical properties of the polyethylene were clearly defined on the data sheets. Any scientist with the background of this paper company research director could easily look at the data and visualize the water impermeability, the flexibility at various temperatures, the toughness and many other useful properties.

Or, if he couldn't visualize the end-use opportunities from the figures and graphs, you would think that holding, feeling, flexing, hammering and tearing the molded pieces of plastic I handed him on the second visit should have been more than enough to excite his interest. I thought the potential value of this new development was more than clear. But that wasn't enough. It wasn't enough for him nor was it enough for any of the paper company research directors.

Demonstration, specific demonstration of what the product could do in an end-use application, was the key. Seeing and feeling the coated paper and the paper bag of water bridged the canyon and did it quickly. Maybe over a long period of time, some of these same scientists would have arrived at the same conclusion, the same result. But, not so soon. Dramatic demonstration achieved a result that had defied conventional approach.

— *Gordon Bethards, "Selling," Agri Marketing Magazine, (Sept. 1982), page 34.*

The salesperson who adds a bit of showmanship to his presentation can often accomplish much where others fail, and get his point across to the customer more successfully.

There is nothing new about showmanship in agri selling. Demonstrating what a product can do, what it feels like to drive, or how well it performs in a field, is as old as agri selling itself. Anytime you can get a prospect to try your product, you've gone a long way toward making the sale.

SUMMARY
Selling Aids
and
Demonstrations

* Selling aids can be a valuable tool in capturing and holding a customer's interest as they give the person several types of information to process during the presentation.

* Aids may be as simple as a company brochure or as complex as a product demonstration. Either way they must be carefully prepared to convey a professional air.

* The most effective aids are usually those personally prepared by a salesperson, as these aids can include specific information of interest to, and often featuring, the local customer.

* Salespeople can take advantage of aids as psychological tools to direct the customer's attention or increase credibility.

* Showmanship is an important aspect of developing aids. The best sellers are showmen who use creativity with enthusiasm to show their product to best advantage.

Reading Twelve
Maintaining Customer Relations

Jim braked hard to avoid the concrete truck bearing down on him as he pulled out of Elliot's Farm Supply. The way he felt, getting hit by a concrete mixer couldn't make a deeper impression than Pete Elliot just had.

Jim was disturbed. Pete had been his largest customer since he'd started selling in this area and one of the most loyal. To find suddenly that Pete had stocked a whole new competitive line was a complete shock. If today's order was any indication, he'd lost most of this year's business.

What had gone wrong? And why hadn't Pete given him any warning? Jim thought he'd given good service. He'd been there every time Pete called. And he knew his company's incentive program was superior to that of the competition. Despite Pete's busy schedule as of late, Jim was certain Pete would let him know if anything was wrong.

As Jim mulled over the situation, he realized that when he last lunched with Pete, Deb Willard's name had come up. Willard was a sales representative who handled a new competitive line. In fact, Pete had specifically asked questions about models that Willard was selling.

By the time Jim returned home, the depression had grown worse. This was the third account in two months that was in jeopardy and Jim's biggest worry seemed to be how he'd explain this one to his manager.

Customer Relations as a Valued Asset

Most agri sales are based on long-term repetitive business. The salesperson and the customer interact professionally, socially and personally and often develop solid relationships over time. Knowing the customer's needs, problems and values is essential to servicing the account. Sound customer relationships are the most valued asset any agri salesperson has.

Although agri selling is often intensely competitive, there is a tendency for farmers or dealers to be loyal to their current supplier. Such a relationship offers security. That is why new customers are so hard to come by, with the exception of those who can be "bought" with low prices.

But, therein lies the problem. The stability of a relationship can lull even the most experienced salesperson into a false sense of security. A customer relationship that becomes routine can dull the aggressiveness and enthusiasm for providing service. As the salesperson begins to take a customer for granted, there is a tendency to be less responsive to the customer's changing needs. As a result, the customer may become vulnerable to a newly assigned competitor who is different, more attractive, has a different accent or is more aggressive.

Further complicating matters is the nature of many rural people to avoid open confrontation when they become dissatisfied with the salesperson. It's easier to change suppliers — gradually or abruptly. By the time a negligent salesperson realizes there's a problem, the business arrangement may be over.

Consequently, it is important for professional salespeople to be sensitive to and continuously monitor the health of their customer relationships. An alerted salesperson can take action to heal a deteriorating relationship and thwart developing problems.

Clues that serve as an early warning that problems are developing are often quite subtle and require a high level of sensitivity and observation. Most are based on knowing the customer through repeated contact and understanding normal behavioral patterns.

CHECKLIST OF EARLY WARNING SYMPTOMS OF DETERIORATING CUSTOMER RELATIONSHIPS

Important: If Any of These Symptoms Are Noted, Corrective Measures Should Begin Immediately.

1. Increase in frequency of complaints.
2. Late payments with no explanation.
3. Purchases from another source.
4. Too busy to talk on two or three consecutive calls or misses two to three appointments consecutively.
5. Has unexpected information about a competitor.

6. Discrepancy of facts or opinion from one call to the next.
7. Movement of competitive products to a more favorable location.
8. Delays in ordering past the normal time.
9. Decreasing market share.
10. Spends more time with competitor.
11. Asks about or mentions a competitor's product.
12. Concentrates on price unexpectedly.
13. Makes important decisions concerning you without consulting you.
14. Deviations from normal behavioral patterns — less friendly, stops kidding, short-tempered, stops asking advice.
15. Tells you straightforwardly, "We have a problem!"

Even though we don't know all the details of Jim's relationship with Pete Elliot, there were several signals that would have concerned Jim had he been more alert. When Pete was busy on three consecutive regular calls, Jim should have wondered why.

But Pete's growing dissatisfaction was masked by their close relationship. Pete's inability to level with Jim gave him an uncomfortable feeling which resulted in his avoidance behavior.

Three Types of Problems   There are three distinct types of relation-related problems common in agri selling. The first and easiest to handle — because customers are more open about it — is dissatisfaction with product performance. Discussing this nonpersonal subject is less threatening because there's no reflection on the salesperson and it can be handled on a factual basis.

The second involves customer dissatisfaction with the company or company's policies. This often comes out when both customer and salesperson begin talking about the company as "they" and normally occurs when the customer and salesperson have a good relationship. Although referring to the company as "they" may help the salesperson feel safer, it also may become a major problem later when the salesperson must represent the company he or she previously disclaimed.

The third and most difficult — considering the personal nature of the one-on-one relationship — is dissatisfaction with the salesperson. Customers may be reluctant to discuss it and salespeople are reluctant to hear it. Yet the salesperson/customer relationship forms the basis for all personal selling and service in agriculture. The relationship must be acceptable before sales can be made.

Improving Customer Relations   The sooner a problem can be detected the more likely it is to be resolved. That's why early detection is so critical. And as soon as a problem is identified it should be dealt with as quickly as possible.

The most potent medication is dealing with the problem in person. A personal visit says, "You are important to me — I value our relationship."

Deal with the issue directly and openly. "The last couple of visits haven't felt quite right, Pete. I'm wondering if there's a problem." If the response indicates there may be a problem but the customer is reluctant to openly discuss it, it may be necessary to move to a more direct line of questioning. But note that the customer may require a great deal of patient encouragement in order to verbalize any personal concerns about his feelings toward the salesperson.

It's important not to overreact to anything the customer says. Becoming defensive or even offensive, will not be helpful and may cause the customer to withdraw from further discussion. The customer should be encouraged to talk with probing but objective or nurturing comments. If the problem doesn't get verbalized, dealing with it will be impossible.

Dealing with the problem does not mean giving concessions. Often misunderstandings are clarified and the matter is resolved. Other times, an honest conflict is uncovered which necessitates additional outside input. Getting the problem out and dealing with it constructively is the hallmark of a skilled professional.

Preventive Measures

Prevention is always the best cure for any illness. Unsatisfactory customer relationships are no exceptions. Most prevention revolves around maintaining good service and being sensitive. Good service means following up on sales and not taking customers for granted — as Jim may have done with his customer, Pete.

Regular follow-up calls and annual in-depth reviews are highly useful in uncovering potential problems.

Some salespeople send letters to customers they don't see as often as they'd like. Although written correspondence may not be frequent, the letter serves to keep goodwill evident and communication open. Brief phone contacts can give additional opportunities to keep communication open and positive.

Professionals Make Relationships Work

Salespeople are busy — so busy that it's easy to become insensitive to the feelings of established customers. These customers can be taken for granted and become vulnerable to more aggressive competitors who will give them the attention they deserve and have been accustomed to receiving.

But conscientious attention to the early warning symptoms of a deteriorating customer relationship can provide the lead time necessary to correct the problem.

Professional agri salespeople recognize that they must intentionally examine each customer on the basis of their own unique personality, problems and needs in order to accurately interpret and maintain the health of their customer relationship.

SUMMARY Maintaining Customer Relations

* Good customer relations are vital to successful selling because of the highly competitive environment. Customers often buy from a seller because of loyalty.

* A steady relationship shouldn't be allowed to deteriorate because the salesperson feels secure and does not continually nurture it. Rural people tend to avoid a confrontation with salespeople to whom they feel close and the situation may result in a lost customer.

* Early warnings may indicate changing relationships and should be looked

for by salespeople. Warnings include an increase in complaints, purchasing from another source, interest in the competition and changes from normal behavior patterns.

* Three types of relationship problems involve dissatisfaction with the products, company or salesperson. Dissatisfaction with the salesperson is probably the most difficult to resolve and the most important.

* The best way of coping with problems is to prevent them. Alert salespeople look for clues of dissatisfaction and maintain frequent contact with customers.

Reading Thirteen

Sales Manager Subordinate Relationships

Sales managers come in all shapes, sizes and ages. Some are insensitive, task-oriented and demanding. Others are warm, understanding and flexible. Some are skillful communicators and effective leaders, while others struggle to accomplish their objectives through subordinates. But regardless of their description, personality or management style, each is still the boss.

There are many effective sales managers in agribusiness. However, excellent performance at one level in a sales organization is certainly no guarantee the person will be an effective boss at some higher level. Since most people in agricultural sales organizations have little to say about who their boss is, they are forced to live with the situation — or quit.

Almost all traditional thinking places the burden of effective sales manager/subordinate relationships squarely on the manager. Companies hold seminars on leadership and supervision. The trade press abounds with articles on motivating employees.

This relegates the subordinate to a position of futility and helplessness, as it suggests the subordinate has no responsibility for the success of the relationship and can do nothing about it. As Scott Stewart, district manager for a major ag chemical company lamented "I don't know what they were thinking when they made Baxter regional manager. He just embarrasses me when we visit my key accounts. But there's nothing I can do but put up with him. I'm stuck!"

Stewart's attitude is common among agricultural salespeople at all levels who are forced to work with a boss with whom they are uncomfortable. While a boss may lack necessary leadership skills, the subordinate is not helpless to improve the situation. There are many things a subordinate can and should do that can have a profound influence on the situation.

Stewart went on to explain he felt a real problem in communicating with his new boss. The newly appointed regional manager was an aggressive fast-talker who had been with a competitive company until three years ago. Stewart was six years older than Baxter and had been with the company since college, working in various parts of the southern region.

"The guy just doesn't understand how we do business down here. My previous boss just let me manage my district, but this guy is on my neck all the time, wanting this or that. And when I go ahead and make a decision, he gives me the third degree. Honestly, if it weren't for the time I've got in this company, I'd quit."

The climate in most agricultural sales organizations is quite conducive to conflict between sales managers and their subordinates at every level.

First, the sales organization is the most critical element of the agribusiness because it is the source of all revenue generated to support the total organization. There is constant pressure for sales performance.

Second, the sales force is the primary interface between the agribusiness and customers, competitors and the public. Information must flow rapidly and accurately. Decisions must be made quickly and often under considerable pressure.

The boss is usually concerned with cost control, setting quotas and controlling sales activities. But the subordinate is usually more concerned with customer relationships.

To further complicate matters, the sales organization is often staffed with aggressive people who feel strongly about the best way to do things. There is often considerable geographical separation and limited face-to-face contact, preventing development of strong personal relationships.

Although everyone in the sales organization is working toward the same overall objective — maximizing profitable sales — each level has particular responsibilities that can easily result in conflict, especially in the heat of battle.

Stewart's attitude — that he is in a box and must simply accept the frustrating relationship with his boss — is most unfortunate and certainly unnecessary. The subordinate has as much responsibility for good "followership" as his boss has for leadership. In fact, there is much he can do to actually manage his boss while fulfilling the subordinate role most respectfully.

There are several important reasons why Stewart should accept responsibility for improving his relationship with his boss. Foremost is the obvious impact his boss can have on his professional success. His manager directs, informs, encourages, evaluates, reprimands, promotes, sets salary, helps him out of jams or gives him grief.

But there are other reasons. His relationship has its own unique characteristics and there are many things the subordinate can do to make a good relationship better — or a poor relationship more acceptable.

Conflict is Inbred in Sales Structure

First, the subordinate must recognize that both he and his boss are part of a management team. Stewart and Baxter work together to manage the total selling effort in their territory. Some responsibilities are separate while others are held jointly. But both are accountable for sales in the area.

Respect is a must. It's highly desirable this be personal as well as professional respect. But as one sales manager for a farm equipment manufactu-

Saving the Conflicts

rer told a new salesman, "I hope we get along well, but remember son, liking me is not one of the requirements of your job." If you can't respect the boss, at least respect the position.

Respect is reflected in everyday activities. Ask the boss's opinion, accept his or her decisions, get assignments done on time (remember the boss has deadlines too), thank him, don't criticize him in conversation with peers and never circumvent your boss unless there is a major relationship crisis. And recognize even then that the consequences may be disastrous.

Attitude is a basic key. The boss is not better than the subordinate — he's just the boss. It's not a matter of personal worth but purely a matter of designated responsibilities. So there is no reason a subordinate should feel unimportant or "less than" another.

Stewart seems to be having attitude problems with his boss. While it is true not all supervisors are as competent as others, a negative attitude seems to magnify troubles. Stewart appears to resent the "young outsider" moving into his territory and conflict is the result.

A poor attitude often results in prior judgments that worsen a difficult relationship. Once Stewart made up his mind Baxter was not a good manager, he began to look for evidence to prove his dislike was justified.

Cooperation is important also. Seldom does a subordinate view himself as being uncooperative. Yet there are many levels of cooperation ranging from aggressive voluntary cooperation, through passive cooperation of doing what you know you must, to reluctant cooperation with grumbling and gnashing of teeth.

Bosses are human too. Everything they do, say or hear is filtered through their values and previous experience. A subordinate who makes an attempt to understand where his boss is coming from has a much better chance of developing a comfortable working relationship. Through conversation and observation, try to become conscious of your boss's:

> Goals and aspirations
> Pressures from his boss and peers
> Background and previous bosses
> Personal situation
> Work habits
> Communication patterns
> Strengths and weaknesses

Had Stewart anticipated some areas of potential conflict with Baxter, he might have done much to avoid many of his frustrations.

Agribusinesses are filled with examples where the promoted bring along those who have helped them succeed. It stands to reason that helping a boss can have highly tangible benefits for the subordinate.

Making One's Superior Look Good   There are many things a subordinate can do to make his boss look good. Most revolve around trying to think of things from your boss's viewpoint and then responding in a helpful way.

Anticipate problems and deal with them early. If local weather conditions cause inventories to build, initiate an informal inventory position report and submit it to your boss for his information. The early warning may help him pinpoint a potential problem for headquarters and make him look insightful. Sales managers are smart enough to know where their best help is coming from.

Support your boss among peers and other management. Casual conversation often makes it clear how you feel about your boss, which is useful information for their formal and informal evaluations. By continually placing your boss in a favorable light, you are developing a favorable impression of him among others. This support, when honest and genuine, will be evident over time and mutually beneficial for both of you.

Compliment your boss. The higher the supervisor, the more lonely it is. Most compliments come from the boss to the subordinate. Consequently, the boss's "stroke bucket" can get pretty empty. When not overdone, compliments are usually welcomed. Occasionally put it in the form of a written thank-you note — after the annual review or salary increase is an excellent and highly appropriate time. If it's particularly complimentary, consider sending your boss's boss a copy of the note.

Make him think he thought of it. Rather than expounding on a great new idea of yours, try planting a seed of the idea in a casual conversation. Carefully nurture the idea on a periodic basis. As the boss discovers your idea, it will likely be well-appreciated. If you are smooth enough, the boss will feel good about "his" idea — but will have even better feelings about you.

Good work is probably the best tool for making your boss look good and improving your relationship with him. There is no substitute for a job well done.

When your boss begins to feel he can count on you to come through, keep him informed and be loyal to his and the company's objectives, you are well on your way to ensuring a good relationship.

When it comes right down to it, the success of your performance is the key factor in the company's evaluation of your boss. When you look bad he looks bad, and when you succeed he succeeds.

Other suggestions for improving relationships with your boss:

DO:

1. Anticipate needs and problems. Bring them to your boss's attention.
2. Send your boss an annual unsolicited report summarizing the year's activities and future outlook. He'll be impressed.
3. Use informal agendas in your meetings with your boss — it improves efficiency and thoroughness.
4. After a lengthy meeting summarize what you think you heard in a brief note and send it to the boss for confirmation.
5. Ask for feedback and don't expect only compliments.
6. Treat your boss's secretary with respect — she probably deserves it and she can be very influential.

7. Tell your boss your failures as well as your successes. The boss should hear about your failures from you before he does from anyone else. This improves your credibility.

8. Do what you're asked to do — then do just a little more. This age-old adage creates much goodwill and leaves a very favorable impression.

DON'T:

1. Expect your boss to always know what you need. It's up to you to initiate communication.

2. Expect constant feedback. Some bosses are just not frequent communicators.

3. Ever surprise a boss, especially with or around his boss, peers or outsiders.

4. Submit messy, incomplete reports.

5. Be late or undependable.

6. Maliciously obey his instructions when you know circumstances no longer warrant the action. Malicious obedience — carrying out instructions to the letter even when they are no longer appropriate — is a way of getting back at the boss that causes much ill will.

Everyone in the agribusiness sales organization has a boss — and they're stuck with him. Fortunately there is a lot the subordinate can do to manage the relationship. In fact, the subordinate has a responsibility to maintain and improve this relationship.

By assuming a positive attitude and aggressively managing the relationship, the subordinate can significantly improve his or her situation and increase the probability of a more satisfying and profitable relationship with the boss.

SUMMARY
Sales Manager
Subordinate
Relationships

* The burden for good sales manager/salesperson relationships should not rest totally on the manager. The salesperson should take a vital role in creating and maintaining a good relationship.

* The company environment offers a breeding ground for conflict since managers are generally more interested in sales while the salesperson is bent on customer relationships.

* The salesperson can take valuable steps to maintain the sales team relationship with respect, cooperation and proper attitude.

* Most managers are gratified by a salesperson's willingness to help ease the management burden, which in turn can improve the performance of everyone involved.

Selling Skills for Ag Lenders

With the evolution of the agricultural marketplace, the lending function is taking on new significance, and with it new challenges.

There are fewer farmers. Operations are larger. Management prowess is the key to profitability, in both production and finance. Farmers want loan packages carefully crafted to their needs as well as up-to-date financial advice. For many of them, the services provided by lending institutions are as important as the product — short- or long-term loans.

With the economic upheaval of the past few years, however, the lender knows he must seek out those customers who can best handle the financial challenges of farm management. And of course, competitive lenders also seek the same customers. When producers have several options for borrowing money and obtaining financial advice, lenders are put into a position in which they must vie for the credit worthy customers.

A lender can attract the kind of customers he needs with solid, service-oriented salesmanship. While many loan officers recoil at the thought of themselves as "selling," it is in their best interest to rethink that philosophy and evaluate how selling principles can help them. Problem solving, targeting high potential prospects and follow-up are but a few of the ideas that have direct application to lending.

There is no doubt that selling in the lending arena is different than selling tractors or chemicals. In lending money, you are offering a product with great emotion attached. Customers may have difficulty making decisions regarding finance because there is often risk involved, as well as the opportunity to spend the money elsewhere.

Selling the lending service is also different because your process is as much one of evaluation as it is one of trying to convince a customer your product is the one for him. Often, you must "unsell" a prospect if you discover an inability to handle a loan. And, following up with customers becomes as crucial in lending as it is in any sale. An ongoing, close relationship is essential in making sure terms are met and success is achieved.

The key to using selling principles in lending then becomes how you apply them. That takes careful evaluation of your customers as well as your institution's philosophy. The skills must be applied in a way that portrays you as a partner and advisor.

You can do this by following a few basic principles.

Target High Potential Customers

Despite the competitive air in lending, the most successful lenders are the ones who pursue producers who are successfully coping with today's economic challenges. These people tend to have larger operations, were conservative in borrowing in the last decade, and are well-informed, efficient managers. The catch is, of course, that these prospects can borrow from whomever they choose and are often well-established with their lenders.

The way to approach these people is with your offer of service. Be visible in organizations and community events. Be well versed in what's going on, and perhaps most importantly, be competent. These people will choose only to work with competent professionals.

Program Approach

This approach means the lender considers himself a marketer. He realizes the many sources of credit available, and that he does his job best when he attracts the borrower who is a stable manager. This lender is pro-active and seeks those prospects who he identifies as being good credit risks. Then he is willing to develop a community image and related programs to appeal to these prospects.

Why is this so important? Careful planning helps you present an image to the community; an image that portrays you in the way you want to be seen.

With economic hardship, lenders have been the source of criticism from all sides. Rightly or wrongly, you must be willing to take responsibility for your community profile and work to improve or maintain it.

Consistency is the key. Advertising, direct mail and other written materials help keep your institution's name in front of the public. The written word can't stand alone, however, and even more important is your ability to appear as a sincere, competent member of the community whose major interest is in making good loans. You can never support your customers too much, and the simplest gestures on your part will do much for your image.

Regular personal contact is essential. A simple "How's it going?" every few weeks shows you are more than a money broker and establishes you as a full-service lender. Realize the value of being a professional friend rather than an aloof business acquaintance.

The contact can take other forms as well: meeting new people, becoming acquainted with prospects, contributing to local events and organizations.

This marketing program effort will pay off in many ways, namely when foreclosures and bankruptcies threaten. Customers and prospects will be more likely to respect your position if you show your allegiance in good times as well as bad.

Your Counselor Role with Customers

Farmers are looking for advice. Despite the glut of written and broadcast information available, proper interpretation can be scarce. You must be available to give advice, and to help point out the options available.

More farmers are realizing the importance of securing a "management team." This team is made up of lender, attorney, technical advisor and accountant. And, farmers say the lender is the member upon whom they rely for financially related production advice. You have the responsibility to know what is going on currently and to have a grasp of the production basics. It is not necessary that you become a farmer, but professional competence *is* a credibility builder.

Despite the old adage, in ag lending "the customer isn't always right."

One of the most difficult parts of your job may be to gently convince a customer or prospect that his plans are not appropriate to the situation.

In counseling, listen carefully to what the customer has to say. Allow him to explain problems or concerns completely. If there are things you do not understand, ask open-ended questions. Be sure to get the full story, from the customer's perspective. Determine facts as well as feelings.

Then suggest alternatives or options. Your attitude should be positive and you should encourage your customer to take the lead in thinking of ideas. It's important that the customer leaves believing that it was his idea to rent more land or sell some livestock. You are simply there to point out alternatives, not to make decisions.

Once an alternative has been chosen, do all you can to help the customer carry out his plan. Stay in contact; offer your assistance.

Remember: You don't have to know all the answers. However, you should know where to find them.

Saying No to Loan Requests

This ability comes primarily from sound business judgment and experience.

Many beginning loan officers may have trouble with the emotional impact of saying no to a request, but they soon discover it is in the customer's interest as well as the lending institution's.

Rejections are inevitable. While unpleasant, they can be turned into positive situations if handled properly. You can set the stage for doing future business, should that be advisable, or for building your credibility as a fair lender.

If you respond honestly from the beginning and do not build false expectations, objective lending will be easier. While there is a tendency to be positive when first working with a customer, you do him no good by leading him on when you know that what he asks isn't feasible.

Be ready to explain why an application must be rejected. Have logical reasons and be prepared to spell them out. You owe it to the customer so that he can look to the future with ideas for improvement.

With such an explanation, the majority of denied borrowers will understand and respect the decision. However, that leaves a minority who will be angry and insult the lender. Don't let this anger become contagious. You can react in a couple of ways. Give the person time to cool off and schedule another meeting. Or send a letter, tactfully explaining your position and expressing your regret in a positive way. You may even wish to suggest other lending alternatives. You don't have to apologize for rejecting a borrower, yet you should make the situation understandable and bearable.

The "Unsell" Technique

Lenders can prevent problem rejections with effective communication prior to taking the application. One way to do that is to "unsell" or to convey honest expectations with your actions.

Start by making if perfectly clear during initial contact that loan action can only be taken after a credit application is completed and analyzed.

Never promise more than you can deliver. Keep in mind that you represent investors who have granted to you their trust and responsibility for making good loans. And remember too, that you are restricted by policies, regulations and procedures. You need not apologize for these. They exist for good reason.

Concentrate on the needs and problems of prospects and explain how you may or may not be able to help. Never oversell yourself.

If you check the background of your prospects in advance, you can prevent many problems. A good method for deciding who makes a good customer is provided on page 102, the Prospect Profile. The Profile helps you objectively look at important aspects of a potential customer's operation and personality.

Maintain a Positive Image

Important to customers of any financial service is the trust they place in their loan officers. These customers need to feel as if their lenders are of the highest moral fiber, and that a matter as important as their financial affairs is in good hands.

The image can be cultivated and maintained with community involvement and interest in agricultural and youth groups. Advertising and promotional materials, used properly, keep your name in front of the public.

Foremost in image making, however, is the idea of confidentiality. How discreet you are goes a long way in cementing a customer relationship. Customers want to feel, and rightly so, that everything they tell you will remain in confidence.

There are several ways to let customers know you respect their confidentiality. Start with intentional discretion. Always shut the office door when discussing financial matters. Never do so in a public place or front office.

Mark your folders "confidential" and go out of your way to remove and file records in the presence of your customer. Going through these motions will impress the customer and protect his information at the same time.

Signs Of a Deteriorating Relationship

Personal commitment is an integral part of the lending relationship. A decrease in commitment can spell trouble for lender and customer alike. There is a remedy, however. If spotted early enough, problems can often be solved before the relationship deteriorates beyond repair. Signs of developing problems are:

Inaccessibility
Personal or operational problems
Disrepair or change in cleanliness
Extended vacations

Any of these may mean that the customer has financial problems. Or it may be that the customer is looking to someone else for advice. If so, you should take it upon yourself to get to the root of the problem, and determine whether or not the situation is worth salvaging.

"Selling" financial products and services is anything but simple. In fact, it is as complex a set of products and programs as can be found when viewed in light of the personal impact it has upon your customer.

Your job is to ease the pressure by offering counsel and support. Properly handled, you can nurture a relationship that will be beneficial for borrower and lender alike.

Reading Fifteen

In-Store Selling

The farm supply market is competitive. When farmers need animal health products, lawn and garden items, feed, seed or any of thousands of products, they have several choices. They can buy from a farm store or cooperative. And, these days, there are chains, independents and convenience stores as well as discount houses from which they can buy.

Farm store managers and salespeople are confronted with a challenge of gigantic proportions. How can they compete and be profitable? Adding more in-store salespeople may or may not be the right answer. More advertising dollars may not necessarily do the job. Expanding the product line or the size of the store may be inappropriate actions.

The most likely answer is improved merchandising and in-store selling techniques. Effective in-store selling involves combining the best of personal and non-personal selling with the right product and service mix for the store's trade area.

While our intent is not to turn you into merchandising experts, it is to help you understand some of the basics. Application of a few simple principles can accentuate the selling activities of any store, and hopefully, increase sales.

Personal Selling In The Store

Every person who works in a farm store is a salesperson. Their attitudes, knowledge and dress are direct reflections upon the stores in which they work. They should be made aware of the importance of their roles as team members and act accordingly. The understanding and application of the selling skills described in *Agri Selling* is as important to in-store salespeople as to those with selling responsibilities outside the walls of the store.

All store employees should watch customers as they shop. There are several reasons for this. One is that if a customer has a problem or question, it can be taken care of before the customer has to search for help.

Another reason is suggestion selling. This is a powerful, simple technique aimed at selling additional, related items to buyers. It works like this: You notice shoppers picking out five gallons of white paint. You say, "Looks like you've got a big job ahead of you." They laugh and say, "Yes, we have been putting off painting the shed for two years." You say, "Got everything you need? An extra brush or two would probably help. In fact, they're on sale this week." With good suggestion selling, you can send the buyer out with new brushes or maybe even a ladder or paint sprayer. And when you know and respond to the personalities of your customer, suggestion selling can be even more effective.

Because in-store salespeople have limited discretionary sales time, they must spend it in areas where the pay-off is greatest. Organize the store so that this sales time is focused in areas where customer support is necessary...and most profitable. These areas may vary somewhat by store, yet seasonal items, hand and power tools, and animal health products generally fit the bill.

Employees should be well informed about products, policies and procedures to be most effective. Staff meetings to discuss these subjects is time well spent as long as the information is relevant to better communication with the customer and to store efficiency. Remember that in-store selling is a highly service oriented process. Service is best rendered through information and effective operations.

Store Design and Layout

Your objective is simple. You want people to walk by your merchandise, notice it, and make purchases. Due to the size and marketing evolution of farm and urban stores, it is impractical to place merchandise on one side of the counter, the customer on the other and utilize a clerk to fill all orders from the stock shelves. The layout, design and environment of a store can enhance cost-effective selling while maintaining a service oriented image.

A self-service orientation has become important in the selling of in-store products. People are used to serving themselves, and become frustrated when not easily able to do so, particularly with routine purchases. Literature displayed in prominent areas with coupons or product descriptions helps customers help themselves.

Customer convenience and common sense are the primary influences which dictate merchandise groupings. People can't buy what they can't find. Related items should be together within "departments." These departments are like "stores within a store." Both departments and related item groupings should be designated by signs, and coupons should be available in the store as well as in publications. Bin or bulk items should be clearly marked with unit prices. Many suppliers offer signage kits to assist in store organization and layout. However, don't overlook making your own, as necessary, with stencils and poster board. Signage and directional markings are critical to in-store sales success.

The store should be attractive, both inside and out. A bright, open atmosphere is essential as it helps to keep the customer in the store longer, which is the major objective for interior and exterior decoration. Studies show that the longer a customer is in the store, the more they purchase.

Cleanliness contributes to the environment as well. Metallic products should be shiny, floors swept and shelves dusted. While this is not always easy when products such as feed and seed are in stock, it is very important to today's farm store customer.

Rearranging the layout periodically helps to give a "new look" to the store and also helps organization. While you don't want to disorient customers, it is possible to make alterations without completely redoing a store, and customers will notice your attempts to make shopping easier for them. Further, by rearranging without disrupting, you make it more likely for customers to see items for purchase which they haven't really noticed before.

Traffic flow through a store is traditionally to the right or counter clockwise. Therefore, plan your store layout to take advantage of the traffic flow. The perimeter selling areas are valuable. Use them for items you wish to have high visibility. Put high demand items in the back so people will have to walk by other items to see them. Use in-aisle and end displays to create flow in the center areas.

You can check how effective your layout is. Watch customers to see where they go and how long they spend there. This will help you spot dead areas in the store and help you evaluate where you should make improvements.

Don't forget about ease of movement in a farm store. Aisle widths are commonly 4½ feet to 6½ feet. They should be wide enough to allow people to navigate through, yet not so wide that you give up valuable selling space. Also use the checkout area wisely. It can be a great display area for impulse items; don't waste it with a soda or gum ball machine.

Technology

Computer systems offer great potential for streamlining processes such as inventory management. Our purpose in mentioning it here is to point out the importance of having processes in place that allow you to most efficiently serve your customer. An unorganized inventory system, for example, may mean out-of-stock items when your customers need them most. Management decisions in pricing and specials can be greatly augmented by data generated by computers, too.

Another innovation taking its place in many rural areas is electronic check-out. Electronic check-out helps in inventory management, and supplier communication. More important, when combined with unit and item pricing at stocking, electronic check-out offers customers a clearer record of their purchases and associated prices.

Displays

Suppliers often provide displays and promotional materials about their products. While their most obvious use is with specials or advertised items, they may be used to promote any item. Displays are especially effective with new products since they often contain additional information.

Make sure displays are neatly maintained and in spots where they will be noticed — at ends of aisles or in aisles next to shelves of related objects.

Shelving

As shoppers walk through a store, they may make impulse decisions about whether or not to look at each aisle. They can be encouraged to do so by the appearance of the shelves. Clean, fully stocked shelves are an invitation to look and are the key to gaining the shopper's attention.

There are several techniques for product arrangement. The top shelf is the prime selling area. Locate the most popular and high-margin products here. The second shelf is the next-best position and the bottom shelf should be the location of large items and back-up stock. Give faster moving products more facings.

Starter gaps should be incorporated at stocking. These are gaps in the products which help shoppers to remove items and also psychologically encourage the shopper to buy what others already have. Typically, starter gaps are placed at the end of the shelf or display. Shelf talkers can also be used to stimulate interest. A shelf talker announcing a sale or special item can easily be made or acquired from suppliers.

Check for damaged merchandise frequently and remove or replace it.

Non-Personal Selling

Advertising is one of the most frequent ways of promoting the use of your products. Suppliers may have "camera-ready" art ready to print that you may simply present to your newspaper or you may need to work with advertising salespeople of newspapers, radio and television stations to formulate your ads.

The use of advertising can be heightened with the addition of games, giveaways, specials and sales. These activities tend to draw customers into a store. If you choose such a special promotion, take care to have plenty of product on hand, along with the personnel to handle its operation.

Specials are generally highlighted by pricing. Having reduced prices or volume discounts lets customers feel as if they are getting a bargain and may help you move larger amounts of product. Most advertising and direct mail is targeted at sale items as a means to attract traffic.

Seasonality

Purchases are often made based upon the time of the year. You can take advantage of this by offering needed products, beginning four to six weeks in advance. Advertising is critical to the success of moving seasonal items.

Be sure to clear the products away during off-season and make every attempt to clear inventory before you have to store it. Storing such items is an expensive alternative in comparison to selling them.

Competition

One way to keep up with the competition is to keep track of where they are. Information about pricing, product lines and merchandising ideas is helpful when formulating your own plans. Simply spend some time in your competitor's stores on a regular basis. Watch local media for advertising or special announcements which could indicate the need for "competitive shopping."

Making It Work

Despite the techniques listed here, how you put them to work is most important. Unless you own and manage a store, you may not be in a position to direct others to do these things. The key is to offer your help in doing them, rather than telling someone to do them.

In many cases, you may have to take the lead in making merchandising improvements. Showing you care enough to do the extra work to move your products may be enough. If not, work to educate fellow employees. It is an investment that will pay off in increased sales.

Index

About Our Other Publications . . .

COORDINATED FINANCIAL STATEMENTS FOR AGRICULTURE INSTRUCTIONAL BOOKLETS

You and Your Balance Sheet Booklet, 48 pages. $6.95. By Thomas L. Frey & Gene Nelson. This booklet is a clear, easy-to-understand booklet explaining how to complete the balance sheet portion of CFS.

Farmers can annually complete accurate balance sheets with the help of step-by-step instructions.

You and Your Cash Flow Booklet, 56 pages. $6.95

You and Your Income Statement Booklet, 36 pages. $6.95
These booklets are based on the same concept as *You and Your Balance Sheet:* The farmer can fill out his own financial forms when he has complete instructions. One booklet explains how to fill out the cash flow statement and the other provides instructions for the income statement.

Quantity prices for the above: 2-4 copies $5.95; 5-9 copies $4.95

Coordinated Financial Statements for Agriculture Manual, 84 pages. Includes one each of 16 Statements/Schedules. $14.95. By Thomas L. Frey and Danny Klinefelter. This reference manual provides complete instructions on preparing and analyzing the 16 statements/schedules. Included are general concepts and advantages underlying the system followed by separate chapters on the balance sheet, income statement, cash flow statement and statement of change in financial position.

Financing Agribusiness by David M. Kohl and David A. Lins. Special booklet for farm suppliers and dealers. 28-pages of practical ideas on how to obtain needed funds to run the business and establish workable credit and financial programs. Also included is practical information on using financial statements to analyze and manage the agribusiness, understanding the farmer's needs for financing and the lender's requirements before providing funds. 1 copy $6.95; 2-5 copies $5.95 each.

Legal And Tax Guide For Agricultural Lenders, by Neil E. Harl helps you apply the ever-changing law to your daily lending practice.

This complete handbook ties together the significant legal and tax aspects of lending with the special preparation needed for agricultural accounts.

Zero in on the key problem areas that affect your farm customers.

Concisely written, easy to read — a must for all new and seasoned loan officers. 1-5 copies $18.95 each.

(more on next page)